Fact File 2009

• Copiable book   • Online   • CD Rom

Digital Fact File
All the Fact File pages as pdfs as well as
the raw data to make your own charts.
Also includes previous editions since 2001.
See website or telephone 01228 538928.

Reference CAREL PRESS
http://www.carelpress.com

Welcome to Fact File 2008

What's new

Fact File has been linked more closely with its companion resource, Essential Articles, which is now published annually. A searchable guide, which matches the statistics in Fact File to relevant discussion or personal accounts in Essential Articles, is available on our website. This means that anyone using the two publications can put together facts and opinions to support an argument or provoke discussion.

Revised sections

In response to the changing demands of the school curriculum we have changed the balance of sections.

Britain & its citizens focuses particularly on the issue of what it means to be British and the changing nature of our population. It also deals with some of the recurring issues – social, moral and political – which we as a nation have to face.

The new section on Financial issues considers personal finance via the issues of affordable housing, poverty, savings and debt, as well as pay. Within it you will find topics to help young people consider how to manage their finances – and even compare their pocket money with the national average!

As in previous years, the impact of technology on our daily lives is examined in detail. The increasing pace of change brought about by digital communication – in particular its effect on our social habits – is reflected in the statistics in the Internet & media section.

In Environmental issues there is a particular emphasis on the environmental impact of air travel. The issue of whether 2007's extreme weather is linked to global warming is also considered.

The Family & relationships section looks at the ways in which a family can be made up in modern Britain. It also considers how relationships start and what causes disagreements.

The majority of the information in Fact File deals with the countries of the UK. There is also a strong representation of EU information. Charts in Wider world focus on international issues.

Live links

Once again we have included links, live in the digital version, to sources and associated websites.

Finding information easily

The structure of Fact File encourages browsing and exploration but we have also tried to meet the needs of those who are seeking specific information. When the information in a chart could be categorised in several different ways the index will help you find it. A good example of this is the final chart *Well-being* which is taken from the UN report on young people. Because it deals with international comparisons it is in the Wider world section but it is also indexed under: *children, family & relationships* and *young people*. Anyone searching for this information has an easy route to it.

Up-to-date statistics

As always, all the charts have been newly created or thoroughly updated. There is, of course, always a gap, sometimes lengthy, between the collection and the publication of statistics and this is particularly the case with international statistics. The link on the page will lead you to the latest updates.

The nations of the UK collect their own statistics on some topics. These may be compiled at slightly different times making it difficult to find and compare across the whole country.

Supporting the whole curriculum

Fact File has been designed to support the whole secondary and further education curriculum and is an essential library resource. Those teaching citizenship and PSHEE will find Fact File invaluable in providing current data related to these subjects. Teachers of business, English, general studies, geography, economics, politics and sociology will also find relevant statistics, attractively presented, to enhance their teaching.

Fact File online & on CD Rom

Fact File is also available digitally. This gives you all the pages in searchable form. In addition, you receive the raw spreadsheet data which we used to create the charts, so you can make your own charts instantly.

The Fact File archive from 2001 is available digitally.

Sample material from the digital version is on our website. Schools can buy the online or CD rom version using Curriculum Online e-learning credits.

The companion publication to Fact File: Essential Articles 10

The Essential Articles series provides thematically arranged journalism covering all of the topics in Fact File and much more. Essential Articles 10 is now available

Publication Information

Fact File 2008 © 2008 Carel Press Ltd
4 Hewson St, Carlisle
Tel 01228 538928
Fax 591816
info@carelpress.com
www.carelpress.com

British Library Cataloguing in Publication Data
Fact File 2008
1. Great Britain – Statistics 314.1
ISBN: 978-1-905600-13-7

Reproduction from this resource is allowed only within the individual purchasing institution.

Research, design and editorial team:
Kevin Burke, Anne Louise Kershaw, Debbie Maxwell, Ross Percival, Sandra Percival, Christine A Shepherd, Faye Sisson, Jan Vernon, Chas White

Subscriptions:
Ann Batey (manager), Brenda Hughes, Anne Maclagan

Printing:
Finemark, Poland

Book cover:
Arthur Procter

Fact File 2008 Contents

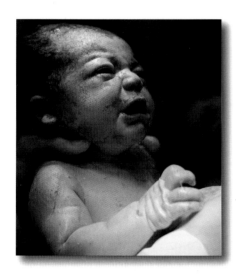

Hit at 40mph Hit at 30mph

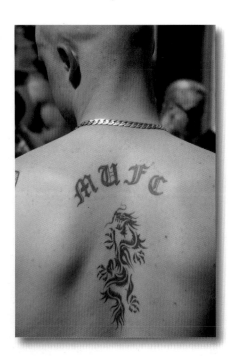

Britain &
its citizens

Facts of life

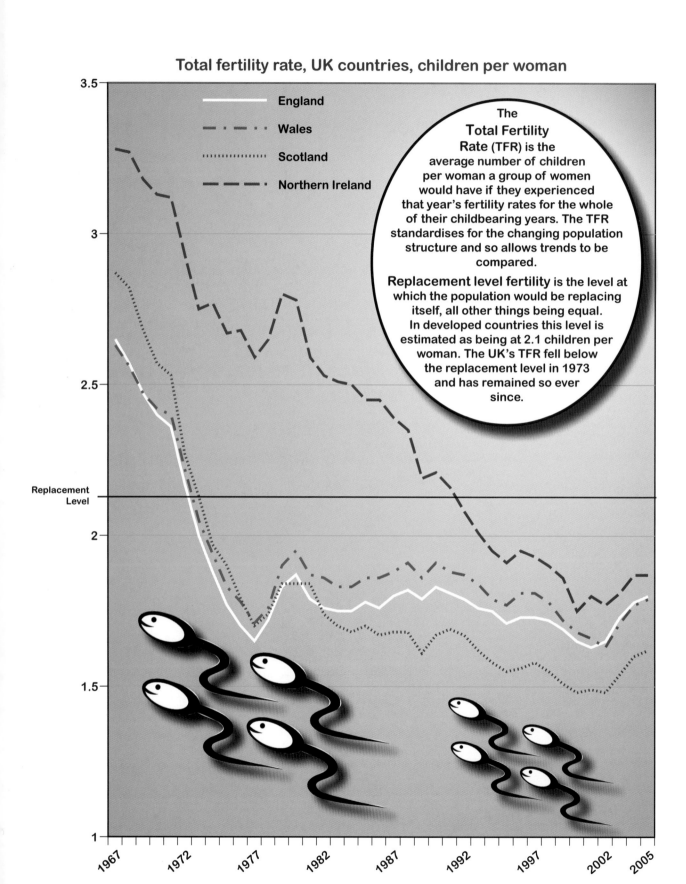

Total fertility rate, UK countries, children per woman

England
Wales
Scotland
Northern Ireland

The Total Fertility Rate (TFR) is the average number of children per woman a group of women would have if they experienced that year's fertility rates for the whole of their childbearing years. The TFR standardises for the changing population structure and so allows trends to be compared.

Replacement level fertility is the level at which the population would be replacing itself, all other things being equal. In developed countries this level is estimated as being at 2.1 children per woman. The UK's TFR fell below the replacement level in 1973 and has remained so ever since.

Source: Office for National Statistics: Social Trends 2007
© Crown copyright 2007

http://www.statistics.gov.uk

Advancing age

Population of the UK, by age and gender, mid 2006 and 2066 (projected)

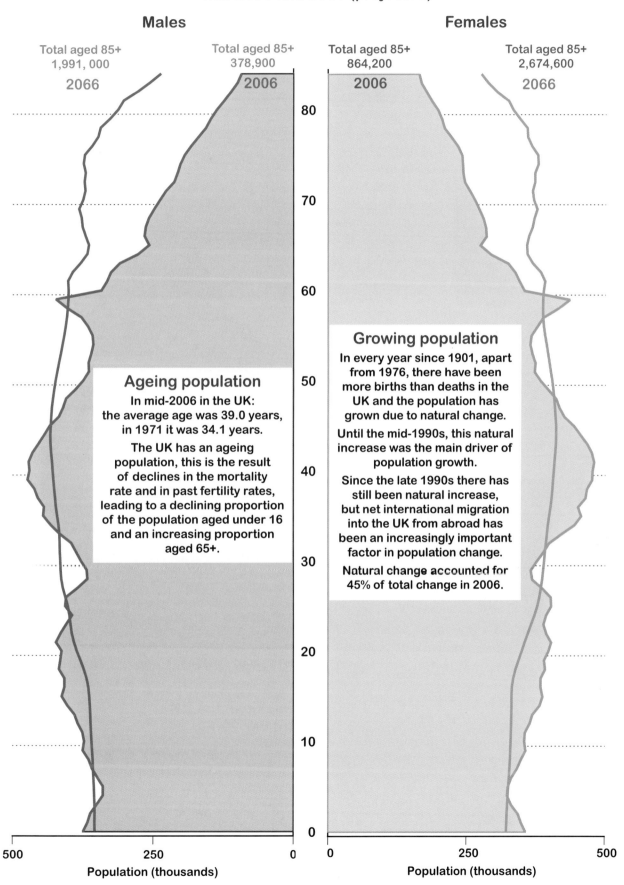

Males

Total aged 85+
1,991,000
2066

Total aged 85+
378,900
2006

Females

Total aged 85+
864,200
2006

Total aged 85+
2,674,600
2066

Ageing population
In mid-2006 in the UK:
the average age was 39.0 years,
in 1971 it was 34.1 years.

The UK has an ageing
population, this is the result
of declines in the mortality
rate and in past fertility rates,
leading to a declining proportion
of the population aged under 16
and an increasing proportion
aged 65+.

Growing population
In every year since 1901, apart
from 1976, there have been
more births than deaths in the
UK and the population has
grown due to natural change.

Until the mid-1990s, this natural
increase was the main driver of
population growth.

Since the late 1990s there has
still been natural increase,
but net international migration
into the UK from abroad has
been an increasingly important
factor in population change.

Natural change accounted for
45% of total change in 2006.

Population (thousands)

Population (thousands)

Source: Office for National Statistics © Crown copyright 2007

http://www.statistics.gov.uk

Becoming Brits

Applications for British citizenship received and decided in the UK, 1996–2006

	Received	Granted	Refused	Refusal as a % of all decisions
1996	61,800	43,070	4,770	10%
1997	66,000	37,010	4,745	11%
1998	68,030	53,935	3,750	7%
1999	67,400	54,900	3,995	7%
2000	62,475	82,210	6,785	8%
2001	109,005	90,295	9,530	10%
2002	115,500	120,125	8,455	7%
2003	147,345	125,535	10,480	8%
2004	132,630	140,705	13,650	9%
2005	219,115	161,700	16,645	9%
2006	149,035	154,095	15,360	9%

NB Each year some applications remain 'in the pipeline' as they are not processed within that year

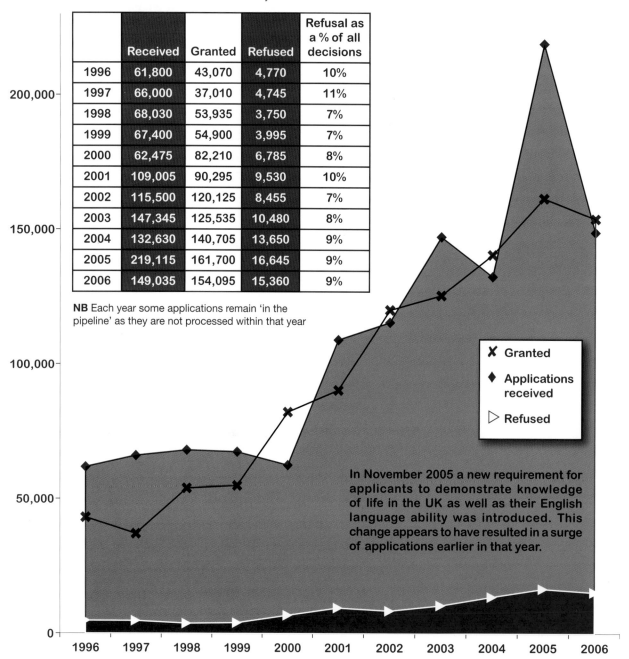

Legend:
- ✘ Granted
- ◆ Applications received
- ▷ Refused

In November 2005 a new requirement for applicants to demonstrate knowledge of life in the UK as well as their English language ability was introduced. This change appears to have resulted in a surge of applications earlier in that year.

Grants of British citizenship in the UK, by previous nationality, 2006

Africa	30%	Americas	8%
Indian sub–continent	19%	Oceania	3%
European Economic Area	2%	Remainder of Asia	16%
Remainder of Europe	13%	Others	2%
Middle East	7%		

Source: Persons Granted British Citizenship, United Kingdom, 2006
Home Office © Crown copyright 2007

http://www.homeoffice.gov.uk

Number's up

Many overseas workers have come to the UK – but not all have stayed

A National Insurance (NI) number is needed by anyone of working age who wants to work legally or claim benefits in the UK

Top 10 countries of origin for overseas workers (thousands) 2003-04	
India	31.3
South Africa	18.4
Australia	17.1
Pakistan	16.8
Portugal	14
China	13.3
France	13.1
Spain	11.9
Poland	11.2
Philippines	10.7

Top 10 countries of origin for overseas workers (thousands) 2006-07	
Poland	222.8
India	49.3
Slovakia	28.8
Pakistan	25.3
Australia	24.4
Lithuania	24.1
France	20.2
South Africa	16.9
Germany	15.2
China	13.2

Bulgaria and Romania joined the EU on 1/1/07. In the first 6 months of 2007, 13,000 NI allocations were made to nationals of these countries, 2 in 3 from Romanians

Overseas Nationals entering the UK and allocated a NI number (thousands)

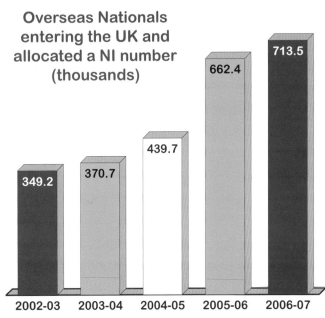

2002-03	2003-04	2004-05	2005-06	2006-07
349.2	370.7	439.7	662.4	713.5

NB The figures do not include dependants such as children

» 81% coming to work in the UK in 2006-07 were aged under 35

» Men accounted for 54%

» The expansion of the EU has been the biggest reason for the increase – 466,000 Polish workers over 4 years have come to Britain

» These figures do not mean there are now 713,000 more foreign workers in the UK than a year earlier, as the figures do not count those who leave the country

» There are a variety of ways in which immigration is measured in the UK, although there is not one definitive one, and none include illegal immigrants

Source: National Insurance Number Allocations to Overseas Nationals Entering the UK, 2006/07, Bulgarian and Roman Accession Statistics, Department for Work and Pensions, Office for National Statistics © Crown copyright 2007

http://www.statistics.gov.uk
http://www.dwp.gov.uk

In & out

International migration to/from the UK
1996-2005

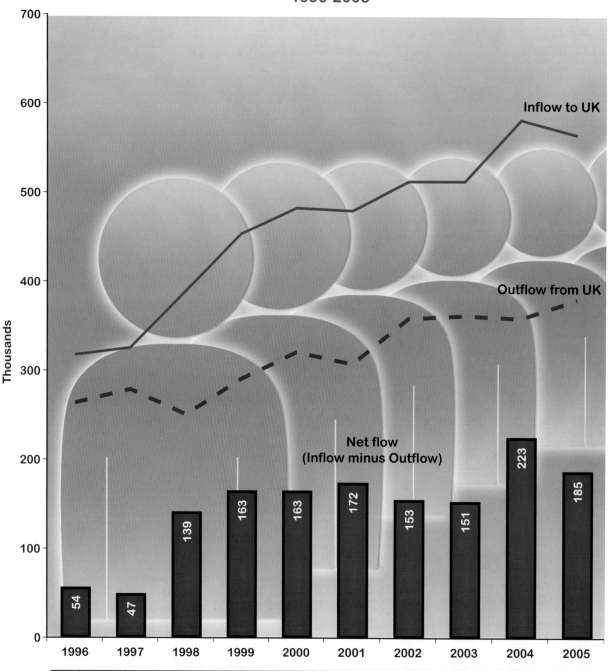

Inflow to UK

Outflow from UK

Net flow
(Inflow minus Outflow)

Thousands

Year	Net flow
1996	54
1997	47
1998	139
1999	163
2000	163
2001	172
2002	153
2003	151
2004	223
2005	185

» The 380,000 people who left the UK in 2005 are the equivalent of 1,000 people a day leaving the UK to live abroad – 198,000 of these were British citizens. Australia was the preferred destination, followed by Spain then France.

» In 2005 the number of people arriving to live in the UK was 565,000, an average of over 1,500 a day.

» An estimated 49,000 Polish citizens migrated into the UK in 2005, almost three times the 2004 estimate of 17,000.

» Mid year figures for 2005-06 suggest an inflow of 559,000 and an outflow of 383,000 leaving a net flow of +176,000.

Source: Total International Migration, International Passenger Survey 2006 © Crown copyright 2006 UK population News Release, August 2007

http://www.statistics.gov.uk

Changing places

Population movement within the UK, by country and English region, 2006, (thousands)

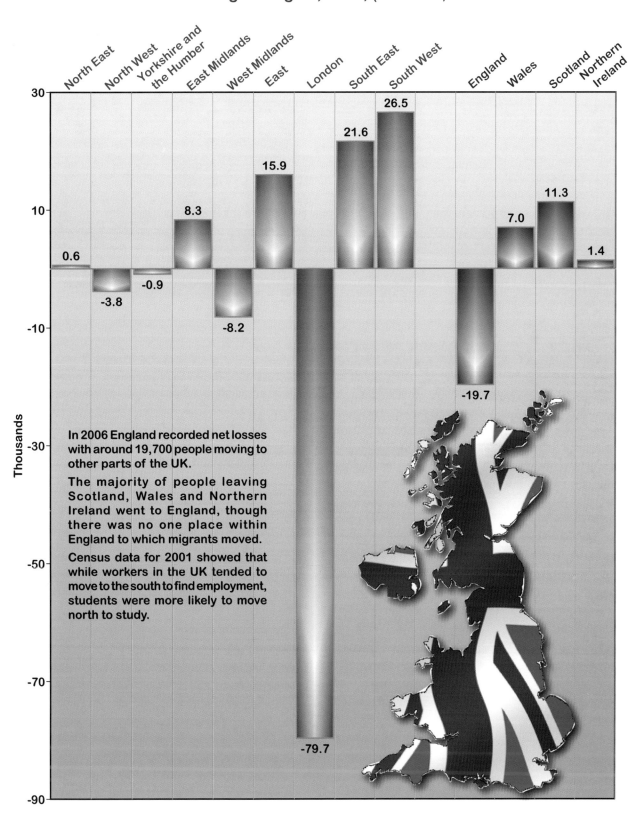

North East **0.6**
North West **-3.8**
Yorkshire and the Humber **-0.9**
East Midlands **8.3**
West Midlands **-8.2**
East **15.9**
London **-79.7**
South East **21.6**
South West **26.5**
England **-19.7**
Wales **7.0**
Scotland **11.3**
Northern Ireland **1.4**

Thousands

In 2006 England recorded net losses with around 19,700 people moving to other parts of the UK.

The majority of people leaving Scotland, Wales and Northern Ireland went to England, though there was no one place within England to which migrants moved.

Census data for 2001 showed that while workers in the UK tended to move to the south to find employment, students were more likely to move north to study.

Source: National Health Service Central Register; General Register Office for Scotland; Northern Ireland Statistics and Research Agency © Crown copyright 2007

http://www.ons.gov.uk

Who do we think we are?

**Britain is an increasingly diverse society –
can it also be an equal one?**

Who are we?

Proportion of the British public who say that 'British' is the best or only way to describe themselves – 44%.

Women make up just over 50% of the UK's population

Minority ethnic groups make up 8%, of which 2% are black and 4% of Asian origin.

People over pensionable age – 18.5%.

Christian – 77%, but an increasing minority (16%) has no religious affiliation. Muslims represent the largest religious minority at 3%.

19% of the population have a long term disability.

Approximately 5-7% of the UK population is gay, lesbian or bisexual.

37% of people say they are middle-class while 57% feel working-class.

Who 'belongs'?

% of people who believe members of different ethnic, racial or religious groups living in Britain are mostly or completely accepted as British by the majority of people in Britain:

Africans	22%
Americans	48%
Arabs	14%
Asians	28%
Christians	84%
Eastern Europeans	24%
Hindus	32%
Jews	55%
Muslims	27%
Non-religious people	62%
Oriental	35%
West Indians	28%
Western Europeans	44%

To what extent are different groups seen as having a common identity in Britain?

One way of judging whether people are fully accepted into society is to ask whether others see them as part of a common group – with shared interests – or as separate groups.

Women, black people and disabled people are likely to be seen as belonging to the mainstream culture. However, gay men and lesbians, people over 70 and

Muslims are viewed as belonging to groups which are separate from the mainstream.

This difference seems not to be based on ethnicity. It is more likely that the 'separateness' that people perceive has something to do with the lifestyle of these groups and the way in which they segregate themselves.

People were asked to assess the following 'threats':

"How do you think *'this group'* are affecting the customs, traditions or general way of life of other people in Britain?"

"How do you think the current situation for *'this group'* in this country affects things like the safety, security or health of other people in Britain?"

"On balance, do you think that *'this group'* take out more from the economy than they put in/put in more than they take out?"

The groups that people believe to pose a combination of threats seem likely to be regarded with contempt, anger, resentment and fear – this may result in prejudice and discrimination.

% who perceived 'threats' of different types from different minority groups within Britain

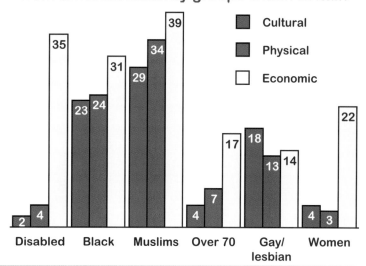

Legend:
- Cultural
- Physical
- Economic

Who is most prejudiced?

Prejudice against women. White respondents were less prejudiced (19%) than Black or Asian respondents (33%). Christian respondents were less prejudiced (16%) than non-Christian respondents (26%).

Prejudice against gay men and lesbians. Men (41%) were more prejudiced than women (33%), the over 70s were more prejudiced (41%) than the under 70s (32%). White respondents were less prejudiced (31%) than Black and Asian (60%) respondents.

Prejudice was also lower among Christian and non-religious people (30%) than among other religions (59%).

Prejudice against people over 70. Prejudice against older people was generally lower than 15%, but was higher among the under 30s (19%) than other age groups

(10%). It was also lower among Christian respondents (9%) than others (19%).

Prejudice against Muslims. Responses were similar across gender, sexuality and age groups. However, Whites were more prejudiced (37%) than Blacks and Asians (21%).

Prejudice against black people. Prejudice was higher among Whites (27%) than among Blacks and Asians (9%). It was also higher among Christians and non-religious people (26%) than among Muslims and other religions (20%). Disabled people were more prejudiced against Blacks (34%) than non-disabled people (23%).

Prejudice against disabled people. There were no group differences in prejudice against disabled people.

Level of prejudice felt towards different minority groups within Britain, %

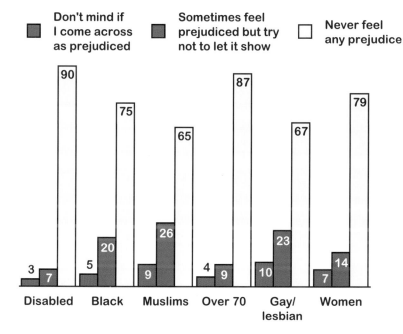

Legend:
- Don't mind if I come across as prejudiced
- Sometimes feel prejudiced but try not to let it show
- Never feel any prejudice

Source: Equality, Diversity and Prejudice in Britain, British Social Attitudes

Victimisation and equality

The Metropolitan Police reported 11,799 incidents of racist and religious hate crime and 1,359 incidents of homophobic hate crime between 2005-06. Nationally, however, the police recorded 50,000 such incidents between 2005-06.

The British Crime Survey, based on interviews with a wide sample of people which picks up unreported crimes, indicated that there were 260,000 such offences.

Most racist and religious hate crime, and as much as 90% of homophobic crime, goes unreported.

Adults from a mixed race or Asian background are more likely than those from other ethnic groups to be victims of crime in England and Wales.

Age Concern England reports that 890,000 people over the age of 50 who are out of work want a job.

One third of people with disabilities are living below the poverty line.

Only 19.8% of MPs are female and only 11% of Board Members of top companies.

http://www.kent.ac.uk
http://www.homeoffice.gov.uk

Comfort zone

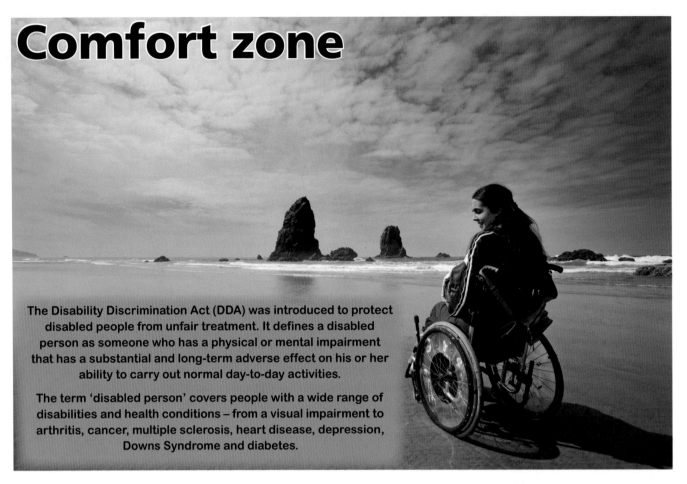

The Disability Discrimination Act (DDA) was introduced to protect disabled people from unfair treatment. It defines a disabled person as someone who has a physical or mental impairment that has a substantial and long-term adverse effect on his or her ability to carry out normal day-to-day activities.

The term 'disabled person' covers people with a wide range of disabilities and health conditions – from a visual impairment to arthritis, cancer, multiple sclerosis, heart disease, depression, Downs Syndrome and diabetes.

How much prejudice do you think there is against different types of disabled people
(percentages)

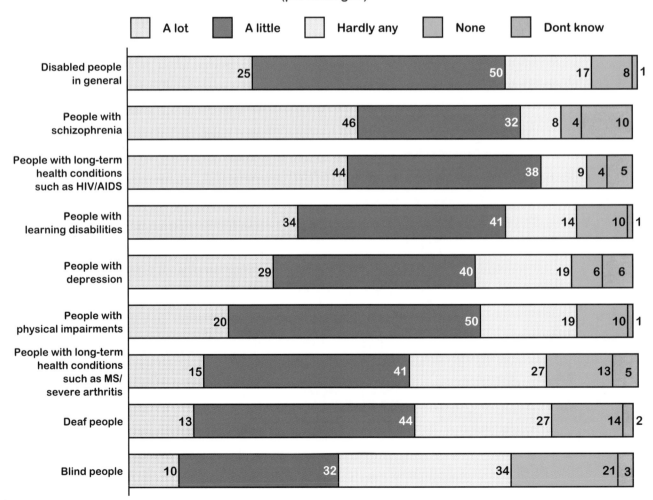

	A lot	A little	Hardly any	None	Dont know
Disabled people in general	25	50	17	8	1
People with schizophrenia	46	32	8	4	10
People with long-term health conditions such as HIV/AIDS	44	38	9	4	5
People with learning disabilities	34	41	14	10	1
People with depression	29	40	19	6	6
People with physical impairments	20	50	19	10	1
People with long-term health conditions such as MS/ severe arthritis	15	41	27	13	5
Deaf people	13	44	27	14	2
Blind people	10	32	34	21	3

People who thought that there was prejudice in society were also likely to be uncomfortable around disabled people.

Responses varied according to the condition. Asked if they would feel comfortable if someone with various disabilities moved in next door, 89% responded positively to someone who uses a wheelchair, 79% to someone who is blind and 83% to someone who is deaf.

People felt least comfortable about those with mental health conditions. Only 44% would feel comfortable with a neighbour suffering from depression and only 29% would be comfortable if the condition was schizophrenia.

Generally speaking, the closer the relationship or the more contact someone would have with a disabled person, the less comfortable they would feel, as can be seen from the figures for marriage to a close relative.

Q How comfortable would respondent feel if someone disabled married a close relative

	Very comfortable %	Fairly comfortable %	Fairly uncomfortable %	Very uncomfortable %	Don't know %
Someone who cannot hear without a hearing aid	62	34	4	1	1
Someone who uses a wheelchair	59	32	7	1	1
Someone who is blind	51	39	7	2	1
Someone with a long-term health condition such as MS or severe arthritis	21	48	24	5	2
Someone who has a diagnosis of schizophrenia	19	38	26	14	3
Someone who had a diagnosis of depression	14	41	35	8	3

24% of people think most disabled people should expect to work rather than rely on benefits yet 3 out of 5 employers readily admit they would not employ someone with a history of mental illness.

There are over 10 million disabled people in Britain, 6.8 million of whom are of working age – 1 in 5 of the total working population.

Only 50% of disabled people of working age are in employment compared to 81% of non-disabled people.

1 million disabled people without a job want to work.

The average gross hourly pay of disabled employees is 10% less than that of non-disabled employees (£9.36 per hour compared to £10.39 per hour).

28% of British workers believed their boss would be unlikely to help them keep their job if they became disabled.

Disabled people with mental health problems have the lowest employment rates of all impairment categories, at only 20%.

Only 17% of people with learning disabilities are in paid work.

Source: Attitudes towards and perception of disabled people – Findings from a module included in the 2005 British Social Attitudes Survey, Disability Rights Commission

http://www.drc-gb.org
http://www.direct.gov.uk

Faithful few?

53% of UK adults belong to the Christian religion. 6% belong to other faiths and 39% say they have no religion

Church attendance in the UK 2006

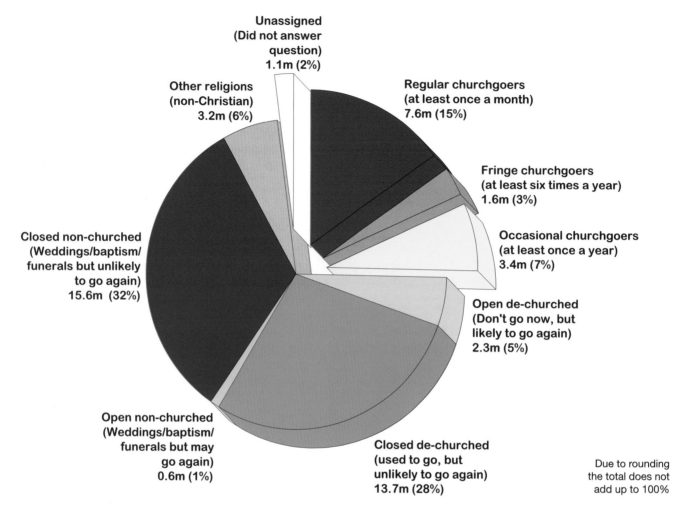

Unassigned (Did not answer question)
1.1m (2%)

Other religions (non-Christian)
3.2m (6%)

Regular churchgoers (at least once a month)
7.6m (15%)

Fringe churchgoers (at least six times a year)
1.6m (3%)

Occasional churchgoers (at least once a year)
3.4m (7%)

Closed non-churched (Weddings/baptism/funerals but unlikely to go again)
15.6m (32%)

Open de-churched (Don't go now, but likely to go again)
2.3m (5%)

Open non-churched (Weddings/baptism/funerals but may go again)
0.6m (1%)

Closed de-churched (used to go, but unlikely to go again)
13.7m (28%)

Due to rounding the total does not add up to 100%

Base:
A representative poll of 7,000 UK adults took place in 2006

Go to church at least:

Once a week or more	10.0%
Less often but at least once in two weeks	2.2%
Less often but at least once a month	3.2%
Less often but at least six times a year	3.4%
Less often but at least twice a year	4.1%
Less often but at least once a year	2.8%
Less often than once a year	5.0%
Varies too much to say	1.4%
Never or practically never	58.7%
Refused to answer/don't know	2.8%
Adults belonging to other religions	6.4%

Characteristics of a UK
Christian churchgoer, 2006

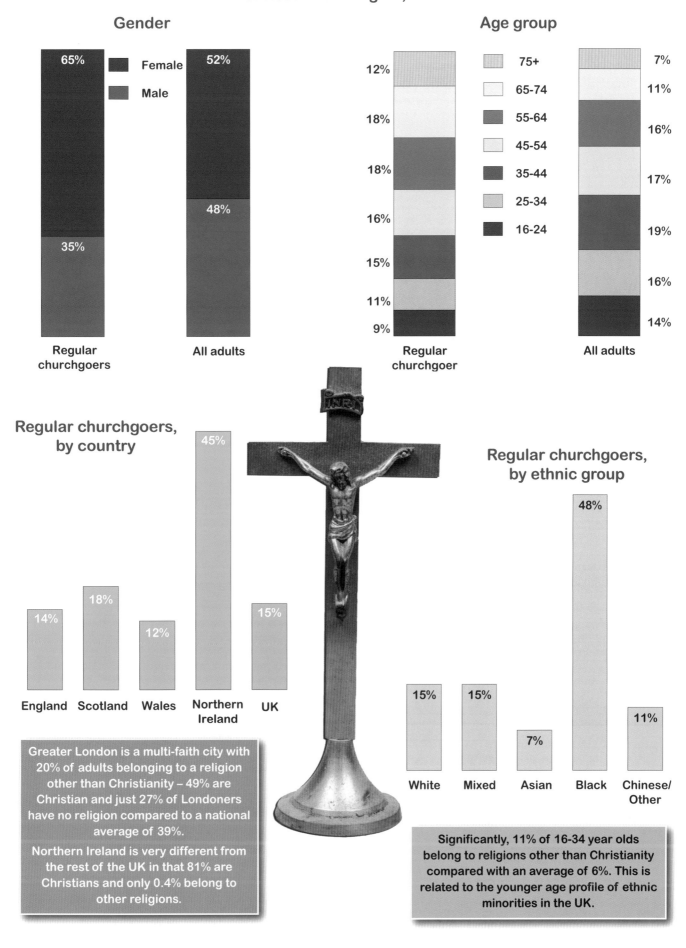

Gender

Regular churchgoers
- 65% Female
- 35% Male

All adults
- 52% Female
- 48% Male

Age group

Legend:
- 75+
- 65-74
- 55-64
- 45-54
- 35-44
- 25-34
- 16-24

Regular churchgoer
- 12%
- 18%
- 18%
- 16%
- 15%
- 11%
- 9%

All adults
- 7%
- 11%
- 16%
- 17%
- 19%
- 16%
- 14%

Regular churchgoers, by country

- England 14%
- Scotland 18%
- Wales 12%
- Northern Ireland 45%
- UK 15%

Greater London is a multi-faith city with 20% of adults belonging to a religion other than Christianity – 49% are Christian and just 27% of Londoners have no religion compared to a national average of 39%.

Northern Ireland is very different from the rest of the UK in that 81% are Christians and only 0.4% belong to other religions.

Regular churchgoers, by ethnic group

- White 15%
- Mixed 15%
- Asian 7%
- Black 48%
- Chinese/Other 11%

Significantly, 11% of 16-34 year olds belong to religions other than Christianity compared with an average of 6%. This is related to the younger age profile of ethnic minorities in the UK.

Source: Churchgoing in the UK, Tearfund charity 2007

http://www.tearfund.org

Homophobia

A survey of gay men found they were often subject to verbal abuse and physical assault

Q In the last 12 months have you been physically attacked or verbally abused because of your sexuality? (percentages)

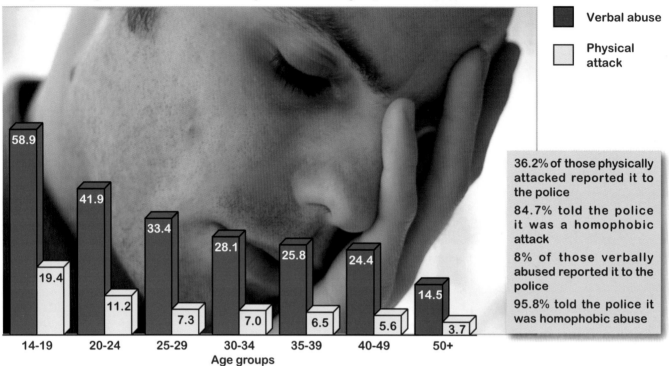

- ■ Verbal abuse
- □ Physical attack

14-19: 58.9 / 19.4
20-24: 41.9 / 11.2
25-29: 33.4 / 7.3
30-34: 28.1 / 7.0
35-39: 25.8 / 6.5
40-49: 24.4 / 5.6
50+: 14.5 / 3.7

Age groups

36.2% of those physically attacked reported it to the police

84.7% told the police it was a homophobic attack

8% of those verbally abused reported it to the police

95.8% told the police it was homophobic abuse

Q Why did you NOT report the homophobic hate crime to the police? (percentages)

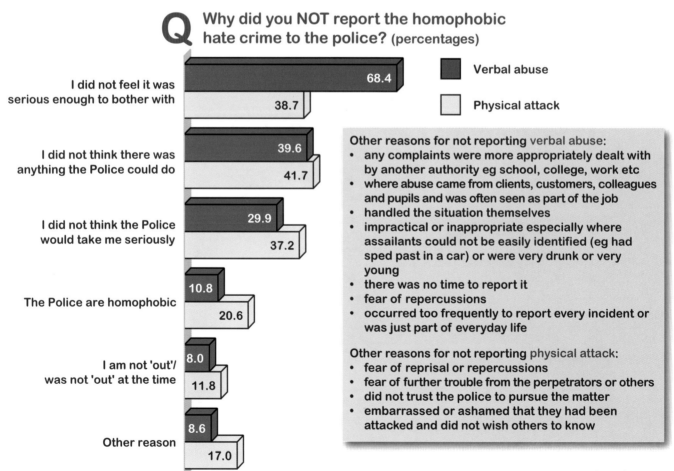

- ■ Verbal abuse
- □ Physical attack

I did not feel it was serious enough to bother with: 68.4 / 38.7

I did not think there was anything the Police could do: 39.6 / 41.7

I did not think the Police would take me seriously: 29.9 / 37.2

The Police are homophobic: 10.8 / 20.6

I am not 'out'/ was not 'out' at the time: 8.0 / 11.8

Other reason: 8.6 / 17.0

Other reasons for not reporting verbal abuse:
- any complaints were more appropriately dealt with by another authority eg school, college, work etc
- where abuse came from clients, customers, colleagues and pupils and was often seen as part of the job
- handled the situation themselves
- impractical or inappropriate especially where assailants could not be easily identified (eg had sped past in a car) or were very drunk or very young
- there was no time to report it
- fear of repercussions
- occurred too frequently to report every incident or was just part of everyday life

Other reasons for not reporting physical attack:
- fear of reprisal or repercussions
- fear of further trouble from the perpetrators or others
- did not trust the police to pursue the matter
- embarrassed or ashamed that they had been attacked and did not wish others to know

Base: Over 16,426, UK men aged 14 years and over

Source: Consuming Passions, Findings from the United Kingdom Gay Men's Sex Survey 2005
http://www.sigmaresearch.org.uk

Dicey business

Problem gambling is a cause for concern. Around 284,000 (0.6%) adults in Britain are seen as problem gamblers. 2.2% of men and 0.4% of women admit to being preoccupied with gambling, 0.4% of adults have tried but failed to cut back on gambling while 0.5% have relied on others to help with a financial crisis caused by gambling.

GamCare is a registered charity, offering advice and practical help in addressing the social impact of gambling.

They provide a Helpline (tel: 0845 600133) to support problem gamblers and their families. 30,247 calls were made to the Helpline in 2006, a 33.9% increase on 2005.

Main gambling location of GamCare callers, 2006
(% using each location)

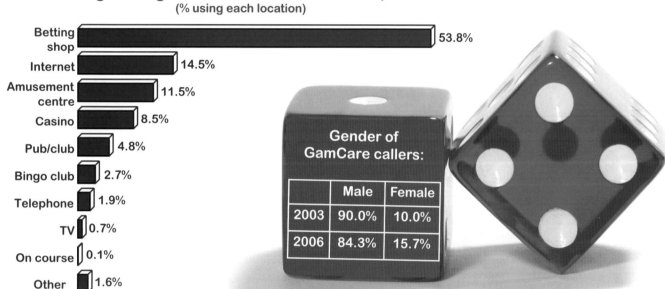

Location	%
Betting shop	53.8%
Internet	14.5%
Amusement centre	11.5%
Casino	8.5%
Pub/club	4.8%
Bingo club	2.7%
Telephone	1.9%
TV	0.7%
On course	0.1%
Other	1.6%

Gender of GamCare callers:

	Male	Female
2003	90.0%	10.0%
2006	84.3%	15.7%

Age of GamCare callers

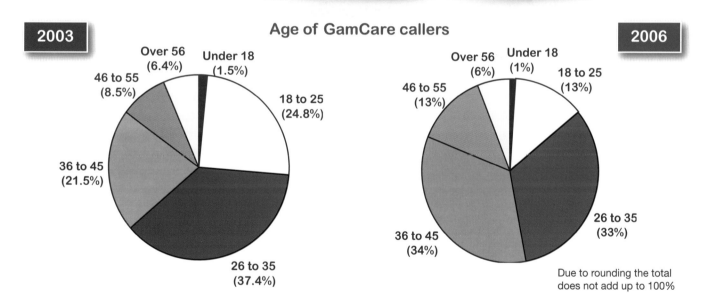

2003

- Over 56 (6.4%)
- Under 18 (1.5%)
- 46 to 55 (8.5%)
- 18 to 25 (24.8%)
- 36 to 45 (21.5%)
- 26 to 35 (37.4%)

2006

- Over 56 (6%)
- Under 18 (1%)
- 46 to 55 (13%)
- 18 to 25 (13%)
- 36 to 45 (34%)
- 26 to 35 (33%)

Due to rounding the total does not add up to 100%

In 2007, about 32m adults aged 16+ had participated in some form of gambling activity within the past year. Men were more likely than women to gamble, 71% compared with 65%. 6% used the internet to gamble in the past year.

Some experts estimate that in 2008 the amount lost by British gamblers will exceed £10bn.

This increase which amounts to 50% over nine years, has come about because of a relaxation in gambling regulations and the emergence of online gambling.

The most worrying trend is in the use of touch screen roulette games in betting shops. These tend to be addictive – one in nine people who played these were classified as problem gamblers and one in four calls to GamCare were about the machines.

It is estimated that there are 24,500 roulette terminals in the UK, taking £650m a year.

Source: Care services report 2003 & 2006, GamCare
Survey data on remote gambling participation, Gambling Commission 2007

http://www.gamcare.org.uk
http://www.gamblingcommission.gov.uk

Alco-teens

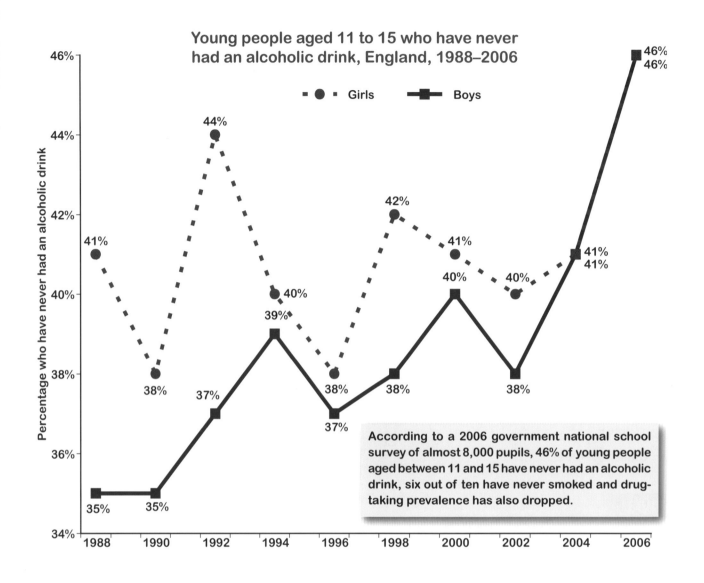

Young people aged 11 to 15 who have never had an alcoholic drink, England, 1988–2006

- ● - Girls   ■— Boys

Percentage who have never had an alcoholic drink

Girls: 41% (1988), 38% (1990), 44% (1992), 40% (1994), 38% (1996), 42% (1998), 41% (2000), 40% (2002), 41% (2004), 46% (2006)

Boys: 35% (1988), 35% (1990), 37% (1992), 39% (1994), 37% (1996), 38% (1998), 40% (2000), 38% (2002), 41% (2004), 46% (2006)

According to a 2006 government national school survey of almost 8,000 pupils, 46% of young people aged between 11 and 15 have never had an alcoholic drink, six out of ten have never smoked and drug-taking prevalence has also dropped.

Recommended units of alcohol

Men: 3-4 units a day
Women: 2-3 units a day

Popular drinks	Units
A large (175 ml) glass of red wine	2
A bottle of wine	8-9
A 330 ml bottle of 4-5% lager or cider	1.5
A pint of 5% export lager	3
A bottle of alcopops	1.5
A can of strong 9% lager	4

Average units of alcohol consumption of those boys who had drunk in the previous week, by age group, 1996 and 2006

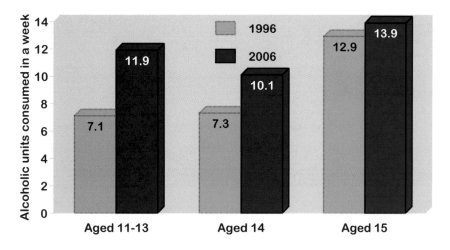

Legend: 1996 | 2006

Aged 11-13: 7.1 (1996), 11.9 (2006)
Aged 14: 7.3 (1996), 10.1 (2006)
Aged 15: 12.9 (1996), 13.9 (2006)

Y-axis: Alcoholic units consumed in a week

The law

It is against the law for anyone under 18 to buy alcohol in a pub, supermarket or other licensed outlet in the UK.

Under 5? It is illegal to give an alcoholic drink to a child under 5 except under medical supervision in an emergency.

Under 14? It is at the landlord's discretion as to whether children are allowed anywhere in a pub. They cannot buy or drink alcohol on the premises.

14 or 15? You can go anywhere in a pub, but cannot buy or drink alcohol.

Under 18? Adults are not allowed to buy alcohol on behalf of under 18s in a licensed premises. The only exception is for 16 or 17 year olds who are allowed to drink beer, wine or cider at a meal out with adults (but they may not buy the alcohol themselves).

It is legal for anyone over 5 to drink alcohol. The restrictions apply to purchasing (under 18) and location – on licensed premises or in alcohol exclusion zones.

Police have powers to confiscate alcohol from under 18s drinking in public spaces (eg in the street or in parks).

Average units of alcohol consumption of those girls who had drunk in the previous week, by age group, 1996 and 2006

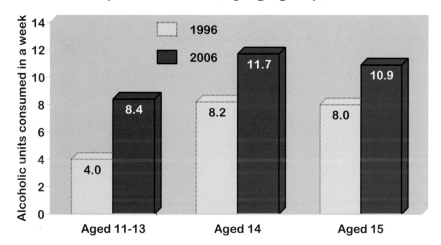

Legend: 1996 | 2006

Aged 11-13: 4.0 (1996), 8.4 (2006)
Aged 14: 8.2 (1996), 11.7 (2006)
Aged 15: 8.0 (1996), 10.9 (2006)

Y-axis: Alcoholic units consumed in a week

Source: Smoking, drinking and drug use among young people in England in 2006, The Information Centre for health and social care, Lifestyle statistics © Crown copyright

http://www.ic.nhs.uk
http://www.drinkingandyou.com

100 years of back street abortions

Before the 1967 Abortion Act women who wanted to end their pregnancies would have had to resort to self-induced or backstreet abortions

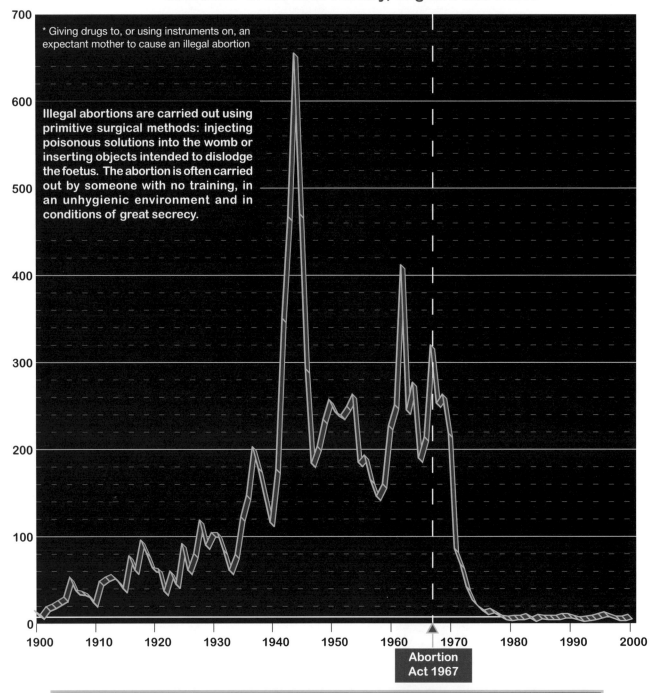

Recorded crime statistics for procuring illegal abortions* in the 20th century, England and Wales

* Giving drugs to, or using instruments on, an expectant mother to cause an illegal abortion

Illegal abortions are carried out using primitive surgical methods: injecting poisonous solutions into the womb or inserting objects intended to dislodge the foetus. The abortion is often carried out by someone with no training, in an unhygienic environment and in conditions of great secrecy.

Abortion
Act 1967

The figures in the graph are for the crime of procuring an illegal abortion, however in 1966 it was estimated that 100,000-150,000 illegal abortions were being carried out each year.

Widespread injury and infection often led to infertility and other permanent health problems, and death by blood poisoning or bleeding was not uncommon.

In the early 1960s 40 women a year in the UK died from the complications of unsafe abortion.

Source: Recorded Crime Statistics 1898–2005/06, Home Office ©
Crown copyright 2006, Education for Choice

http://www.homeoffice.gov.uk
http://www.efc.org.uk

Changing attitudes?

Legend

- **Agree very strongly**
- **Agree strongly**
- **Agree**
- **Neither agree nor disagree**
- **Disagree**
- **Disagree strongly**
- **Disagree very strongly**
- **No opinion**

Q: Should abortion be made legally available for all who want it (%)

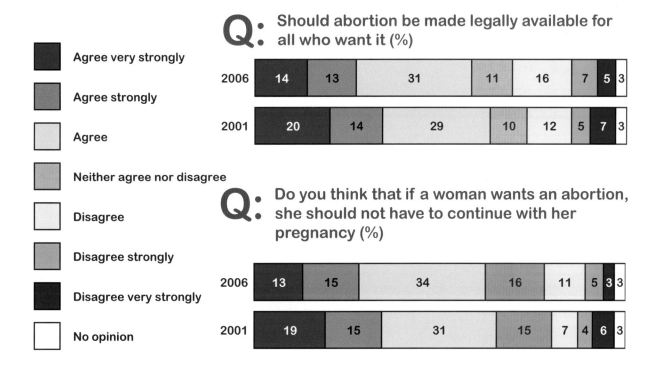

Year	Agree very strongly	Agree strongly	Agree	Neither	Disagree	Disagree strongly	Disagree very strongly	No opinion
2006	14	13	31	11	16	7	5	3
2001	20	14	29	10	12	5	7	3

Q: Do you think that if a woman wants an abortion, she should not have to continue with her pregnancy (%)

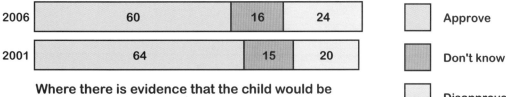

Year	Agree very strongly	Agree strongly	Agree	Neither	Disagree	Disagree strongly	Disagree very strongly	No opinion
2006	13	15	34	16	11	5	3	3
2001	19	15	31	15	7	4	6	3

Q: Do you approve or disapprove of abortion under the following circumstances: (%)

Where the woman is under 16

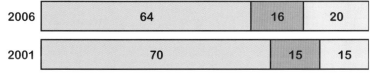

Year	Approve	Don't know	Disapprove
2006	60	16	24
2001	64	15	20

Approve
Don't know
Disapprove

Where there is evidence that the child would be born with serious learning difficulties

Year	Approve	Don't know	Disapprove
2006	55	17	28
2001	64	15	21

Where there is evidence that the child would be born with serious physical disabilities

Year	Approve	Don't know	Disapprove
2006	64	16	20
2001	70	15	15

Where a woman does not wish to have a child

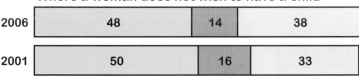

Year	Approve	Don't know	Disapprove
2006	48	14	38
2001	50	16	33

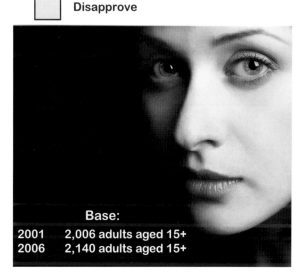

Base:
2001   2,006 adults aged 15+
2006   2,140 adults aged 15+

NB Totals may not add up to 100% due to rounding

Source: Attitudes to Abortion, Ipsos MORI, 2006
http://www.ipsos-mori.com/

Tired traditions

There is extensive debate about what it means to be British and where,
if anywhere, our loyalties lie.

In 2007, a sample of 2,359 British people were asked which traditions they felt were
outdated and they would be prepared to give up.

Q What traditional British customs would you give up?

Custom	%
Watching the Queen's speech	62%
Going to church on Sundays	60%
Rivalry with France/Germany	51%
Fried breakfast	45%
Pints of beer	32%
Sunday lunch	29%
Talking about the weather	26%
Cup of tea	20%
Trip to the seaside	14%

Q Where do your loyalties lie?

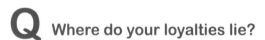

Under 25s   Over 55s

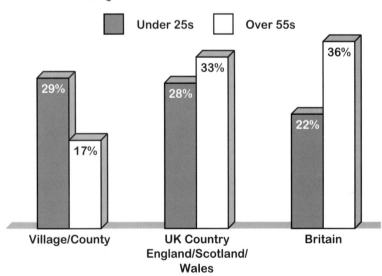

	Under 25s	Over 55s
Village/County	29%	17%
UK Country England/Scotland/Wales	28%	33%
Britain	22%	36%

◊ 49% of Scots define their loyalties to their country

◊ the Welsh were broadly split between loyalty to the Welsh dragon and the Union Jack (32% vs 30%)

◊ in England people were relatively more likely to claim loyalty to Britain or their county – but not England

◊ when it comes to national identity, less than a third (30%) defined themselves first of all as British. Their allegiance is more likely to be to their UK country if they are over 55 or to a smaller locality – region, town or county – if they are under 25

Within English regions, loyalty to the local community was stronger the further from London people lived. Regions with the greatest sense of community, identity and loyalty were the North East (32%), Yorkshire (30%) and the South West (27%).

Source: YouGov survey for Combined Insurance 2007
http://www.combinedinsurance.co.uk

Education

School stress

The number of teachers taking sick leave rose to 57% in 2006. Most teachers blame stress

In a survey of teachers in England and Wales, 57% of respondents said that pressure to improve attainment is having a negative effect on their wellbeing.

Teachers and teaching assistants in primary and secondary schools in England, 2001-2007
(thousands)

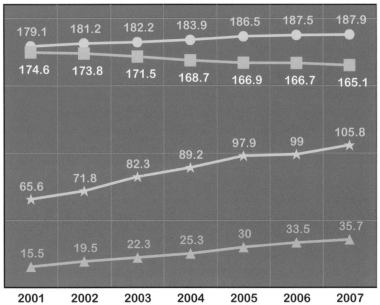

Secondary teachers: 179.1, 181.2, 182.2, 183.9, 186.5, 187.5, 187.9

Nursery & primary teachers: 174.6, 173.8, 171.5, 168.7, 166.9, 166.7, 165.1

Nursery & primary teaching assistants: 65.6, 71.8, 82.3, 89.2, 97.9, 99, 105.8

Secondary teaching assistants: 15.5, 19.5, 22.3, 25.3, 30, 33.5, 35.7

Years: 2001 2002 2003 2004 2005 2006 2007

NB includes special needs and ethnic minority support staff

The number of regular teachers fell by 600 while the total number of support staff rose by 17,900

In a poll, 61% of teachers said they felt stressed as a result of teaching, even when not in school, while 48% stated they experienced stress during lesson time.

Teachers are also working long hours, with 13% of all teachers – rising to 18% of teachers at independent schools – working on average seven hours longer a week than the European stipulated allowance.

The research also revealed:

» 60% of teachers blamed stress at school on the amount of administration expected of them

» 49% of secondary teachers felt stressed in the classroom as a result of pupils using electronic gadgets during lessons

» 44% of teachers blamed stress during lessons on large class sizes

» 38% of teachers blamed stress on poor resources in the classroom

» 37% of all primary teachers felt stressed as a result of unreasonable interference from parents within school

Number of teachers taking sickness absence, England

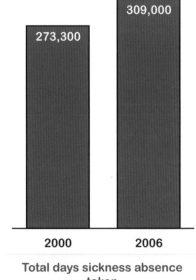

2000: 273,300
2006: 309,000

Total days sickness absence taken	
2000	2,694,400
2006	2,880,400

Source: Department for Education and Skills, School workforce in England January 2007 © Crown copyright 2007, Teacher Support Network

http://www.dfes.gov.uk/rsgateway
http://www.teachersupport.info/

Dress code

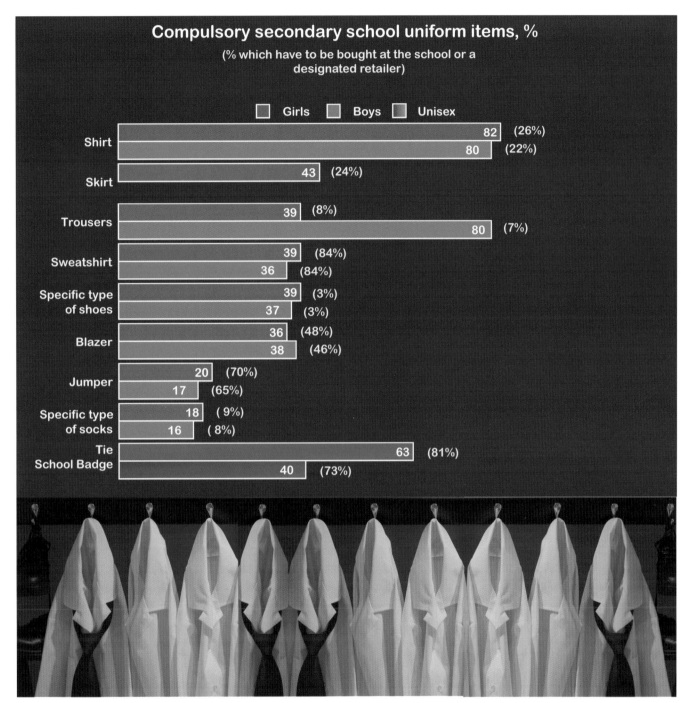

Compulsory secondary school uniform items, %

(% which have to be bought at the school or a designated retailer)

☐ Girls   ☐ Boys   ☐ Unisex

Shirt	82 (26%)	80 (22%)
Skirt	43 (24%)	
Trousers	39 (8%)	80 (7%)
Sweatshirt	39 (84%)	36 (84%)
Specific type of shoes	39 (3%)	37 (3%)
Blazer	36 (48%)	38 (46%)
Jumper	20 (70%)	17 (65%)
Specific type of socks	18 (9%)	16 (8%)
Tie School Badge	63 (81%)	40 (73%)

The vast majority (82%) of State schools in the UK specify that their pupils must wear a uniform of some kind.

84% of schools with uniforms impose restrictions on choice of supplier for some uniform items.

Compulsory uniform items supplied by designated retailers or schools themselves tend to be on average 23% more expensive than from general retailers.

Supermarkets offer the lowest prices, meaning restricted outlets can cost on average 150% more, 108% for primary school items and 173% for secondary school items.

Some larger supermarkets are now selling a complete uniform for as little as £13.96 for 10-12 year olds.

If all secondary uniform items could be purchased from supermarkets, parents could save approximately £27 a year. Over the school life of a child this could equate to £200.

Compulsory items can vary largely in price:
- girls' shirts/blouses £1.75 to £18.00
- boys' trousers £4.00 to £27.00
- girls' blazers £8.00 to £50.99
- boys' blazers £6.00 to £53.00

A third of schools with a designated retailer benefit financially from this. When the school supplies the uniform it makes marginally higher profits than those received through exclusive retailer contracts.

Source: Office of Fair Trading, Supply of School Uniforms review © Crown copyright 2006

http://www.oft.gov.uk

Excluded

The number of fixed period exclusions in secondary schools rose by 4% to 343,840 last year. Pupils with Special Education Needs (SEN) statements are three times more likely to be excluded

A fixed period exclusion means that a pupil is excluded from school but remains on the register because they are expected to return when the exclusion period is completed.

A permanent exclusion means that a pupils' name is removed from the school register. In 2005/06 there were 7,990 permanent exclusions.

Boys account for nearly four-fifths of all permanent exclusions, with pupils aged 12-14 most likely to be excluded. Certain ethnic groups are more likely to be excluded.

Pupils with special educational needs include those with moderate and severe learning difficulties, specific learning difficulties (such as dyslexia) and profound and multiple learning difficulties which are often combined with a physical disability or medical condition.

Pupils with special educational needs may need extra help in areas such as: learning, communicating and relating to others, behaviour, being able to move around school.

If the LEA believes a school can cater for a pupil's special educational needs they will not issue an SEN statement.

Number of fixed period exclusions in maintained secondary schools 2005/06, England

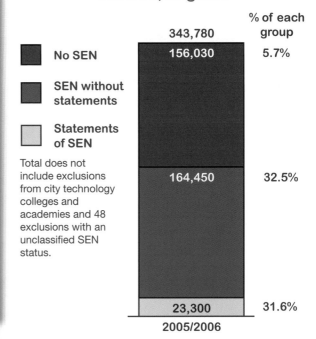

343,780

% of each group

- ■ No SEN
- ■ SEN without statements
- □ Statements of SEN

Total does not include exclusions from city technology colleges and academies and 48 exclusions with an unclassified SEN status.

156,030	5.7%
164,450	32.5%
23,300	31.6%

2005/2006

Reasons for fixed period exclusion, England 2005/06

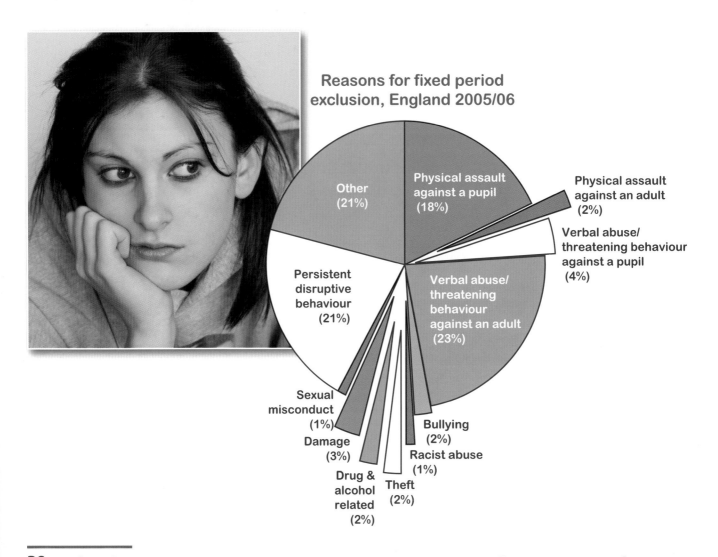

- Other (21%)
- Physical assault against a pupil (18%)
- Physical assault against an adult (2%)
- Verbal abuse/ threatening behaviour against a pupil (4%)
- Persistent disruptive behaviour (21%)
- Verbal abuse/ threatening behaviour against an adult (23%)
- Sexual misconduct (1%)
- Damage (3%)
- Drug & alcohol related (2%)
- Theft (2%)
- Bullying (2%)
- Racist abuse (1%)

Fixed period exclusions, maintained secondary schools, % of each ethnic group and gender excluded, 2005/06, England

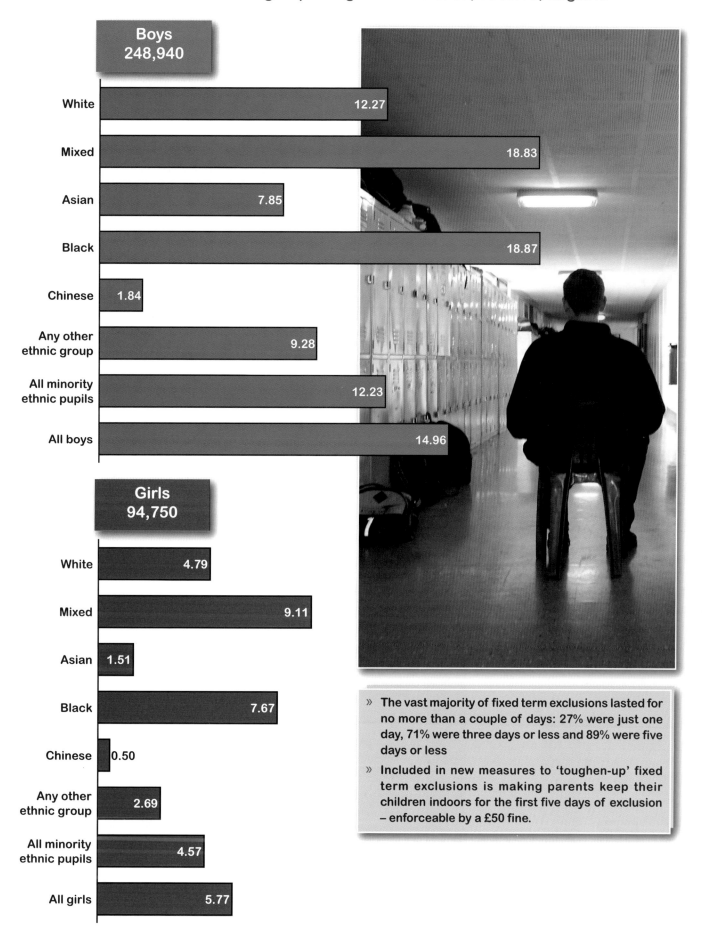

Boys 248,940

	%
White	12.27
Mixed	18.83
Asian	7.85
Black	18.87
Chinese	1.84
Any other ethnic group	9.28
All minority ethnic pupils	12.23
All boys	14.96

Girls 94,750

	%
White	4.79
Mixed	9.11
Asian	1.51
Black	7.67
Chinese	0.50
Any other ethnic group	2.69
All minority ethnic pupils	4.57
All girls	5.77

» The vast majority of fixed term exclusions lasted for no more than a couple of days: 27% were just one day, 71% were three days or less and 89% were five days or less

» Included in new measures to 'toughen-up' fixed term exclusions is making parents keep their children indoors for the first five days of exclusion – enforceable by a £50 fine.

Source: Department for Education & Skills © Crown copyright 2007

http://www.dfes.gov.uk
http://www.direct.gov.uk

Class distinction

The social class attainment gap at GCSE is measured by the difference between those eligible/not eligible for free school meals

The social class attainment gap at Key Stage 4 (as measured by percentage point difference of those eligible/not eligible for free schools meals) is three times as wide as the gender gap. Some minority ethnic groups attain significantly below the national average and their under-achievement is much greater than the gap between boys and girls. Social class and ethnicity appear to have a greater impact on achievement than gender, yet within these subgroups, girls still perform better than boys.

% of pupils gaining 5+ A*-C GCSEs, by Free Schools Meals (FSM), gender and ethnicity, England, 2006

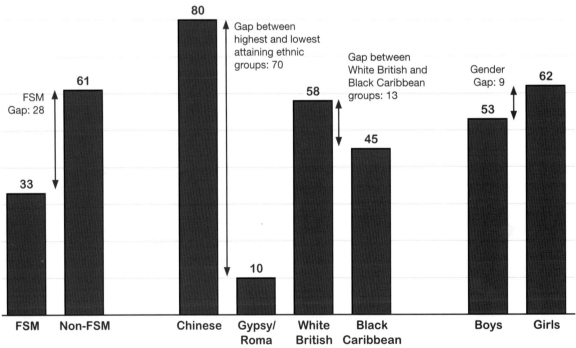

Gap between highest and lowest attaining ethnic groups: 70

Gap between White British and Black Caribbean groups: 13

Gender Gap: 9

FSM Gap: 28

- FSM: 33
- Non-FSM: 61
- Chinese: 80
- Gypsy/Roma: 10
- White British: 58
- Black Caribbean: 45
- Boys: 53
- Girls: 62

% of FSM pupils gaining 5+ A*-C GCSEs, by gender and ethnicity, England, (2006)

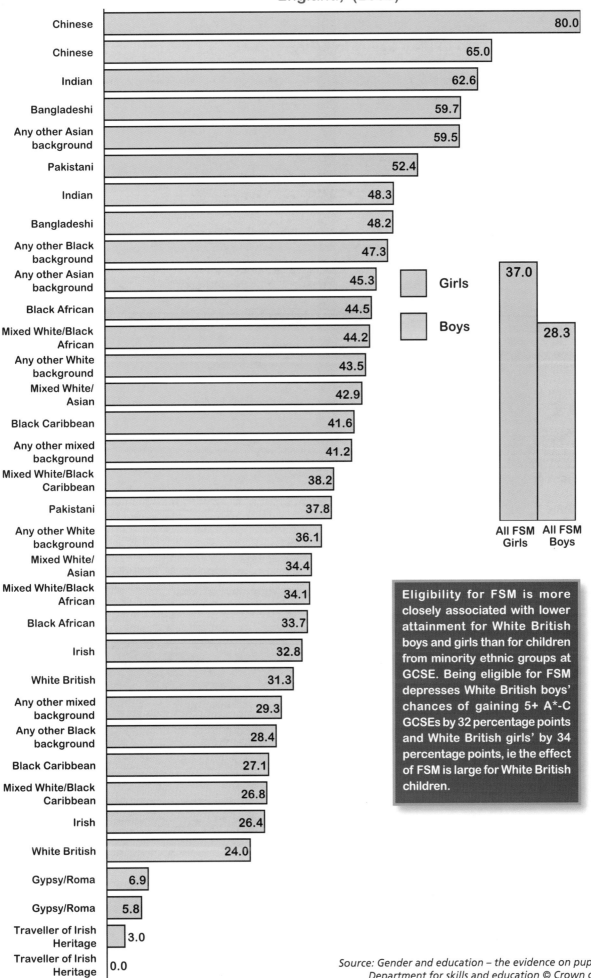

Ethnicity	%
Chinese	80.0
Chinese	65.0
Indian	62.6
Bangladeshi	59.7
Any other Asian background	59.5
Pakistani	52.4
Indian	48.3
Bangladeshi	48.2
Any other Black background	47.3
Any other Asian background	45.3
Black African	44.5
Mixed White/Black African	44.2
Any other White background	43.5
Mixed White/Asian	42.9
Black Caribbean	41.6
Any other mixed background	41.2
Mixed White/Black Caribbean	38.2
Pakistani	37.8
Any other White background	36.1
Mixed White/Asian	34.4
Mixed White/Black African	34.1
Black African	33.7
Irish	32.8
White British	31.3
Any other mixed background	29.3
Any other Black background	28.4
Black Caribbean	27.1
Mixed White/Black Caribbean	26.8
Irish	26.4
White British	24.0
Gypsy/Roma	6.9
Gypsy/Roma	5.8
Traveller of Irish Heritage	3.0
Traveller of Irish Heritage	0.0

Girls
Boys

All FSM Girls: 37.0
All FSM Boys: 28.3

Eligibility for FSM is more closely associated with lower attainment for White British boys and girls than for children from minority ethnic groups at GCSE. Being eligible for FSM depresses White British boys' chances of gaining 5+ A*-C GCSEs by 32 percentage points and White British girls' by 34 percentage points, ie the effect of FSM is large for White British children.

Source: Gender and education – the evidence on pupils in England, Department for skills and education © Crown copyright 2007
http://www.dfes.gov.uk

High achievers

Chinese girls achieved the best GCSE results in 2006. Both gender and ethnicity seem to play a part in achievement

Students getting five or more Grade A*-C GCSEs including Maths and English, 2006, %

Boys   Girls

Ethnicity	Boys	Girls
Chinese	59.2	72.0
Mixed background: White and Asian	55.8	62.5
Indian	54.0	64.2
Irish	46.2	53.4
Other Asian background	43.1	60.5
Other White background	42.2	51.0
Other Mixed background	40.9	48.9
White British	40.2	48.2
Mixed background: White and Black African	38.4	47.2
Other ethnic group	37.1	46.2
Bangladeshi	35.1	42.1
Black African	31.3	43.0
Pakistani	30.4	38.8
Mixed background: White and Black Caribbean	27.4	37.3
Other Black background	24.7	38.1
Black Caribbean	22.5	35.7
Traveller (Irish heritage)	7.0	14.5
Gypsy / Roma	2.3	5.8
All pupils	39.7	48.0

Although results for 2006/07 have yet to be analysed, independent schools appear to have done particularly well.

Some reports have suggested that their success has been inflated by the significant number of pupils from China who make up 40% of all foreign students in independent schools.

Source: Department for Education and Skills: National Curriculum Assessment, GCSE and Equivalent Attainment and Post-16 Attainment by Pupil Characteristics in England 2005/06 © Crown copyright 2007

http://www.dfes.gov.uk

Learning on the job

Attitudes towards vocational qualifications, GB, %

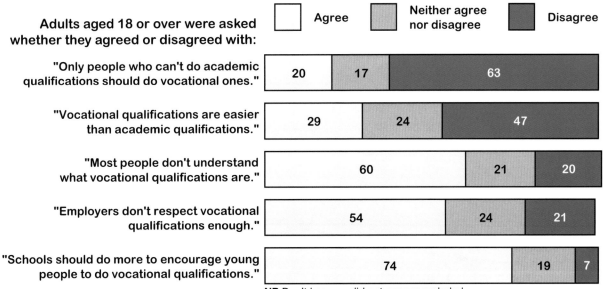

☐ Agree	☐ Neither agree nor disagree	■ Disagree

Adults aged 18 or over were asked whether they agreed or disagreed with:

"Only people who can't do academic qualifications should do vocational ones."
20 | 17 | 63

"Vocational qualifications are easier than academic qualifications."
29 | 24 | 47

"Most people don't understand what vocational qualifications are."
60 | 21 | 20

"Employers don't respect vocational qualifications enough."
54 | 24 | 21

"Schools should do more to encourage young people to do vocational qualifications."
74 | 19 | 7

NB Don't know or did not answer excluded
Figures do not add up to 100% due to rounding

16-24 year olds in work-based learning, by area of learning, England

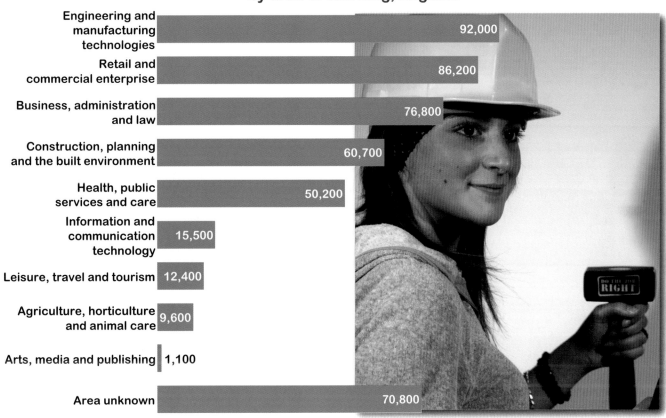

- Engineering and manufacturing technologies — 92,000
- Retail and commercial enterprise — 86,200
- Business, administration and law — 76,800
- Construction, planning and the built environment — 60,700
- Health, public services and care — 50,200
- Information and communication technology — 15,500
- Leisure, travel and tourism — 12,400
- Agriculture, horticulture and animal care — 9,600
- Arts, media and publishing — 1,100
- Area unknown — 70,800

Work-based learning for young people comprises:
Advanced Apprenticeships at NVQ level 3
Apprenticeships at NVQ level 2
NVQ Learning
Entry to Employment

Source: Office for National Statistics: Social Trends 2007
© Crown copyright 2007

http://www.statistics.gov.uk

Aim high

Higher education initial participation rate (HEIPR) for first-time participants aged 17-30 in higher education courses at UK institutions. England, 1999/00-2005/06, %

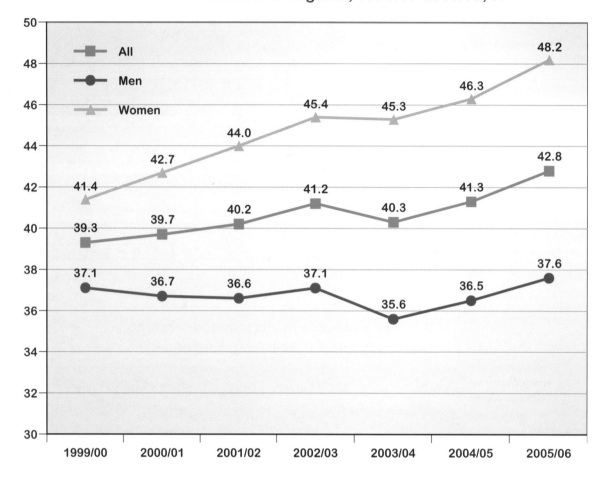

The HEIPR is the statistic that the Government uses to measure progress towards its target of 50% of those aged 18-30 entering Higher Education by 2010.

The HEIPR includes students who live in England and who study at UK universities. It also includes students on Higher Education courses (NVQ level 4) in Further Education colleges.

Source: Department for Education and Skills, Participation rates in higher education 1999/2000-2005/2006 © Crown copyright 2007

http://www.dfes.gov.uk

Why not apply?

Applications to university, by age, UK 2002-2006

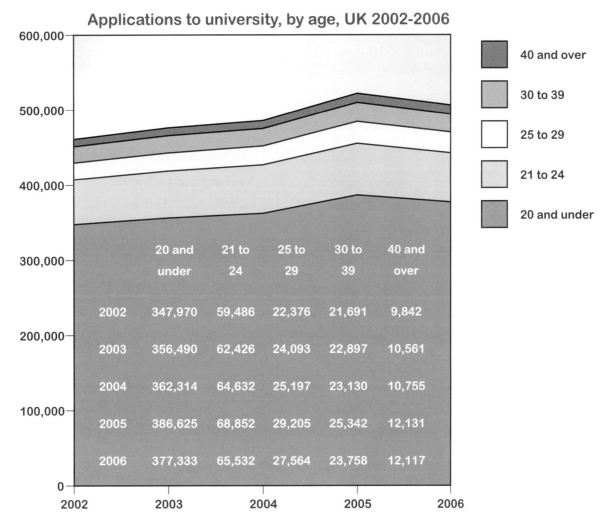

	20 and under	21 to 24	25 to 29	30 to 39	40 and over
2002	347,970	59,486	22,376	21,691	9,842
2003	356,490	62,426	24,093	22,897	10,561
2004	362,314	64,632	25,197	23,130	10,755
2005	386,625	68,852	29,205	25,342	12,131
2006	377,333	65,532	27,564	23,758	12,117

Legend: 40 and over, 30 to 39, 25 to 29, 21 to 24, 20 and under

Applications to university, by gender, UK 2002-2006

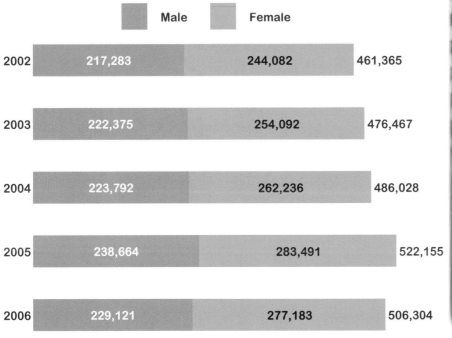

Male / Female

Year	Male	Female	Total
2002	217,283	244,082	461,365
2003	222,375	254,092	476,467
2004	223,792	262,236	486,028
2005	238,664	283,491	522,155
2006	229,121	277,183	506,304

Source: UCAS Data

http://www.ucas.com

Learning & earning

Although more women are attaining higher educational qualifications, they still earn less than their male counterparts

Level of highest qualification held by economically active adults, England 2006, %

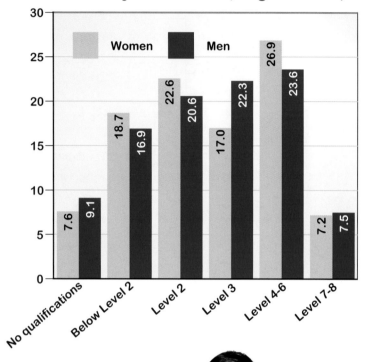

Legend: Women, Men

	Women	Men
No qualifications	7.6	9.1
Below Level 2	18.7	16.9
Level 2	22.6	20.6
Level 3	17.0	22.3
Level 4-6	26.9	23.6
Level 7-8	7.2	7.5

What do the levels mean?

Level 7-8: Higher degrees, postgraduate-level professional qualifications, NVQ level 5

Level 4-6: First or Foundation degrees, degree-level professional qualifications, NVQ level 4, teaching or nursing qualifications, HE diploma, HNC/HND or equivalent vocational qualification

Level 3: 2 A-levels grades A-E, 4 AS-levels grades A-E, Advanced GNVQ, NVQ level 3 or equivalent vocational qualification

Level 2: 5 GCSEs grades A*-C, Intermediate GNVQ, 2 AS-levels, NVQ level 2 or equivalent vocational qualification

Below level 2: One or two GCSEs but less than five A*-C or equivalent, BTEC general certificate, YT certificates, other RSA certificates, other City and Guilds Certificates or NVQ level 1. Key Skills and Basic Skills qualifications are also classified here

Trade apprenticeships fall between levels 2 and 3; in this graph they have been divided equally between the two levels.

Average gross hourly earnings of working-age full-time employees, England, 2006

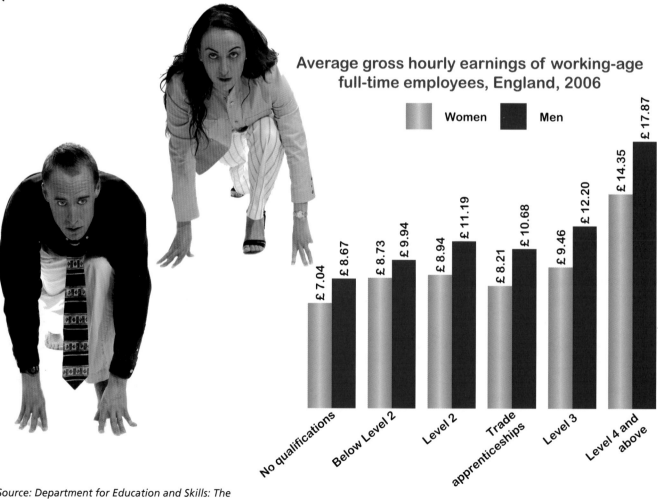

Legend: Women, Men

	Women	Men
No qualifications	£7.04	£8.67
Below Level 2	£8.73	£9.94
Level 2	£8.94	£11.19
Trade apprenticeships	£8.21	£10.68
Level 3	£9.46	£12.20
Level 4 and above	£14.35	£17.87

Source: Department for Education and Skills: The level of highest qualification held by adults in England 2006 © Crown copyright 2007

http://www.dfes.gov.uk
http://www.statistics.gov.uk

Environmental issues

Endangered

Polar Bear

Key Issues: Climate change and human/ wildlife conflict

Sea ice is a crucial hunting habitat for polar bears; without it, their numbers may fall by some 30% in the next 50 years. The polar bear's habitat is shrinking so fast that the summer sea ice, so critical to its survival, may disappear entirely by 2080. At this rate, the species could be extinct within 100 years.

Save energy and switch off lights when you don't need them, and don't leave the TV, computer or stereo on standby – switch them off!

Reduce your CO_2 emissions by using public transport, cycling or walking.

Try to use organic and environmentally friendly fertilisers and pesticides – organic gardening reduces pollution and is better for wildlife.

Giant Panda

Key Issues: Habitat loss, bamboo die-off, poaching and conversion of forests to farmland

Between 1974 and 1989, 50% of panda habitat was lost. There are now only around 1,600 giant pandas left in the world.

Take action – join WWF!

Bengal Tiger

Key Issues: Poaching, deforestation and habitat fragmentation

The tiger is now found only in small, isolated protected areas in Bangladesh, Bhutan, Burma, India and Nepal.

These areas are not large enough to sustain long-term, viable tiger populations and, since 1990, there has been a drastic, Asia-wide increase in tiger poaching. In the last 100 years, 94% of tigers disappeared and three subspecies became extinct.

If you use alternative Chinese homeopathic medicines read the label! These products often contain tiger bone and other ingredients from endangered species.

Asian Elephant

Key Issues: Human/wildlife conflict, habitat loss and poaching

There are only 30,000 Asian elephants in the wild. They share their habitat with a fifth of the world's human population.

Refuse to buy animal souvenirs when on holiday. If there are people willing to buy these goods then animals, like the elephant, will continue to be poached.

Orang-utan

Key Issues: Palm oil plantations, logging, and loss and fragmentation of habitat due to agricultural expansion

In the last 10 years, the orang-utan population has declined by 30-50%. Of the 44 forested areas inhabited by orang-utans registered in 1999, four have disappeared and five have been subjected to extensive logging. There are no orang-utans left in seven of the original 44 areas.

Look for the Forest Stewardship Council (FSC) logo when buying wood products – from paper to raw timber. This ensures the wood comes from well-managed forests. B&Q, The Body Shop, Boots the Chemist, Sainsbury's, Tesco, Homebase and many other stores all stock FSC-certified products.

Mountain Gorilla

Key Issues: Habitat loss and war

When you are going on holiday, on safari or visiting relatives around the world, if you must travel by air, think about reducing CO2 in other ways – air travel uses large amounts of fossil fuels and creates greenhouse gases which add to the serious impacts of climate change.

And if you have flown for a holiday this year, think about cutting down on work air travel, or taking your next holiday in the UK.

Photo: The Gorilla Organisation (formerly the Dian Fossey Gorilla Fund)

Hyacinth Macaw

Key Issues: Habitat destruction and capture for the pet trade

The species is very sensitive to changes in its habitat. For example, 95% of nests in the Pantanal wetland of Brazil are in a single type of tree, the manduvi, making them particularly vulnerable to human activities. Populations once numbered hundreds of thousands but now there are just 6,500 in the wild, of which 5,000 are found in just one region of Brazil.

Try to ensure that you buy responsible soya products which promote the economically viable and environmentally sustainable production of soy.

Leatherback Turtle

Key Issues: Unsustainable fishing practices and poaching

The species has declined by more than 95% in the last 20 years. Part of the cause is the often unintentional killing of marine turtles on hooks and nets set by fishermen. This is compounded by harvesting turtles and their eggs for food by coastal communities. Development along shore areas also creates light pollution that can seriously disorient young hatchlings on their way to the sea. Turtle numbers have plummeted to the point where fewer than 2,000 females are now found in the eastern Pacific Ocean.

When buying fish, look out for 'eco-labelling' such as the Marine Stewardship Council (MSC) logo wherever possible as this means that it is certified as being sourced from sustainable, well managed fisheries. If possible try to buy local fish.

Source: WWF
http://extinct.wwf.org.uk/species/index.htm
http://www.gorillas.org

Trading in danger

The legal trade in wildlife products worldwide is worth 239.5 billion euros but the illegal trade is probably worth much more

The trade in wildlife covers not only live animals but also animal and plant resources, extracts used in medicine and perfume, natural ornamental products and timber.

Trade can be a significant threat to species and environments – but it can sometimes be a benefit. If products have a high value the legal trade can be an incentive to local people to protect the species and the environment, to maintain trade. Illegal trade, however, generates huge profits for traders, who are prepared to wipe out species and habitats.

The legal trade is controlled by CITES (the Convention on International Trade in Endangered Species) which lists 30,000 species as protected whether they are traded alive, dead or as parts – such as ivory or leather – or as products such as medicines.

The EU and USA are major importing regions for CITES listed species.

Where the wildlife products are going, in major categories, 2000-2005

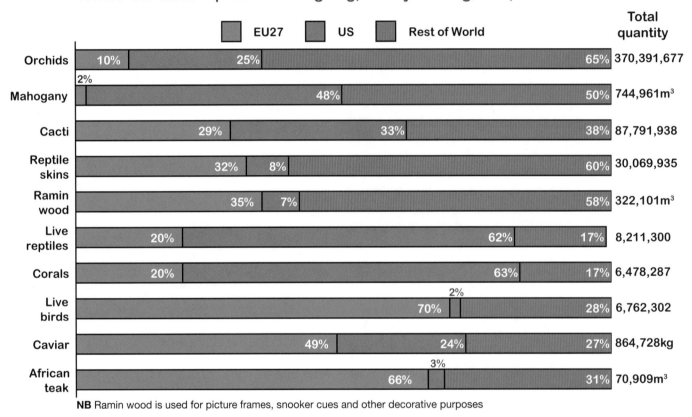

Legend: EU27 | US | Rest of World

Category	EU27	US	Rest of World	Total quantity
Orchids	10%	25%	65%	370,391,677
Mahogany	2%	48%	50%	744,961m³
Cacti	29%	33%	38%	87,791,938
Reptile skins	32%	8%	60%	30,069,935
Ramin wood	35%	7%	58%	322,101m³
Live reptiles	20%	62%	17%	8,211,300
Corals	20%	63%	17%	6,478,287
Live birds	70%	2%	28%	6,762,302
Caviar	49%	24%	27%	864,728kg
African teak	66%	3%	31%	70,909m³

NB Ramin wood is used for picture frames, snooker cues and other decorative purposes

The difficulties of controlling trade become evident when you look at the trade in ramin wood, which is on the CITES protected list. This tropical hardwood grows in swamps and cannot be cultivated in plantations. Many of the last specimens are in national parks in Indonesia which are also the habitat of endangered species such as the orang-utan.

Indonesia recorded NO legal exports to neighbouring Malaysia, yet Malaysia, which doesn't have any ramin left, exported large quantities. These must have come from Indonesia. Huge profits encourage illegal loggers to destroy habitats regardless of trade control or the environmental consequences.

Estimated value of global and EU wildlife trade, 2005
(billion euros)

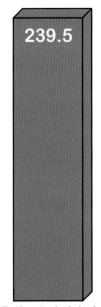

239.5

The world total includes:
- Primates €75m
- Cage birds €38m
- Birds of prey €5m
- Reptiles €31m
- Ornamental fish €257m
- Furs and fur products €4bn
- Frogs legs €40m

93.0

Estimated global value

Estimated EU value

It is obviously difficult to estimate the size of the illegal trade as it is, by definition, a hidden activity. It is likely that the enlargement of the EU has expanded the size of the market and the demand for products.

For example, the value of the illegal trade in caviar is thought to be several times greater than the value of the legal trade which was estimated at over 244 million euros in 2005.

The demand for rare specimens and products means that black market values can be very high: certain species of tortoise can fetch 30,000 euros per specimen. In turn the high value creates a significant incentive for people, especially the rural poor, to become involved in illegal trade.

Over half of 41 premises surveyed by Customs and Excise in the UK in 2000 stocked traditional Asian medicine ingredients claiming to contain protected species including leopard bone and bear bile. In the Netherlands, eight sea containers of medicinal derivatives of tiger, rhino, bears, musk deer, saiga antelope and pangolin were seized along with hawksbill turtle shell and dried orchid roots.

Between 2003 and 2004, the EU made over 7,000 seizures of shipments without legal permits, totalling over 3.5 million specimens listed under CITES. In the UK in 2005 Customs seized 7,846 live birds and animals, 332,043 animal parts and 192 ivory objects.

Selected recent wildlife seizures by EU Member States, 2005-2007

Country	Quantity	Specimen
Austria	35	Live Indian Star Tortoises
Estonia	5,484	Seahorse specimens in jars
Hungary	400 201	Tins of repacked Russian caviar Live Hermann's Tortoises
Romania	210	Kg of sturgeon meat
France	1,839	Live orchids
Italy	10 9,000 815	Live Ploughshare Tortoises Items of traditional Asian medicine products, including rhino, tiger, leopard, musk deer, pangolin, sea turtle, seahorse, and orchid root derivatives Live Egyptian Tortoises

Source: Opportunity or threat: The role of the European Union in the global wildlife trade, a Traffic Europe Report © 2007 Traffic Europe; The Timber Mafia

http://www.panda.org/
http://abc.net.au/4corners

Birdwatch

The Big Garden Birdwatch is the world's biggest bird survey and provides a vital snapshot of the UK's birds each winter

The results are made up of more than 6.5 million birds counted in 236,000 gardens.

The survey has recorded the huge declines in some of our most familiar birds since it began in 1979.

The UK's birds can be split in to three categories of conservation importance – red, amber and green.

- Red is the highest conservation priority, with species needing urgent action.
- Amber is the next most critical group
- Green which means there is no identified threat to the population status.

1 House Sparrow

Average 4.4 per garden.
Numbers declined by 56%

Conservation priority: **RED**

2 Starling

Average 3.67 per garden.
Numbers declined by 76%

Conservation priority: **RED**

3 Blue tit

Average 2.82 per garden.
Numbers increased by 16%

Conservation priority: **GREEN**

4 Blackbird

Average 2.26 per garden.
Although numbers declined by 44%, it is a widespread and common bird and not listed under any conservation designations

Conservation priority: **GREEN**

5 Chaffinch

Average 1.9 per garden.
Numbers declined by 36%

Conservation priority: **GREEN**

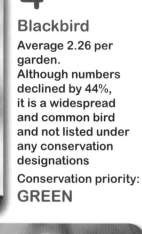

January 2007 was one of the mildest on record. This has meant a bumper crop of fruits in woodlands and hedgerows, which may have kept birds well fed and contributed to their absence at garden feeders.

These results show how changes in climate created changes in bird behaviour and trends. Further changes to our climate will inevitably see the disappearance of many familiar birds in our gardens.

7 Woodpigeon

Average 1.53 per garden.
Numbers increased by 666%

Conservation priority: **GREEN**

6 Collared dove

Average 1.56 per garden.
Numbers increased by 456% since 1979

Conservation priority: **GREEN**

9 Robin

Average 1.26 per garden.
Numbers declined by 37%
Conservation priority: **GREEN**

8 Great tit

Average 1.37 per garden.
Numbers increased by 52%
Conservation priority: **GREEN**

10 Greenfinch

Average 1.2 per garden.
Numbers increased by 21%
Conservation priority: **GREEN**

Base: Over 400,000 people took part, by counting the birds in their garden for an hour on 27 or 28 January 2007

Source: RSPB

http://www.rspb.org.uk/birdwatch/results/

Eco-footprint

We are using up the earth's resources at a faster rate than they can be replaced

Biggest Ecological Footprint
(number of hectares used to support each person)

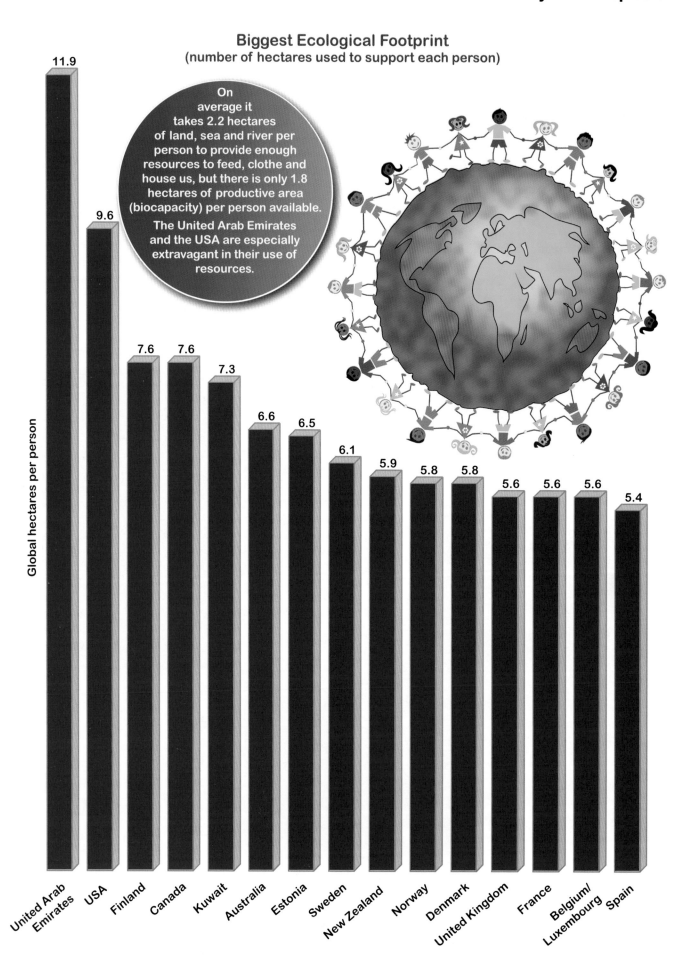

On average it takes 2.2 hectares of land, sea and river per person to provide enough resources to feed, clothe and house us, but there is only 1.8 hectares of productive area (biocapacity) per person available.

The United Arab Emirates and the USA are especially extravagant in their use of resources.

Global hectares per person

United Arab Emirates	11.9
USA	9.6
Finland	7.6
Canada	7.6
Kuwait	7.3
Australia	6.6
Estonia	6.5
Sweden	6.1
New Zealand	5.9
Norway	5.8
Denmark	5.8
United Kingdom	5.6
France	5.6
Belgium/Luxembourg	5.6
Spain	5.4

The Ecological Footprint measures humanity's demand on the biosphere – how much productive land and sea are required to provide the resources we use and to absorb our waste.

The footprint of a country includes all the cropland, grazing land, forest and fishing grounds required to produce the food, fire and timber it consumes, to absorb the wastes emitted in generating the energy it uses and to provide space for its infrastructure.

In theory, we should not take out any more resources than the earth can renew. In practice, we use up assets in a year which take one year and three months for the earth to produce. Over time the earth builds up a bank of assets – like forests and fishing stocks – which we can draw on. However, if we continue to over-consume, as we have for three decades, we will reach the stage where biological resources are so depleted that the planet is unable to renew them.

- Countries like Afghanistan, Somalia and Bangladesh are the leading ecological creditors, using up fewer resources per capita than the global average

- The UK is one of the world's main ecological debtors consuming far more of the Earth's resources than we can contribute, it takes 5.59 hectares to supply the needs of each person living here

- On average carbon dioxide (CO_2) accounts for over 80% of global warming. Atmospheric levels of CO_2 are now higher then ever and this is all due to human action

Smallest Ecological Footprint
(number of hectares used to support each person)

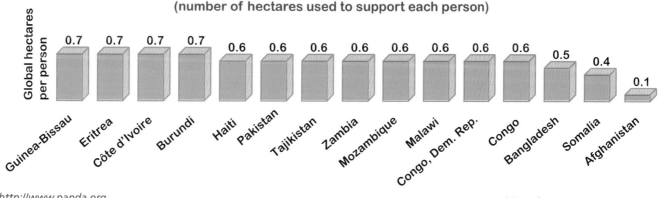

Guinea-Bissau	Eritrea	Côte d'Ivoire	Burundi	Haiti	Pakistan	Tajikistan	Zambia	Mozambique	Malawi	Congo, Dem. Rep.	Congo	Bangladesh	Somalia	Afghanistan
0.7	0.7	0.7	0.7	0.6	0.6	0.6	0.6	0.6	0.6	0.6	0.6	0.5	0.4	0.1

Global hectares per person

http://www.panda.org

Source: Living Planet Report 2006 WWF

Dirty thirty

All of Europe's 30 biggest climate polluting power stations are coalfired, a third of these are in the UK

Worst climate polluting power stations, Europe 2006, by relative emissions – grams of CO_2 per Kilowatt hour

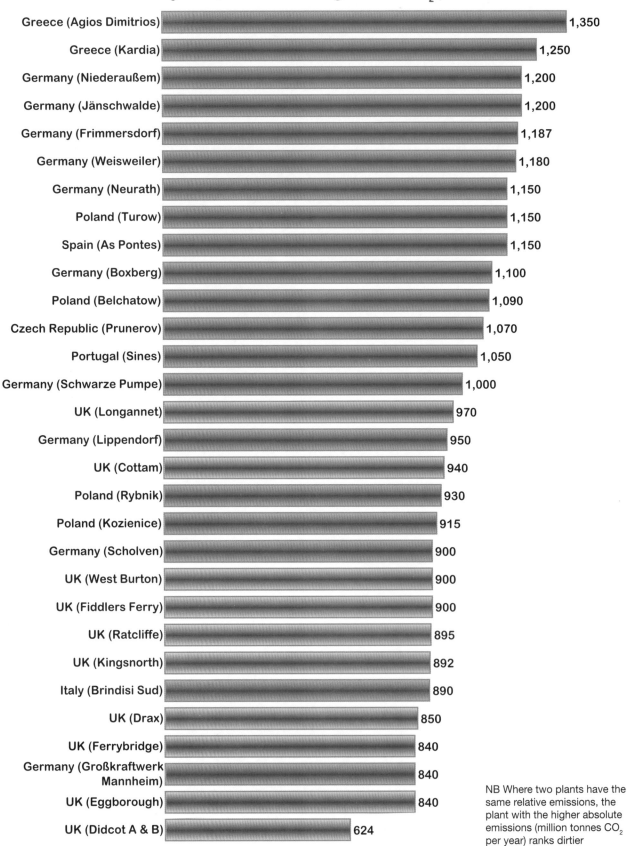

Power station	grams of CO_2 per Kilowatt hour
Greece (Agios Dimitrios)	1,350
Greece (Kardia)	1,250
Germany (Niederaußem)	1,200
Germany (Jänschwalde)	1,200
Germany (Frimmersdorf)	1,187
Germany (Weisweiler)	1,180
Germany (Neurath)	1,150
Poland (Turow)	1,150
Spain (As Pontes)	1,150
Germany (Boxberg)	1,100
Poland (Belchatow)	1,090
Czech Republic (Prunerov)	1,070
Portugal (Sines)	1,050
Germany (Schwarze Pumpe)	1,000
UK (Longannet)	970
Germany (Lippendorf)	950
UK (Cottam)	940
Poland (Rybnik)	930
Poland (Kozienice)	915
Germany (Scholven)	900
UK (West Burton)	900
UK (Fiddlers Ferry)	900
UK (Ratcliffe)	895
UK (Kingsnorth)	892
Italy (Brindisi Sud)	890
UK (Drax)	850
UK (Ferrybridge)	840
Germany (Großkraftwerk Mannheim)	840
UK (Eggborough)	840
UK (Didcot A & B)	624

NB Where two plants have the same relative emissions, the plant with the higher absolute emissions (million tonnes CO_2 per year) ranks dirtier

48 **Environmental issues**

Fact File 2008 • www.carelpress.com

The WWF believes that the world can produce enough sustainable energy to meet global demand and curb climate change, but only if world leaders act by 2012. The six key solutions are:

- Improving energy efficiency
- Stopping forest loss
- Accelerating the development of low-emissions technologies
- Developing flexible fuels
- Replacing high-carbon coal with low-carbon gas
- Equipping fossil-fuel plants with carbon capture and storage technology

By 2030 most of Europe's 'Dirty Thirty' will reach the end of their technical lifetime and will have to be replaced. This presents a great opportunity to drastically reduce CO_2 emissions depending on which replacement scenario they choose.

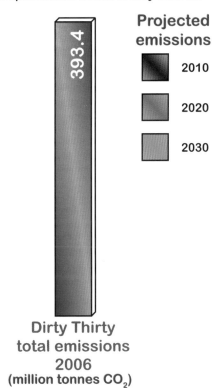

Projected emissions

- 2010
- 2020
- 2030

393.4

Dirty Thirty total emissions 2006
(million tonnes CO_2)

Projected emissions under each scenario
(million tonnes CO_2)

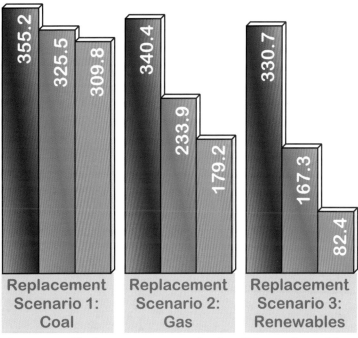

Replacement Scenario 1: Coal	Replacement Scenario 2: Gas	Replacement Scenario 3: Renewables
355.2 / 325.5 / 309.8	340.4 / 233.9 / 179.2	330.7 / 167.3 / 82.4

Assumes that every power plant unit is replaced by:

| A modern plant with the same fuel. 2030 would see a 21.3% reduction in CO_2 emissions compared to 2006 | A new, highly efficient gas fired combined cycle power plant with an emission level of 365g CO_2 per kilowatt hour. 2030 would see a 54.4% reduction in CO_2 emissions compared to 2006. | CO_2-free power generation capacities from renewable energies. 2030 would see a 79.1% reduction in CO_2 emissions compared to 2006. |

Source: Dirty Thirty: Ranking of the most polluting power stations in Europe. World Wide Fund for Nature, 2007 © WWF, 2007

http://www.wwf.org.uk

Warmer world

2007 proved to be a year of extreme weather events, is this because of global warming?

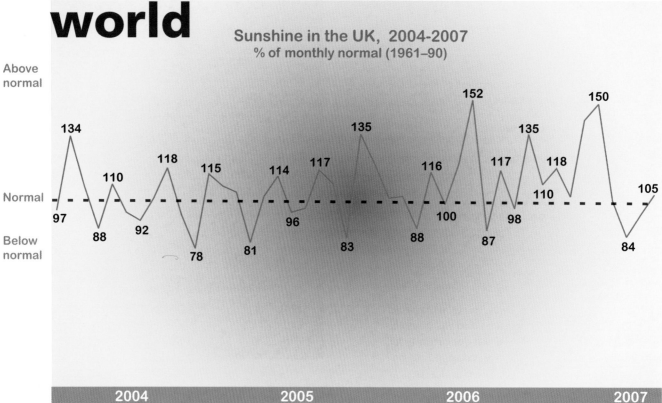

Sunshine in the UK, 2004-2007
% of monthly normal (1961–90)

Above normal

Normal

Below normal

2004 2005 2006 2007

J F M A M J J A S O N D J F M A M J J A S O N D J F M A M J J A S O N D J F M A M J J A

Global warming

Although global temperatures gradually rise over time, over the past 50 years they have increased dramatically. It is thought that during the second half of the 20th century the average Northern Hemisphere temperatures were possibly the highest in the past 1,300 years.

A warmer atmosphere contains more water vapour leading to higher rainfall. A consequence of global warming as predicted by computer models is increased 'extreme weather events' from freak rainfalls to heatwaves, as has been the trend during the last 50 years both in the UK and globally.

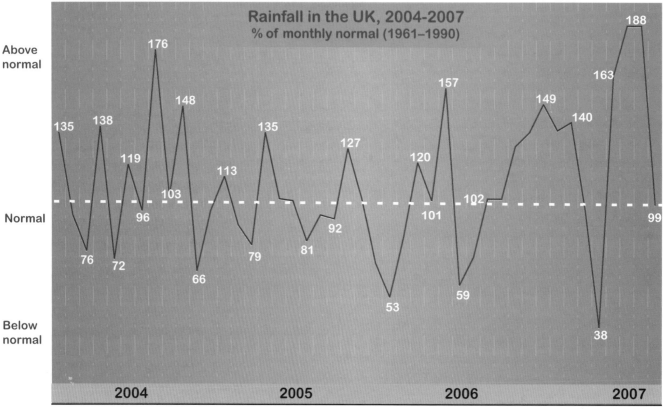

Rainfall in the UK, 2004-2007
% of monthly normal (1961–1990)

Above normal

Normal

Below normal

2004 2005 2006 2007

J F M A M J J A S O N D J F M A M J J A S O N D J F M A M J J A S O N D J F M A M J J A

22nd July 2007 – view from the air of Tewkesbury Abbey, Gloucestershire, surrounded by flood waters

Photo: Barry Batchelor/PA/PA Photos

Human fingerprint

Recent scientific studies have for the first time linked global warming caused by human emissions of greenhouse gases to the rise in extreme weather, suggesting that there is a distinct 'human fingerprint' on such events, as seen over several areas of the world.

Global extremes

The global land surface temperatures in January and April 2007, ranked as the warmest since records began in 1880. In many European countries April peaked 4°C above the long-term mean.

In May a heatwave brought record temperatures to central and western Russia.

In June, the first ever documented cyclone in the Arabian Sea hit Oman with sustained winds of 148 km/h. This affected 20,000 people and caused 50 deaths. In Southern China flooding caused by heavy rains affected 13.5 million people and caused 120 deaths.

In June and July, monsoon season in India, there were four monsoon depressions rather than the normal two. This caused large scale flooding all over South Asia resulting in 500 deaths, the displacement of 10 million people and major destruction of crops, livestock and property. In south-eastern Europe two heat waves struck, breaking previous records with temperatures exceeding 40°C.

The Met Office prediction for 2014 is that it will be 0.3°C warmer than 2004 and that half the years after 2009 will exceed the current warmest records.

Hitting home

In England and Wales, May to July 2007 was the wettest (406mm) since records began in 1766, breaking the previous record of 349mm in 1789.

Extreme rainfall in June brought 103.1mm of rain in 24 hours (24-25 June) in North East England, followed by a similar event in July with 120.8mm of rain (20 July) in central England. These caused extensive flooding across parts of England and Wales in which at least nine people died.

Rainfall for the summer months was 154% of the average in the UK as a whole – 170% in England and in Wales, 157% in Northern Ireland and 132% in Scotland.

The figures for some English regions are even more extreme. Rainfall was 185% of the average in the Midlands, 178% in East and North East England, 167% in South West England and South Wales.

Although it is not possible to attribute individual events to global warming, scientists have urged the government to take account of such extreme events in planning.

Source: Met Office © Crown copyright 2007, World Meteorological Organization

http://www.metoffice.gov.uk

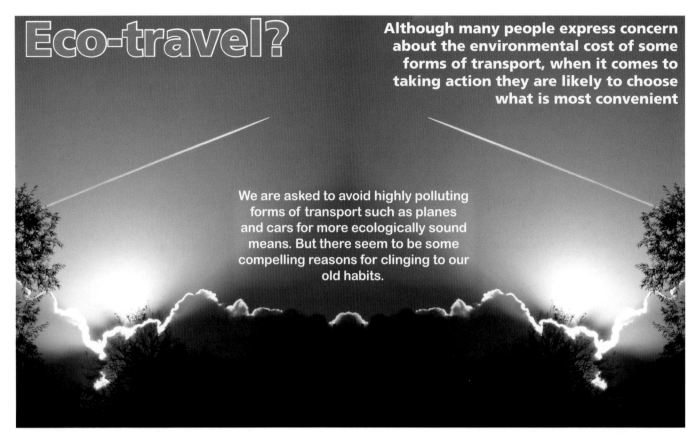

Eco-travel?

Although many people express concern about the environmental cost of some forms of transport, when it comes to taking action they are likely to choose what is most convenient

We are asked to avoid highly polluting forms of transport such as planes and cars for more ecologically sound means. But there seem to be some compelling reasons for clinging to our old habits.

Lonely Planet's annual Travellers' Pulse survey, polled over 24,500 people in 144 countries. It revealed that:

- 36% of people had never purposefully considered the environment in their past travels, but 93% said they would or might in the future

- Most were worried about carbon emissions from flying, with only 7% saying that they did not think aircraft carbon emissions were a concern.

- Offsetting was the top option for dealing with the problem of emissions, with a quarter of all votes, but 43% chose one of the more radical options: boycotting flying; airlines reducing the number of flights; increasing flying costs via a carbon tax; or everyone having an annual carbon allowance into which they must fit their travel.

- 84% said they would consider offsetting their emissions in the future, but only 31% had done so in the past.

Train travel is often promoted as better for the environment but a comparison between train and plane travel costs from London to Madrid found:

Train £259.50 17 hours
Plane £ 67.90   2 hours

Even for local travel the train loses out. Only 9% of adults are frequent rail travellers.

Main reasons for NOT using short-distance rail services, UK non-users, 2006,%

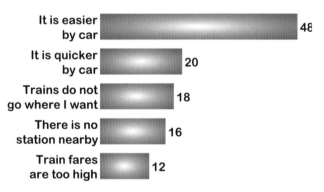

It is easier by car	48
It is quicker by car	20
Trains do not go where I want	18
There is no station nearby	16
Train fares are too high	12

What improvements would encourage you to use rail services for short distance trips? UK non- and infrequent users, 2006, %
(respondents could choose three responses)

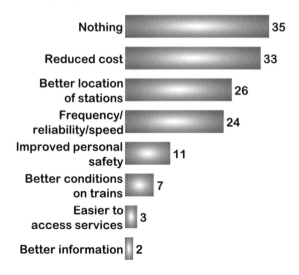

Nothing	35
Reduced cost	33
Better location of stations	26
Frequency/reliability/speed	24
Improved personal safety	11
Better conditions on trains	7
Easier to access services	3
Better information	2

Attitudes towards flying and car use, %

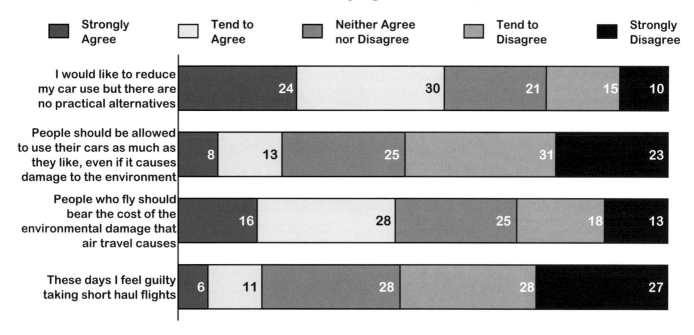

Legend: ■ Strongly Agree | □ Tend to Agree | ▨ Neither Agree nor Disagree | ▨ Tend to Disagree | ■ Strongly Disagree

Statement	Strongly Agree	Tend to Agree	Neither Agree nor Disagree	Tend to Disagree	Strongly Disagree
I would like to reduce my car use but there are no practical alternatives	24	30	21	15	10
People should be allowed to use their cars as much as they like, even if it causes damage to the environment	8	13	25	31	23
People who fly should bear the cost of the environmental damage that air travel causes	16	28	25	18	13
These days I feel guilty taking short haul flights	6	11	28	28	27

In a 2007 survey, over 50% of people believed that *using a car less* and *using a more fuel efficient car* would have a major impact on the UK's contribution to climate change, if most people in the UK were prepared to do them.

Although 29% of people said they were already making an effort to *use their car less* and/or *fly less*, 24% and 32% respectively said they *don't really want to use a car less* and/or *fly less*. 19%, *hadn't really thought about flying less*, 13% *hadn't really thought about using their car less*.

Once again, however, an analysis of behaviour shows that concerns do not necessarily translate into actions.

Main method of travel to work or study in the past year, 2007

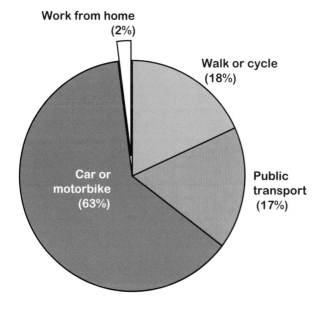

Work from home (2%)
Walk or cycle (18%)
Public transport (17%)
Car or motorbike (63%)

Proportion of people taking non-business return flights in the last year, 2007, %

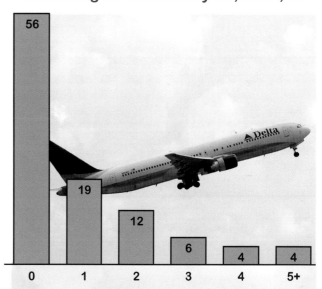

0	1	2	3	4	5+
56	19	12	6	4	4

Over 50% of those questioned had not flown at all on non-business trips. On the other hand, the 4% of the population who flew 5 or more times accounted for one third of all return flights.

58% of flights were within Europe and 17% were within the UK. The main reason for choosing to fly was that it was quicker, though for some it was also cheaper and easier.

Source: Lonely Planet, Public experiences of and attitudes towards rail travel, Department for Transport © Crown copyright 2006, Survey of Public Attitudes and Behaviour Towards the Environment 2007 © Crown copyright 2007

http://www.lonelyplanet.com
http://www.dft.gov.uk
http://www.defra.gov.uk

Green cars

Which models of car would meet the European target for CO$_2$ emissions?

Carbon dioxide emissions of new cars, petrol engines, 2006, grams per kilometre

Top ten 'greenest' models compared with other makes

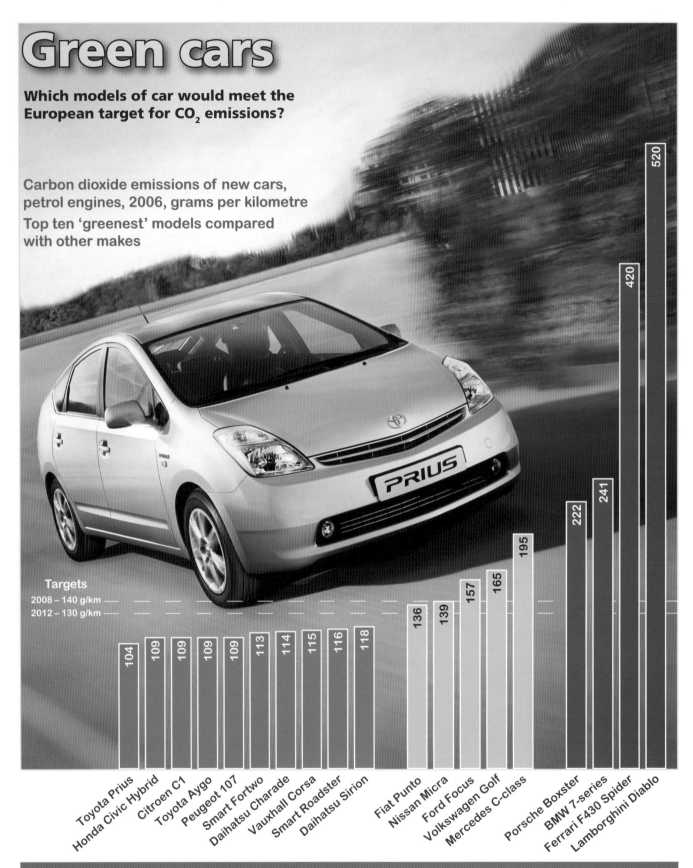

Targets
2008 – 140 g/km
2012 – 130 g/km

Model	g/km
Toyota Prius	104
Honda Civic Hybrid	109
Citroen C1	109
Toyota Aygo	109
Peugeot 107	109
Smart Fortwo	113
Daihatsu Charade	114
Vauxhall Corsa	115
Smart Roadster	116
Daihatsu Sirion	118
Fiat Punto	136
Nissan Micra	139
Ford Focus	157
Volkswagen Golf	165
Mercedes C-class	195
Porsche Boxster	222
BMW 7-series	241
Ferrari F430 Spider	420
Lamborghini Diablo	520

The European Commission and the European Automobile Manufacturers Association (ACEA) agreed in July 1998 to reduce the CO$_2$ emissions from new cars to an average of 140 grams per kilometre (g/km) by 2008. This average is to be reduced to 130 g/km by 2012.

A car's carbon dioxide emissions are proportional to the amount of fuel it uses. Fuel emissions had reduced very little since the 1980s, despite more efficient engines. This is because safety features, power steering and air conditioning had made cars heavier. Fuel consumption is now starting to drop, following the agreement to reduce carbon dioxide emissions.

When choosing a new car you should select the most appropriate size car for your needs and then choose the most fuel-efficient car from that range. The most efficient way of reducing carbon dioxide levels, however, is to walk, cycle or use public transport!

Source: Vehicle Certification Agency: Car fuel data tables © Crown copyright 2006

http://www.vcacarfueldata.org.uk

Lights out

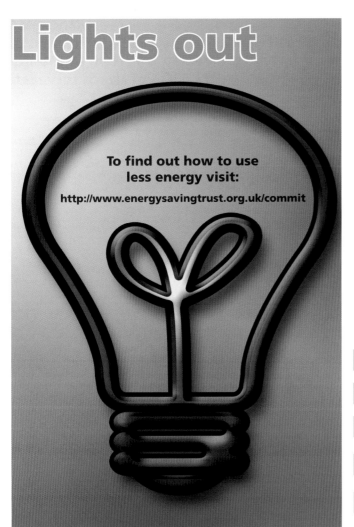

To find out how to use less energy visit:

http://www.energysavingtrust.org.uk/commit

If we all turned the thermostat down by one degree we could save enough energy to heat 1.7 million households for a year

Megawatt hours (MWh) used per UK household, 1999 and 2005

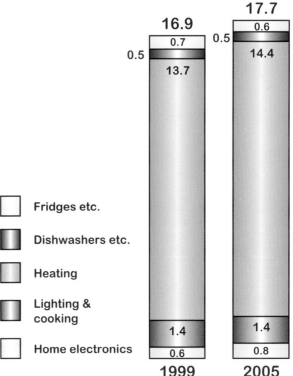

Legend:
- Fridges etc.
- Dishwashers etc.
- Heating
- Lighting & cooking
- Home electronics

1999 — 16.9: 0.7, 0.5, 13.7, 1.4, 0.6

2005 — 17.7: 0.6, 0.5, 14.4, 1.4, 0.8

% of householders who admit to habitually carrying out these actions on a weekly basis

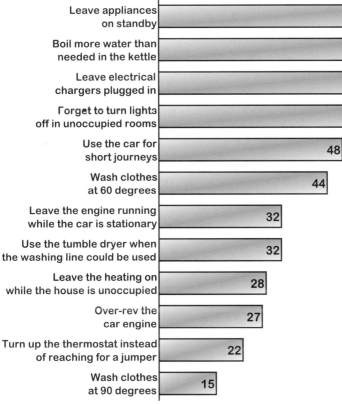

Action	%
Leave appliances on standby	71
Boil more water than needed in the kettle	67
Leave electrical chargers plugged in	65
Forget to turn lights off in unoccupied rooms	63
Use the car for short journeys	48
Wash clothes at 60 degrees	44
Leave the engine running while the car is stationary	32
Use the tumble dryer when the washing line could be used	32
Leave the heating on while the house is unoccupied	28
Over-rev the car engine	27
Turn up the thermostat instead of reaching for a jumper	22
Wash clothes at 90 degrees	15

If everyone in the UK turned appliances off and avoided using standby, we would save enough electricity to power 2.7 million homes for a year.

If we all turned off lights when not needed, we could save enough money to pay the wages of 10,000 new nurses.

If all UK households replaced one ordinary lightbulb with an energy saving efficient one, we would save enough money to pay around 75,000 family fuel bills for a year.

If everyone in the UK upgraded their appliances to *Energy Saving Recommended* models, enough energy would be saved to run all UK street lighting for over 6 years.

Laziness comes top of the list for Brits as an explanation for their inefficient energy habits, with 42% giving it as one of the main reasons for their careless attitude towards energy.

Source: The environment in your pocket 2006, DEFRA
© Crown copyright 2006, Source: Habits of a lifetime, Energy Saving Trust 2006

http://www.defra.gov.uk

Beachwatch

Since 1994, the average density of UK beach litter has increased by 90%. Statistically, one item of litter is found every 50cm of beach surveyed

Top 20 litter items recorded in Beachwatch 2006, UK, % of total litter

Item	%
Plastic pieces 1cm-50cm	13.2
Cotton bud sticks	8.6
Plastic pieces smaller than 1cm	6.2
Crisp / sweet / lolly wrappers	5.6
Polystyrene pieces	5.5
Plastic caps / lids	5.4
Rope	4.3
Cigarette stubs	4.2
Plastic drinks bottles	3.9
Fishing net smaller than 50cm	3.3
Glass pieces	2.8
Cloth pieces / string	2.5
Fishing line	2.5
Metal drink cans	2.2
Plastic bags (inc supermarket)	2
Paper pieces	1.8
Plastic cutlery / trays / straws	1.6
Rubber pieces less than 50cm	1.2
Foam / sponge	1.2
Metal pieces	1.1

Beachwatch is an annual UK beach litter clean-up and survey, organised by the Marine Conservation Society. It was launched in 1993 and aims to promote awareness of the quantities and effects of coastal litter and encourage action to reduce coastal litter pollution.

The four key sources of beach litter were beach visitors (33.9%), fishing debris (11.2%), sanitary waste (10.4%) and shipping litter (2.0%).

The survey takes place on a single day. 4,223 people combed 187km of beach and found nearly 2,000 items per kilometre. Among the items found were false teeth, a TV, fridges, a road sign and a plastic toilet seat.

Litter items found on beaches, UK 1994-2006, average items per km

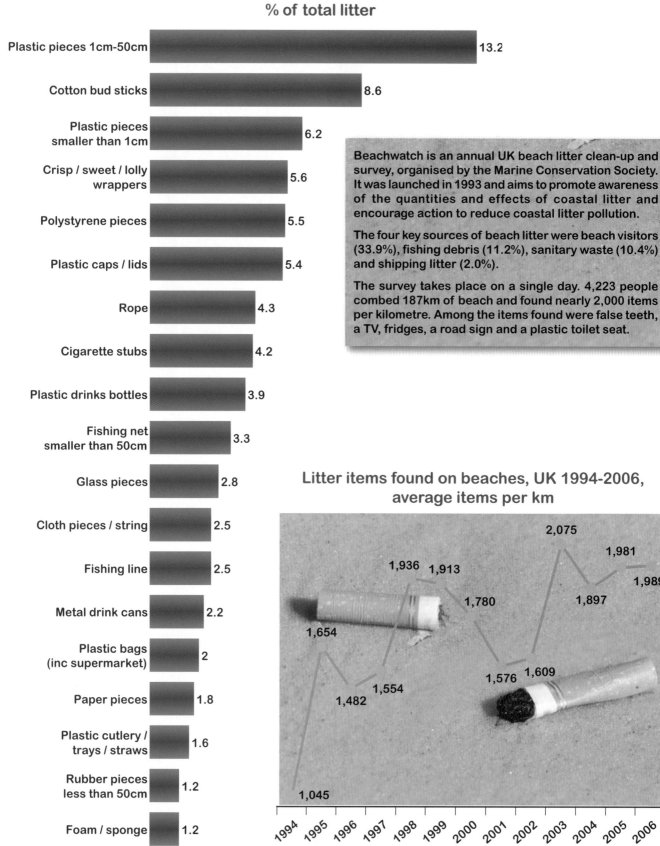

Year	Items per km
1994	1,045
1995	1,654
1996	1,482
1997	1,554
1998	1,936
1999	1,913
2000	1,780
2001	1,576
2002	1,609
2003	2,075
2004	1,897
2005	1,981
2006	1,989

Source: Marine Conservation Society; Beachwatch 2006 © MCS 2007

http://www.mcsuk.org

Bags of waste

We produce and use 20 times more plastics than we did 50 years ago and in our throwaway society disposal is a big issue

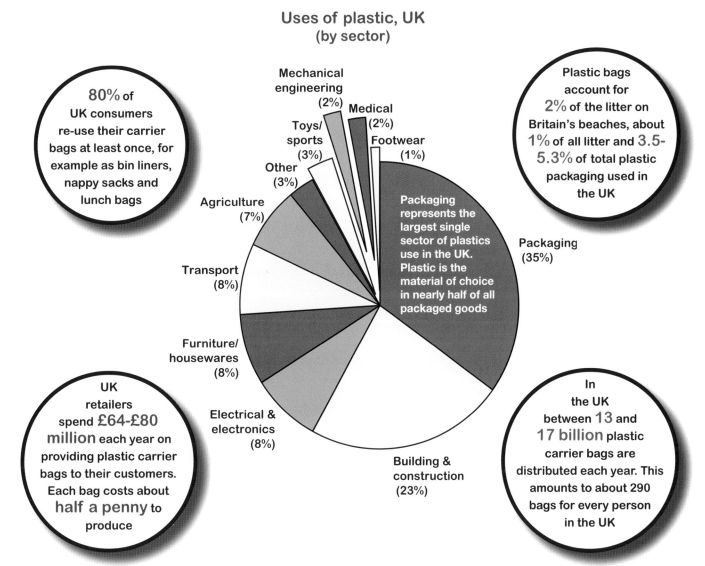

Uses of plastic, UK (by sector)

80% of UK consumers re-use their carrier bags at least once, for example as bin liners, nappy sacks and lunch bags

Plastic bags account for 2% of the litter on Britain's beaches, about 1% of all litter and 3.5-5.3% of total plastic packaging used in the UK

Mechanical engineering (2%)
Medical (2%)
Toys/sports (3%)
Footwear (1%)
Other (3%)
Agriculture (7%)
Transport (8%)
Furniture/housewares (8%)
Electrical & electronics (8%)
Building & construction (23%)
Packaging (35%)

Packaging represents the largest single sector of plastics use in the UK. Plastic is the material of choice in nearly half of all packaged goods

UK retailers spend £64-£80 million each year on providing plastic carrier bags to their customers. Each bag costs about half a penny to produce

In the UK between 13 and 17 billion plastic carrier bags are distributed each year. This amounts to about 290 bags for every person in the UK

Plastic production can be harmful to the environment. Most plastics are non-biodegradable and, with plastic packaging being thrown away almost immediately after purchase, the landfill space needed is a growing concern. All types of plastic are recyclable but plastics currently make up only 1% of recycled waste in the UK.

In February 2007, UK retailers agreed to reduce the environmental impact of their carrier bags by 25% by the end of 2008. They agreed to:

- encourage customers to use fewer carrier bags
- use less plastic or use recycled material
- recycle more bags

The 25% reduction could reduce carbon dioxide emissions by 58,500 tonnes a year – which is equivalent to taking 18,000 cars off the road for a year

Source: Waste Online – Plastic recycling information sheet

http://www.wasteonline.org.uk

Fact File 2008 • www.carelpress.com

Environmental issues **57**

Sort it

In the UK, we produce about 300 million tonnes of waste per year. It has been calculated that if everyone in the world lived like we do, we would need three planets to survive

Composition of household waste, England
(Percentages)

Category	Percentage
Garden waste	20
Paper & board	18
Kitchen waste	17
General household sweepings	9
Glass	7
Wood/furniture	5
Scrap metal/white goods	5
Dense plastic	4
Soil	3
Plastic film	3
Textiles	3
Metal cans/foil	3
Disposable nappies	2

Why does waste matter?

Less than 100 years ago, most waste would have been recycled in some form: ash, food, human and animal waste returned to the land; metals and other minerals reclaimed and reused; paper and wood used as fuel.

However, humans have changed ecosystems more rapidly and extensively in the last 50 years than in any other period. This was done largely to meet rapidly growing demands for food, fresh water, timber, fibre and fuel. The buried detritus from a 21st-century community would include computers, washing machines, fridges, phones, nappies, carrier bags, plastic bottles, milk cartons, cling-film and a hundred-odd other items that have been drawn from resources all over the world, and which will still be there centuries later.

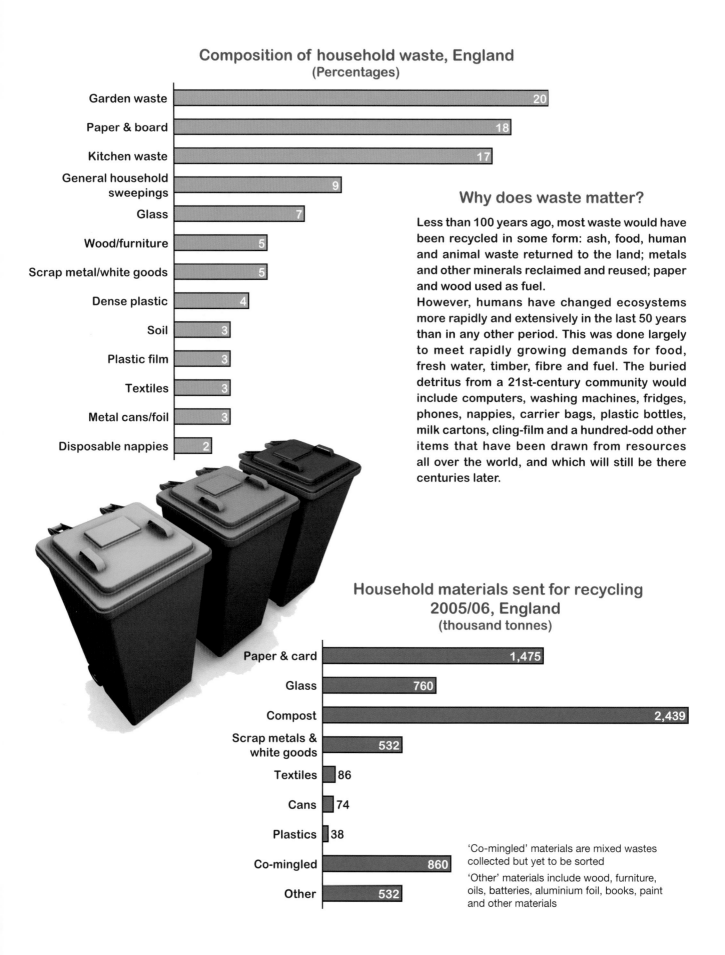

Household materials sent for recycling 2005/06, England
(thousand tonnes)

Material	Thousand tonnes
Paper & card	1,475
Glass	760
Compost	2,439
Scrap metals & white goods	532
Textiles	86
Cans	74
Plastics	38
Co-mingled	860
Other	532

'Co-mingled' materials are mixed wastes collected but yet to be sorted

'Other' materials include wood, furniture, oils, batteries, aluminium foil, books, paint and other materials

Household waste and recycling, England
(kg per person, per year)

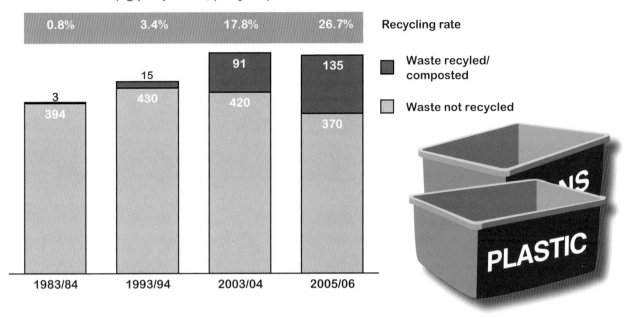

	1983/84	1993/94	2003/04	2005/06	
Recycling rate	0.8%	3.4%	17.8%	26.7%	
Waste recycled/composted	3	15	91	135	
Waste not recycled	394	430	420	370	

The luxury of waste

As dwellers in a 'developed' nation, we have the luxury of consumer goods of every kind, and, consequently, we have the luxury of waste. In poorer communities, or in bad times such as war, there is less to waste and one person's rubbish is another person's usable resource. Modern nations waste more because they have less need to re-use things.

Recently there has been a movement towards a goal of zero waste. Yet in the UK, we are a long way from adopting such a goal at a national level. Most resources stay in the economy for less than six months before they become waste.

The WWF has successfully publicised the notion of 'one-planet living', arguing that our current way of life will require three planets' worth of resources to sustain it, but most people still haven't changed their buying or consuming habits.

Household waste recycling, England
(thousand tonnes)

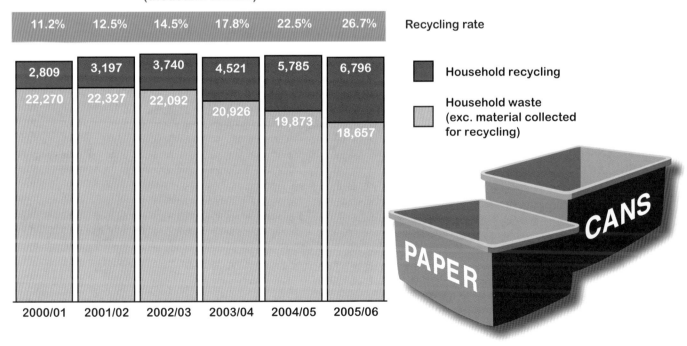

	2000/01	2001/02	2002/03	2003/04	2004/05	2005/06
Recycling rate	11.2%	12.5%	14.5%	17.8%	22.5%	26.7%
Household recycling	2,809	3,197	3,740	4,521	5,785	6,796
Household waste (exc. material collected for recycling)	22,270	22,327	22,092	20,926	19,873	18,657

Sources: A Zero Waste UK November 2006 © ippr and Green Alliance 2006, Municipal Waste Statistics, Department for Environment, Food and Rural Affairs © Crown copyright 2006

http://www.defra.gov.uk
http://www.panda.org

Stop the rot

Q. How much uneaten food do you throw away?

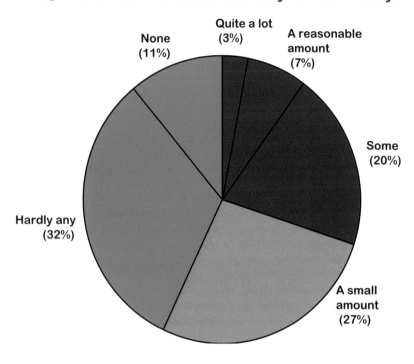

None (11%)

Quite a lot (3%)

A reasonable amount (7%)

Some (20%)

Hardly any (32%)

A small amount (27%)

Food waste is a big problem in the UK yet over half of us don't see it as an issue.

We throw away a third of the food we buy. At least half of what we waste could have been eaten, if we managed our food better. The rest is inedible, eg vegetable peelings, tea bags and meat carcasses.

Food waste accounts for a fifth of our domestic waste.

We are all concerned about the amount of packaging that we have to deal with, but in reality the amount of food wasted by households in the UK is even greater.

In the UK, the vast majority of food waste ends up in landfill. As food rots in landfill it can produce methane, one of the most potent greenhouse gases and a significant contributor to climate change.

Q. How much does throwing away uneaten food bother you?

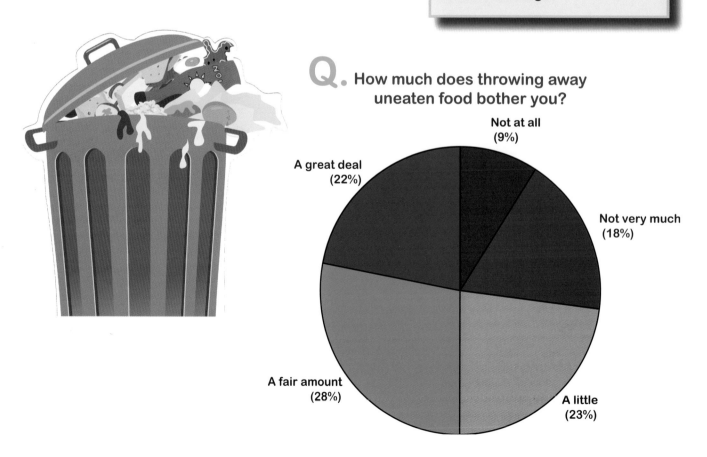

Not at all (9%)

A great deal (22%)

Not very much (18%)

A fair amount (28%)

A little (23%)

Who says they waste food?

Young working people/professionals

- 42% are 'high' food wasters
- Age 16-34, in full time work
- "Lifestyle barriers" often mentioned: more likely to buy too much, be swayed by what they fancy at the time (including takeaways) and change plans day to day
- Waste most unopened food and partly used packs

Young families

- 45% are 'high' food wasters
- Age 25-44, children aged under 16, parent either working or at home
- Very sensitive to food hygiene, more likely to burn food, try to buy more fresh food and throw away because dislike meal
- Waste most cooked food, especially from plates

When we throw food away, we also waste all the carbon generated as it was produced, processed, transported and stored.

This is particularly important given that the whole food supply chain accounts for around 20% of the UK's greenhouse gas emissions.

We could make carbon savings equivalent to taking an estimated 1 in 5 cars off the road if we avoided throwing away all the food that we could have eaten.

Apart from damage to the environment, throwing away food that could have been eaten is also a considerable waste of money.

Each week a typical household throws away between £4.80 and £7.70 of food that could have been eaten.

This is equivalent to £250-£400 a year or £15,000-£24,000 in a lifetime.

Q. Why do you throw food away?

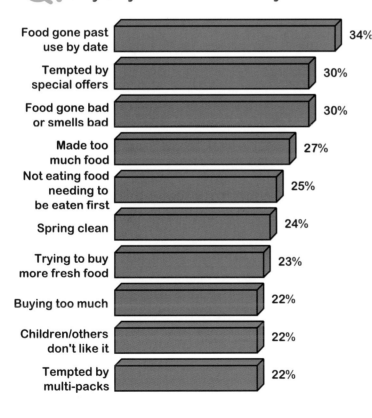

Food gone past use by date	34%
Tempted by special offers	30%
Food gone bad or smells bad	30%
Made too much food	27%
Not eating food needing to be eaten first	25%
Spring clean	24%
Trying to buy more fresh food	23%
Buying too much	22%
Children/others don't like it	22%
Tempted by multi-packs	22%

Source: Why we don't eat our food, WRAP, 2007
http://www.wrap.org.uk

Greenhouse gases

Between 2004 and 2005 emissions from UK companies and the public sector rose by 0.8% but this was offset by a 2.9% reduction in household emissions

Greenhouse gases produce by major sectors, UK

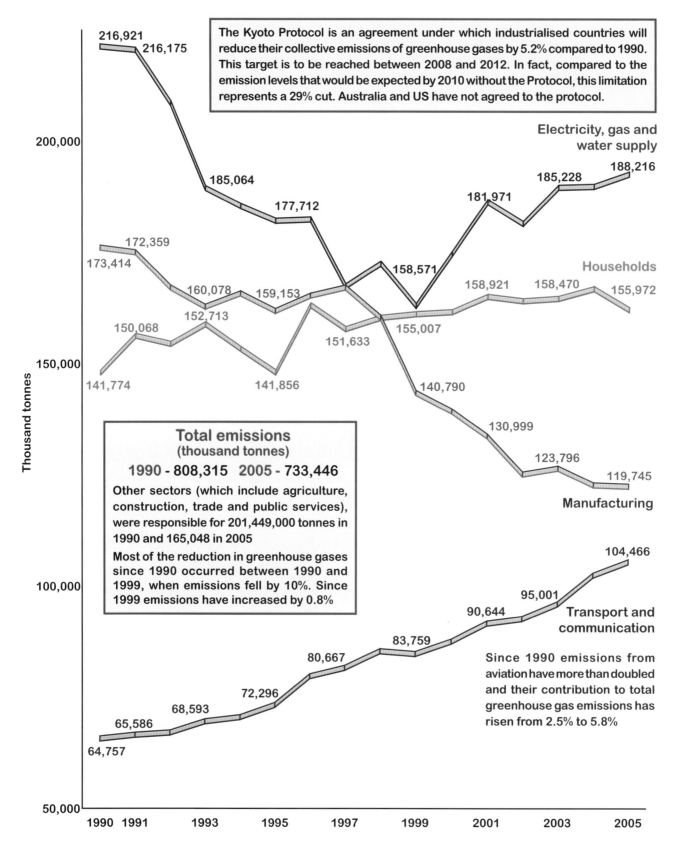

The Kyoto Protocol is an agreement under which industrialised countries will reduce their collective emissions of greenhouse gases by 5.2% compared to 1990. This target is to be reached between 2008 and 2012. In fact, compared to the emission levels that would be expected by 2010 without the Protocol, this limitation represents a 29% cut. Australia and US have not agreed to the protocol.

Electricity, gas and water supply

216,921
216,175
185,064
177,712
181,971
185,228
188,216
158,571

Households

172,359
173,414
160,078
159,153
152,713
158,921
158,470
155,972
150,068
151,633
155,007
141,774
141,856

140,790
130,999
123,796
119,745

Manufacturing

Total emissions
(thousand tonnes)
1990 - 808,315   2005 - 733,446

Other sectors (which include agriculture, construction, trade and public services), were responsible for 201,449,000 tonnes in 1990 and 165,048 in 2005

Most of the reduction in greenhouse gases since 1990 occurred between 1990 and 1999, when emissions fell by 10%. Since 1999 emissions have increased by 0.8%

104,466
95,001
90,644
83,759
80,667
72,296
68,593
65,586
64,757

Transport and communication

Since 1990 emissions from aviation have more than doubled and their contribution to total greenhouse gas emissions has risen from 2.5% to 5.8%

Thousand tonnes

200,000
150,000
100,000
50,000

1990 1991 1993 1995 1997 1999 2001 2003 2005

Source: Environmental Accounts Spring 2007, Netcen, ONS © Crown copyright 2006
http://www.statistics.gov.uk

Disturbing decibels

Noise not only annoys, it causes stress that can have an impact on our health and well-being. Our cities and even our small towns are becoming noise hubs

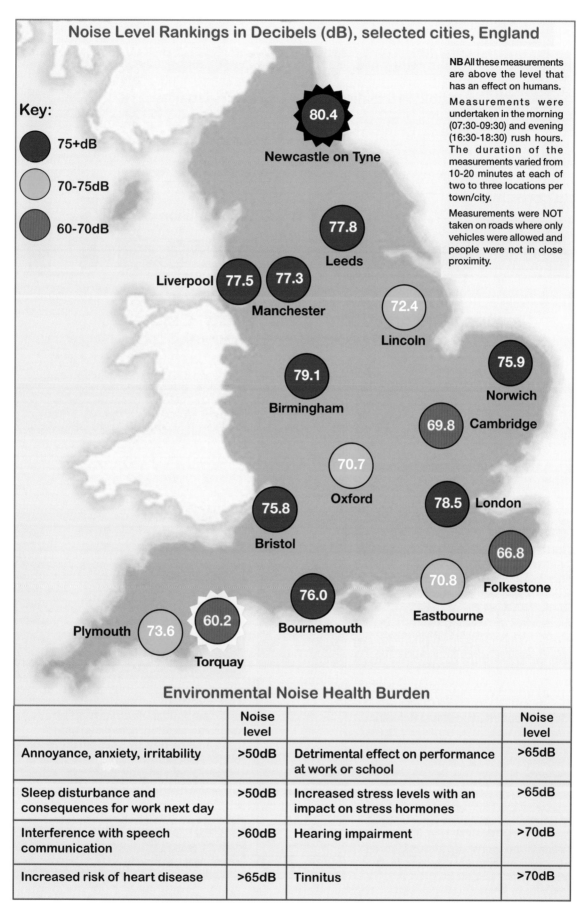

Noise Level Rankings in Decibels (dB), selected cities, England

NB All these measurements are above the level that has an effect on humans.

Measurements were undertaken in the morning (07:30-09:30) and evening (16:30-18:30) rush hours. The duration of the measurements varied from 10-20 minutes at each of two to three locations per town/city.

Measurements were NOT taken on roads where only vehicles were allowed and people were not in close proximity.

Key:

- 75+dB
- 70-75dB
- 60-70dB

80.4 — Newcastle on Tyne

77.8 — Leeds

77.5 — Liverpool
77.3 — Manchester

72.4 — Lincoln

79.1 — Birmingham

75.9 — Norwich

69.8 — Cambridge

70.7 — Oxford

78.5 — London

75.8 — Bristol

66.8 — Folkestone

70.8 — Eastbourne

76.0 — Bournemouth

73.6 — Plymouth

60.2 — Torquay

Environmental Noise Health Burden

	Noise level		Noise level
Annoyance, anxiety, irritability	>50dB	Detrimental effect on performance at work or school	>65dB
Sleep disturbance and consequences for work next day	>50dB	Increased stress levels with an impact on stress hormones	>65dB
Interference with speech communication	>60dB	Hearing impairment	>70dB
Increased risk of heart disease	>65dB	Tinnitus	>70dB

Source: Widex Noise Report – Traffic Noise in England 2007

http://www.widex.co.uk

Ethical spend

Spending on ethical products still only makes up about 3.91% of our total spending

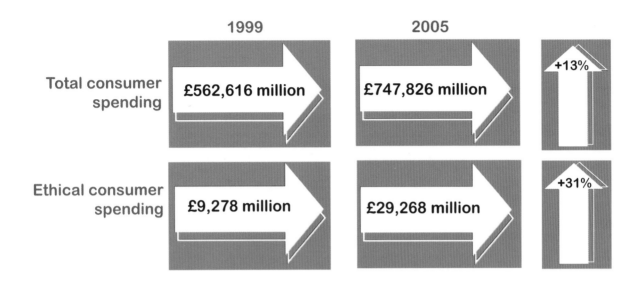

	1999	2005	
Total consumer spending	£562,616 million	£747,826 million	+13%
Ethical consumer spending	£9,278 million	£29,268 million	+31%

Spending on ethical products, UK, £ million
(% increase over 2004-2005 in brackets)

29,268

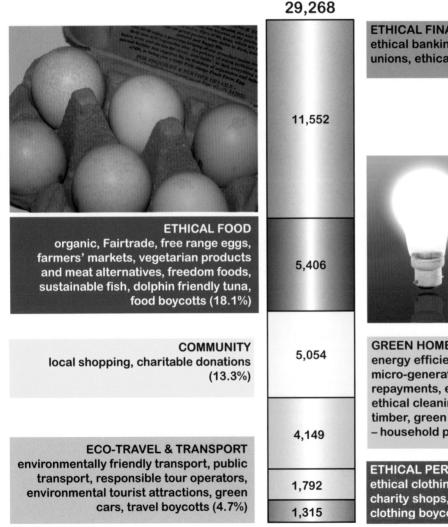

ETHICAL FINANCE
ethical banking, ethical investment, credit unions, ethical share holdings (8.7%)

11,552

ETHICAL FOOD
organic, Fairtrade, free range eggs, farmers' markets, vegetarian products and meat alternatives, freedom foods, sustainable fish, dolphin friendly tuna, food boycotts (18.1%)

5,406

COMMUNITY
local shopping, charitable donations (13.3%)

5,054

GREEN HOME
energy efficient electrical appliances, micro-generation, green mortgage repayments, energy efficient light-bulbs, ethical cleaning products, sustainable timber, green energy, buying for re-use – household products (10.6%)

4,149

ECO-TRAVEL & TRANSPORT
environmentally friendly transport, public transport, responsible tour operators, environmental tourist attractions, green cars, travel boycotts (4.7%)

1,792

ETHICAL PERSONAL PRODUCTS
ethical clothing, humane cosmetics, charity shops, buying for re-use – clothing, clothing boycotts (4.9%)

1,315

Source: Co-operative Bank, Ethical Consumer Report 2006

http://www.co-operativebank.co.uk

Family &
relationships

Mr & Mrs

Despite a rise in the number of marriages in recent years, in 2005 the UK marriage rate fell to its lowest level since 1896

Civil and religious marriages, England & Wales

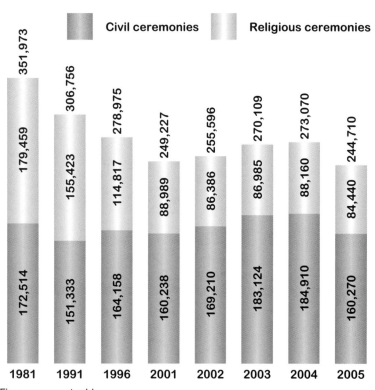

Civil ceremonies | Religious ceremonies

Year	Religious	Civil
1981	179,459 (351,973)	172,514
1991	155,423 (306,756)	151,333
1996	114,817 (278,975)	164,158
2001	88,989 (249,227)	160,238
2002	86,386 (255,596)	169,210
2003	86,985 (270,109)	183,124
2004	88,160 (273,070)	184,910
2005	84,440 (244,710)	160,270

Figures may not add precisely due to rounding

The immigration laws which came into force in 2005 to prevent "marriages of convenience" may have contributed to the decline in marriages.

In the 10 years since 1995, the average age for marriage increased by just over three years for men to 36.2 years and just under three years for women to 33.6 years.

Marriage rate per 1,000 of the unmarried population aged 16 and over, England & Wales

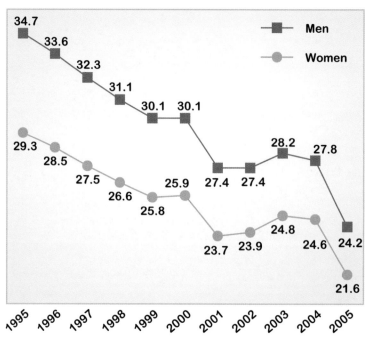

Men — 34.7, 33.6, 32.3, 31.1, 30.1, 30.1, 27.4, 27.4, 28.2, 27.8, 24.2

Women — 29.3, 28.5, 27.5, 26.6, 25.8, 25.9, 23.7, 23.9, 24.8, 24.6, 21.6

1995, 1996, 1997, 1998, 1999, 2000, 2001, 2002, 2003, 2004, 2005

Figures for 2005 are provisional

Source: Marriages in 2005, Department for National Statistics
© Crown copyright, 2007

http://www.statistics.gov.uk

I do... I don't

Marital status by gender
(percentages)

Men ☐ Women

	Men	Women
Married	53	49
Cohabiting	10	10
Single	27	21
Widowed	3	11
Divorced	5	7
Separated	2	2

2.2 million unmarried couples living together

(Great Britain, 2005)

Number of people in civil partnerships by year and gender, UK

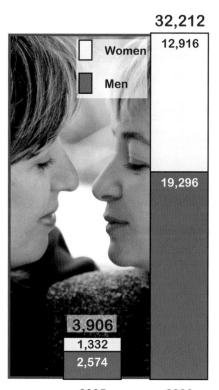

32,212

	2005 (From 5th December)	2006
Women	1,332	12,916
Men	2,574	19,296
(total)	3,906	

I do...

While marriage is the most popular status for couples, it continues to decline. In 2005 there were 283,730 weddings in the UK, a decline of 10% from 2004.

The introduction of the Civil Partnership Act on the 5th of December 2005, enabled gay and lesbian couples to register their partnerships, allowing them important legal rights in the areas of inheritance, pensions and children, among others.

There were 18,059 civil partnerships formed in the UK between December 2005 and the end of December 2006. More men than women formed civil partnerships. In 2006, 60% of all civil partnerships were male.

In 2005, the number of divorces in the UK fell by 7% to 155,052. While this seems like good news, the fall in divorces is believed to reflect the drop in marriages as increasing numbers of couples choosing to cohabit.

...I don't

Official figures show there are more than 2.2 million unmarried couples living together in England and Wales. Government forecasts show that there will be 3.8 million cohabiting couples by 2031.

No matter whether you are straight or gay, if you aren't about to walk up any kind of aisle, you have very few legal rights automatically.

Siblings, descendants and straight couples who live together are not allowed to register as civil partners, and so are not eligible for the tax or inheritance rights.

Straight couples who do not wish to marry, but want equal legal rights, have now begun to campaign for 'gay marriage' rights. Equal Partnership is a group campaigning for the removal of a clause in the Civil Partnership Act which prohibits straight couples.

Recently two sisters who had lived together their whole life appealed to have the same right to inheritance and tax as a lesbian couple.

Source: ONS © Crown copyright 2007, You Gov
http://www.statistics.gov.uk
http://www.yougov.com

Couples & squabbles

Q. How important are these factors in a successful marriage? % of respondents in each category answering "Very important"

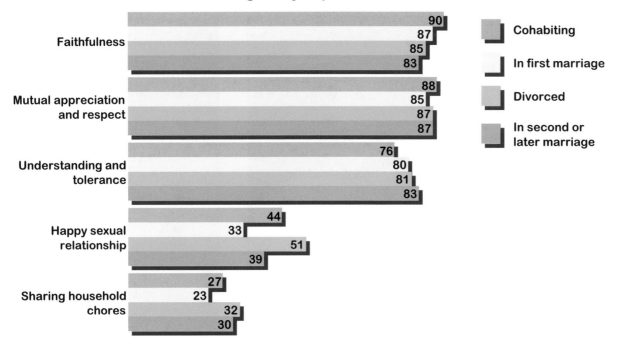

Faithfulness
- 90
- 87
- 85
- 83

Mutual appreciation and respect
- 88
- 85
- 87
- 87

Understanding and tolerance
- 76
- 80
- 81
- 83

Happy sexual relationship
- 44
- 33
- 51
- 39

Sharing household chores
- 27
- 23
- 32
- 30

Legend:
- Cohabiting
- In first marriage
- Divorced
- In second or later marriage

Faithfulness, respect and understanding are the most important factors to people whether married or not. Differences occur however, when it comes to chores.
Cooking is shared equally among 37% of cohabitees, 24% of those in their first marriage and 26% of those in their second. Similar differences occurred with cleaning with 47%, 31% and 33% respectively sharing the chore equally. Dealing with finances is shared equally between 42% of cohabitees, 31% of those in their first marriage and 34% in their second, yet it's the main thing all couples argue about.

Q. Which of these statements comes closest to your view of marriage? % of respondents by category

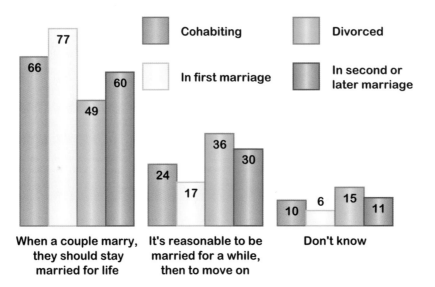

Legend:
- Cohabiting
- Divorced
- In first marriage
- In second or later marriage

When a couple marry, they should stay married for life
- 66
- 77
- 49
- 60

It's reasonable to be married for a while, then to move on
- 24
- 17
- 36
- 30

Don't know
- 10
- 6
- 15
- 11

Q. What do you and your partner argue about?
Top 10 responses %
(respondents could select as many answers as applicable)

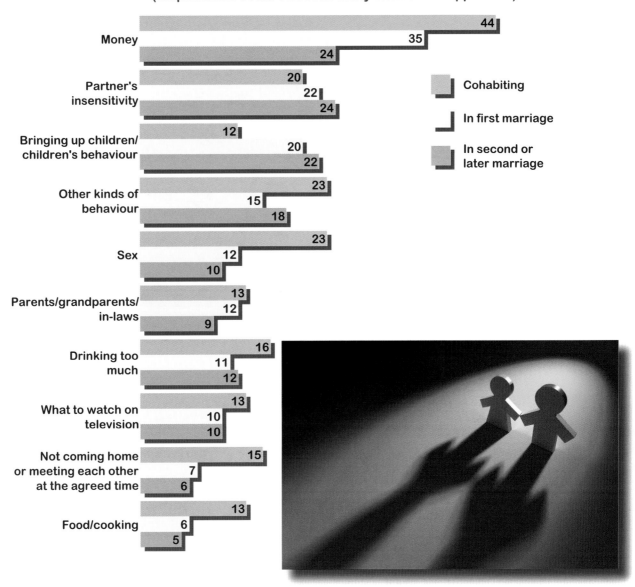

Money
- 44 (Cohabiting)
- 35 (In first marriage)
- 24 (In second or later marriage)

Partner's insensitivity
- 20
- 22
- 24

Bringing up children/children's behaviour
- 12
- 20
- 22

Other kinds of behaviour
- 23
- 15
- 18

Sex
- 23
- 12
- 10

Parents/grandparents/in-laws
- 13
- 12
- 9

Drinking too much
- 16
- 11
- 12

What to watch on television
- 13
- 10
- 10

Not coming home or meeting each other at the agreed time
- 15
- 7
- 6

Food/cooking
- 13
- 6
- 5

Legend:
- Cohabiting
- In first marriage
- In second or later marriage

Q. How often do you and your partner argue? % of respondents

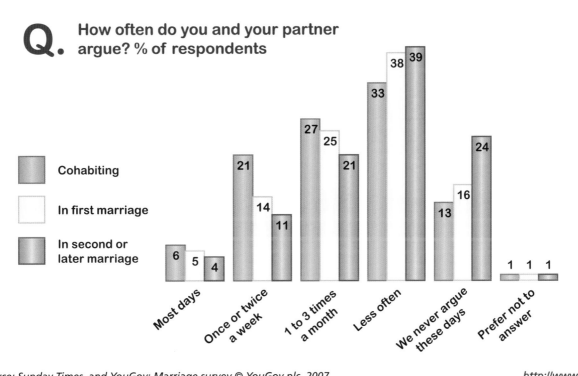

Legend:
- Cohabiting
- In first marriage
- In second or later marriage

Most days: 6, 5, 4
Once or twice a week: 21, 14, 11
1 to 3 times a month: 27, 25, 21
Less often: 33, 38, 39
We never argue these days: 13, 16, 24
Prefer not to answer: 1, 1, 1

Source: Sunday Times and YouGov: Marriage survey © YouGov plc. 2007

http://www.yougov.com

Hurt at home

In a survey, 31% of women and 18% of men said they had been victims of some form of domestic violence

Q: Has a partner ever physically hurt you?

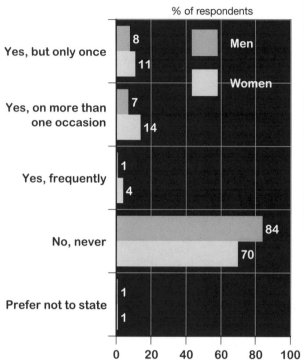

% of respondents

	Men	Women
Yes, but only once	8	11
Yes, on more than one occasion	7	14
Yes, frequently	1	4
No, never	84	70
Prefer not to state	1	1

0 20 40 60 80 100

NB Figures may not add up to 100% due to rounding
Sample size: 2,302

25% of men believed that domestic violence only affects a small percentage of the population, compared to only 8% of women.

71% of men would involve the police if they or a friend were a victim of domestic violence, compared to only 59% of women.

Q: Has a partner ever mentally or physically bullied you?

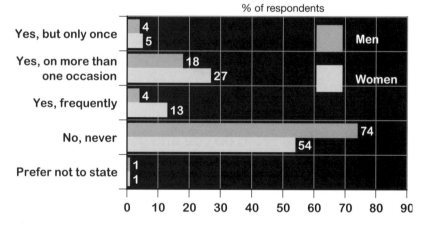

% of respondents

	Men	Women
Yes, but only once	4	5
Yes, on more than one occasion	18	27
Yes, frequently	4	13
No, never	74	54
Prefer not to state	1	1

0 10 20 30 40 50 60 70 80 90

Q: Which, if any, of these do you regard as domestic violence?

% of respondents
(respondents could choose more than one option)

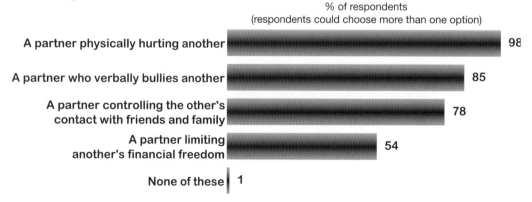

A partner physically hurting another	98
A partner who verbally bullies another	85
A partner controlling the other's contact with friends and family	78
A partner limiting another's financial freedom	54
None of these	1

Source: YouGov / This Morning survey, January 2007 © YouGov plc 2007

http://www.yougov.com

Fact File 2008 • www.carelpress.com

Pulling power

Q: Which of these methods have you used at any time to find a date or partner? UK, 2007, %
(Respondents could choose more than one option)

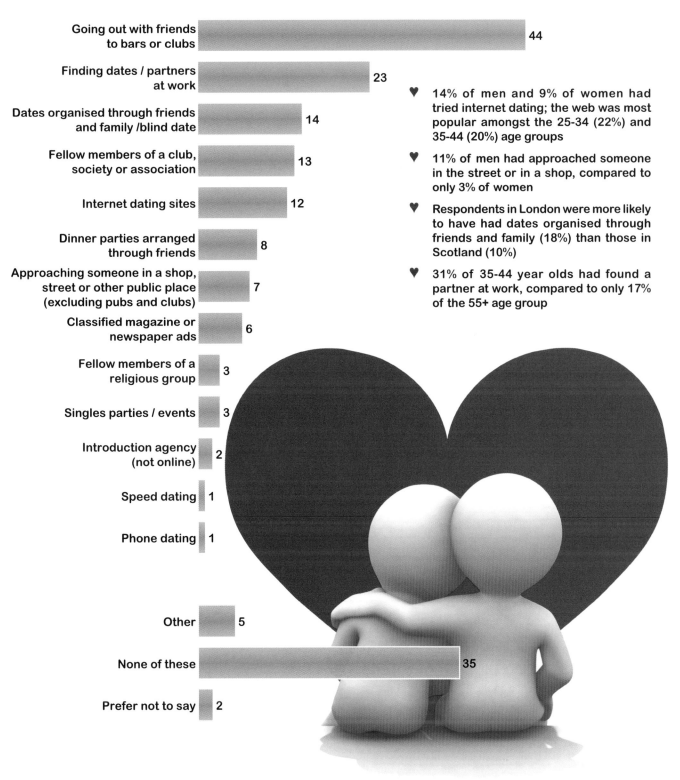

Method	%
Going out with friends to bars or clubs	44
Finding dates / partners at work	23
Dates organised through friends and family /blind date	14
Fellow members of a club, society or association	13
Internet dating sites	12
Dinner parties arranged through friends	8
Approaching someone in a shop, street or other public place (excluding pubs and clubs)	7
Classified magazine or newspaper ads	6
Fellow members of a religious group	3
Singles parties / events	3
Introduction agency (not online)	2
Speed dating	1
Phone dating	1
Other	5
None of these	35
Prefer not to say	2

♥ 14% of men and 9% of women had tried internet dating; the web was most popular amongst the 25-34 (22%) and 35-44 (20%) age groups

♥ 11% of men had approached someone in the street or in a shop, compared to only 3% of women

♥ Respondents in London were more likely to have had dates organised through friends and family (18%) than those in Scotland (10%)

♥ 31% of 35-44 year olds had found a partner at work, compared to only 17% of the 55+ age group

Source: YouGov: Dating survey © 2007

http://www.yougov.com

Modern families

The Millennium Cohort Survey, the most comprehensive study of its kind, surveyed nearly 30,000 parents at the start of the millennium and again in 2003.*
An analysis of the results was published in 2007.

Partnership and economic status of families surveyed when the child was 3 years old, UK

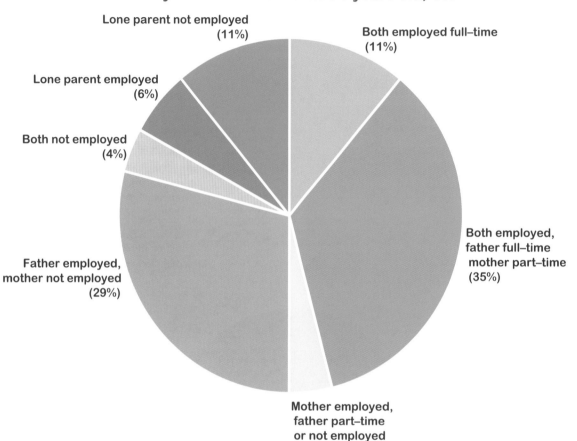

Lone parent not employed (11%)

Both employed full–time (11%)

Lone parent employed (6%)

Both not employed (4%)

Both employed, father full–time mother part–time (35%)

Father employed, mother not employed (29%)

Mother employed, father part–time or not employed (4%)

- Both parents today often want to contribute to the family income and be more closely involved with their children.

- 4 out of 5 new fathers said they would be happy to stay at home and look after their baby.

- 70% of new dads want to spend more time with their children.

- 44% of mothers with babies believed that women are naturally better than men at childcaring.

- The study also found that there is no link between a mother working and developmental problems for their children.

*The MCS follows the lives of a sample of nearly 19,000 babies born between 1 September 2000 and 31 August 2001 in England and Wales, and between 22 November 2000 and 11 January 2002 in Scotland and Northern Ireland. Information has been collected from parents when the children were aged nine months and at around three years of age.

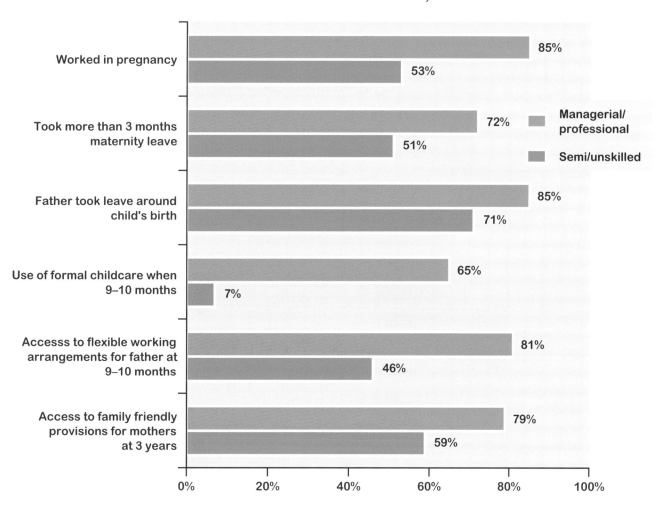

Access to family support, professional families and low–skilled families, UK

- Worked in pregnancy: 85% (Managerial/professional), 53% (Semi/unskilled)
- Took more than 3 months maternity leave: 72% (Managerial/professional), 51% (Semi/unskilled)
- Father took leave around child's birth: 85% (Managerial/professional), 71% (Semi/unskilled)
- Use of formal childcare when 9–10 months: 65% (Managerial/professional), 7% (Semi/unskilled)
- Accesss to flexible working arrangements for father at 9–10 months: 81% (Managerial/professional), 46% (Semi/unskilled)
- Access to family friendly provisions for mothers at 3 years: 79% (Managerial/professional), 59% (Semi/unskilled)

Legend: Managerial/professional, Semi/unskilled

Income divides are creating families of 'haves' and 'have-nots' – low-income families were less likely to have:

- Both parents in employment
- Adequate income during maternity and paternity leave that is topped up by their employer
- Access to formal childcare
- A range of family friendly provisions offered by their employer

80% of dads took time off around the birth of their child.

76% of working dads in high-income families took at least two weeks paternity leave compared to 64% in low-income families.

57% of Pakistani and Bangladeshi working mothers used grandparents for childcare, compared to 45% of white working mothers.

Formal childcare was most popular where both parents worked full-time, while fathers were the most popular carers of children where the mother was the main earner in the family.

A DfES report found that the number of families using formal childcare and early years provision increased from 31% in 2001 to 41% in 2004.

Source: The State of the Modern Family 2007, Equal Opportunities Commission © EOC 2007

http://www.eoc.org.uk

Depends on mum

The Millennium Cohort Study is a longitudinal survey of the lives of 11,500 babies born at the turn of the 21st century.

Selected demographic characteristics of surveyed mothers, by ethnic group, England

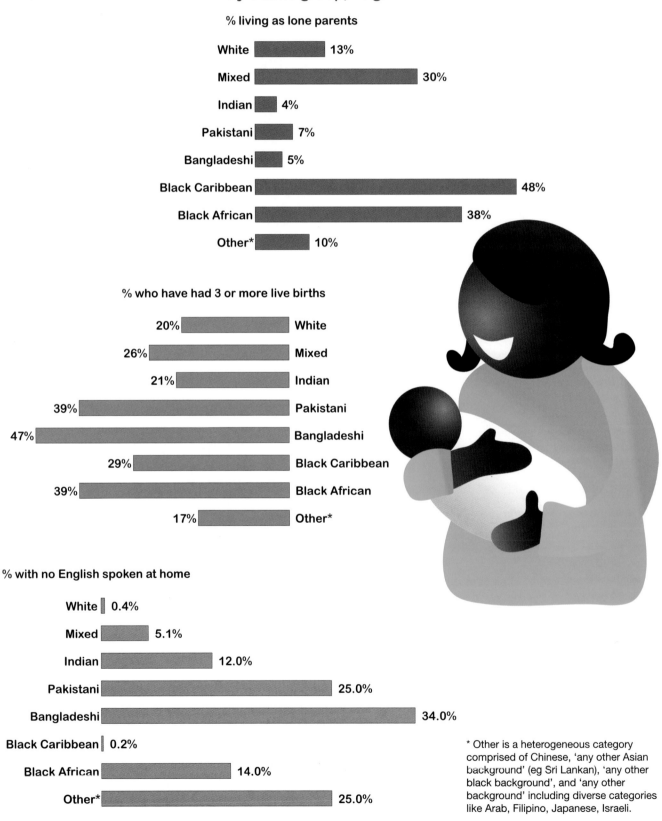

% living as lone parents

Ethnic group	%
White	13%
Mixed	30%
Indian	4%
Pakistani	7%
Bangladeshi	5%
Black Caribbean	48%
Black African	38%
Other*	10%

% who have had 3 or more live births

%	Ethnic group
20%	White
26%	Mixed
21%	Indian
39%	Pakistani
47%	Bangladeshi
29%	Black Caribbean
39%	Black African
17%	Other*

% with no English spoken at home

Ethnic group	%
White	0.4%
Mixed	5.1%
Indian	12.0%
Pakistani	25.0%
Bangladeshi	34.0%
Black Caribbean	0.2%
Black African	14.0%
Other*	25.0%

* Other is a heterogeneous category comprised of Chinese, 'any other Asian background' (eg Sri Lankan), 'any other black background', and 'any other background' including diverse categories like Arab, Filipino, Japanese, Israeli.

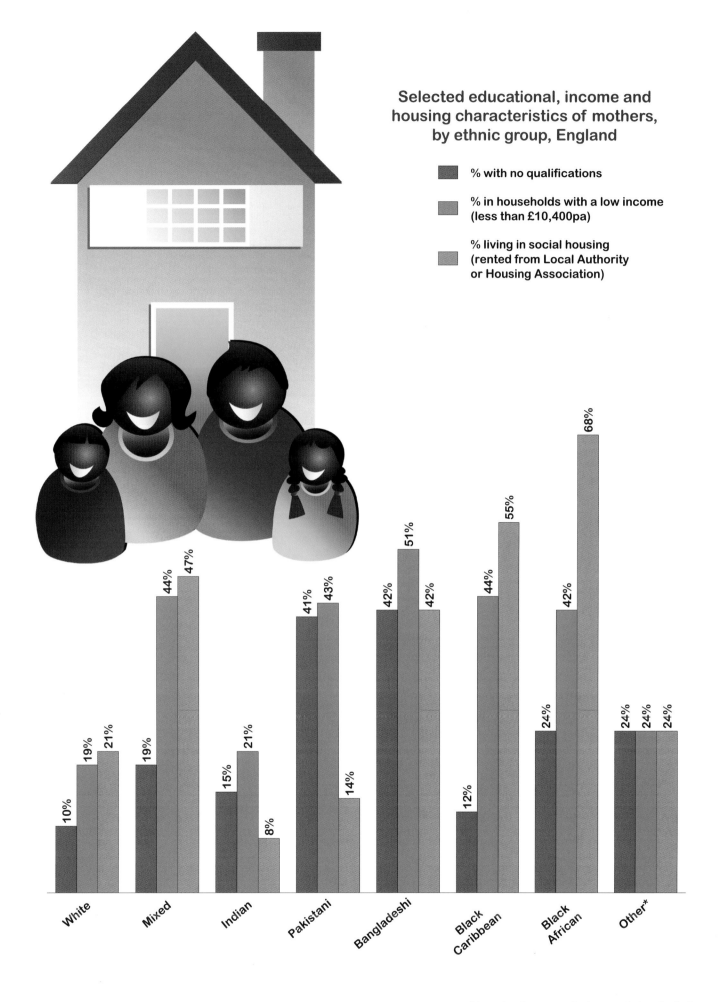

Selected educational, income and
housing characteristics of mothers,
by ethnic group, England

■ % with no qualifications

■ % in households with a low income
(less than £10,400pa)

■ % living in social housing
(rented from Local Authority
or Housing Association)

White
10% 19% 21%

Mixed
19% 44% 47%

Indian
15% 21% 8%

Pakistani
41% 43% 14%

Bangladeshi
42% 51% 42%

Black Caribbean
12% 44% 55%

Black African
24% 42% 68%

Other*
24% 24% 24%

Source: Demographic and socio-economic characteristics of ethnic
minority mothers in England, Millennium Cohort Study, First
Survey, Centre for Longitudinal Studies 2007

http://www.cls.ioe.ac.uk

Early start

The vast majority of teenage pregnancies are unplanned. Young parents and their children often suffer problems with their health, finances, education and social integration

Conceptions among under 20s, by age group, England and Wales
(thousands)

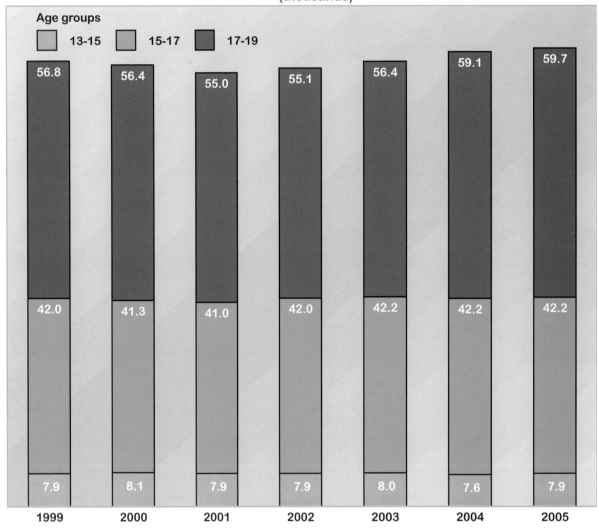

Age groups
13-15   15-17   17-19

	1999	2000	2001	2002	2003	2004	2005
17-19	56.8	56.4	55.0	55.1	56.4	59.1	59.7
15-17	42.0	41.3	41.0	42.0	42.2	42.2	42.2
13-15	7.9	8.1	7.9	7.9	8.0	7.6	7.9

The overwhelming majority of under-18 conceptions are unintended and around half lead to an abortion.

In 2005, 57.1% of conceptions among 13-15 year olds led to abortion and 40.4% among 15-19 year olds.

The media's focus on very young mothers can be misleading. In reality, over half of mothers aged under 20 were aged 19, with only 6% aged 16 or under.

Of the estimated 50,000 mothers aged under 20 living in England in 2005, over 80% were aged 18 or 19; over 60% were lone parents; 70% were not in education, employment or training and they were much more likely to live in deprived neighbourhoods.

Live births by age of mother, England and Wales

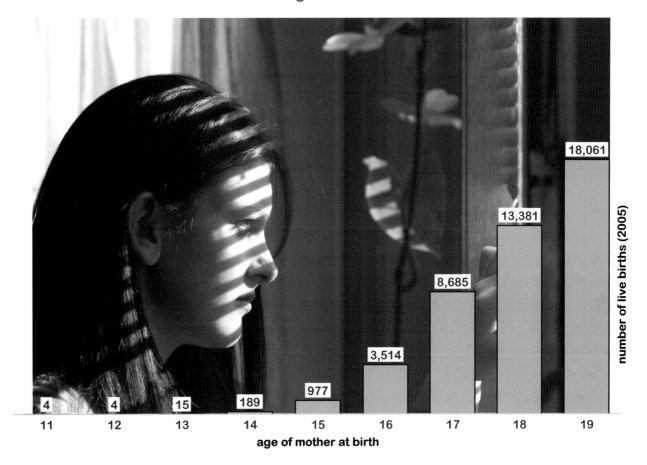

number of live births (2005)

age of mother at birth	
11	4
12	4
13	15
14	189
15	977
16	3,514
17	8,685
18	13,381
19	18,061

The cost of teenage pregnancy places significant burdens on the NHS and wider public services:

- The cost of teenage pregnancy to the NHS alone is estimated to be £63m a year
- Benefit payments to a teenage mother who does not enter employment in the three years following birth can total between £19,000 and £25,000 over 3 years
- Teenage mothers are more likely than older mothers to require targeted support from a range of local services, for example to help them access supported housing and/or re-engage in education, employment and training

The poor outcomes experienced by teenage mothers and their children include a range of factors such as:

- higher rates of relationship breakdown
- a greater likelihood of living in a workless household and in social housing
- lower levels of emotional support

The children of teenage mothers tend to have poorer health and poorer social outcomes. For example, they have higher rates of accidents, such as falls and swallowing dangerous substances and are more likely to experience behavioural problems, such as conduct, emotional and hyperactivity problems. Research shows the higher incidence of these problems are – at least in part – due to higher levels of poor emotional health among teenage mothers.

61% of mothers under 20 giving birth in the preceding three years were lone parents. Although 66% of birth registrations for children born to teenage mothers are joint registrations, almost half of fathers are resident at a different address at the time of the child's birth.

Not being in a stable relationship at and immediately after the time of the birth also contributes to young mothers' poor emotional health and well-being. Only a third of young mothers report having a stable relationship during their pregnancy and in the following three years, compared to nearly 90% of older mothers.

Children born to teenage mothers have a 63% higher risk of living in poverty, compared to babies born to mothers in their 20s. They have lower academic attainment and are at higher risk of economic inactivity in later life.

Source: Office for National Statistics 2007 © Crown copyright,
Teenage Parents Next Steps, Department for children, schools
and families © Crown copyright,
Birth Statistics 2006, ONS © Crown copyright

http://www.statistics.gov.uk
http://www.dcsf.gov.uk
http://www.everychildmatters.gov.uk

Late start

With more women waiting before they start a family, the number of multiple births has increased, mainly due to IVF

Average age of mother, by birth order, England and Wales

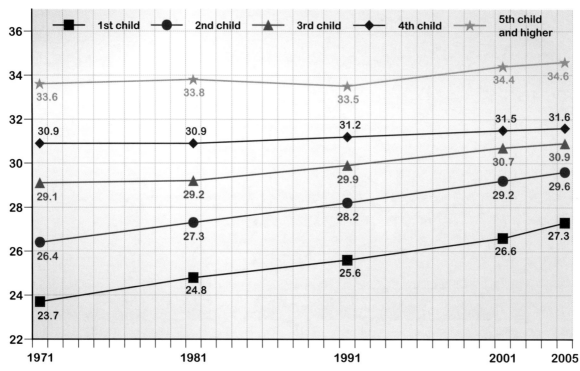

Legend: ■ 1st child ● 2nd child ▲ 3rd child ◆ 4th child ★ 5th child and higher

Data points:
- 5th child and higher: 33.6 (1971), 33.8 (1981), 33.5 (1991), 34.4 (2001), 34.6 (2005)
- 4th child: 30.9 (1971), 30.9 (1981), 31.2 (1991), 31.5 (2001), 31.6 (2005)
- 3rd child: 29.1 (1971), 29.2 (1981), 29.9 (1991), 30.7 (2001), 30.9 (2005)
- 2nd child: 26.4 (1971), 27.3 (1981), 28.2 (1991), 29.2 (2001), 29.6 (2005)
- 1st child: 23.7 (1971), 24.8 (1981), 25.6 (1991), 26.6 (2001), 27.3 (2005)

x-axis: 1971, 1981, 1991, 2001, 2005

Multiple births by age of mother, UK 2005, rate per 1,000 maternities

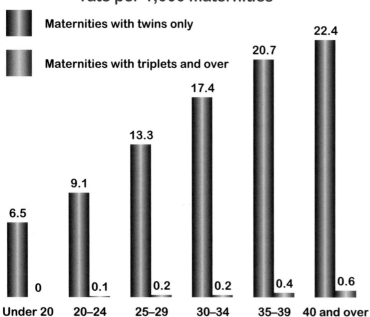

- Maternities with twins only
- Maternities with triplets and over

Age	Twins only	Triplets and over
Under 20	6.5	0
20–24	9.1	0.1
25–29	13.3	0.2
30–34	17.4	0.2
35–39	20.7	0.4
40 and over	22.4	0.6

The rate of multiple births has increased from 9.9 per 1,000 maternities in 1975 to 14.9 per 1,000 in 2005. This is likely to be a result of the increased use of fertility treatment. The chances of a multiple birth through natural conception are low (approximately 1 in 80), but 1 in 4 IVF deliveries in 2005 were twins.

Source: Office for National Statistics: Social Trends 2007
© Crown copyright 2007

http://www.statistics.gov.uk

Who's in the house?

The proportion of children living in lone–parent families has more than tripled in the 34 years 1972–2006

Families with dependent children, GB, 1972 to 2006

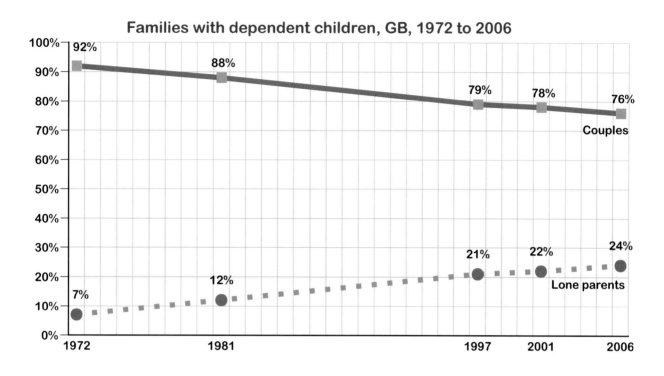

Couples: 92% (1972), 88% (1981), 79% (1997), 78% (2001), 76% (2006)

Lone parents: 7% (1972), 12% (1981), 21% (1997), 22% (2001), 24% (2006)

People in households, by type of household and family, GB, 2006

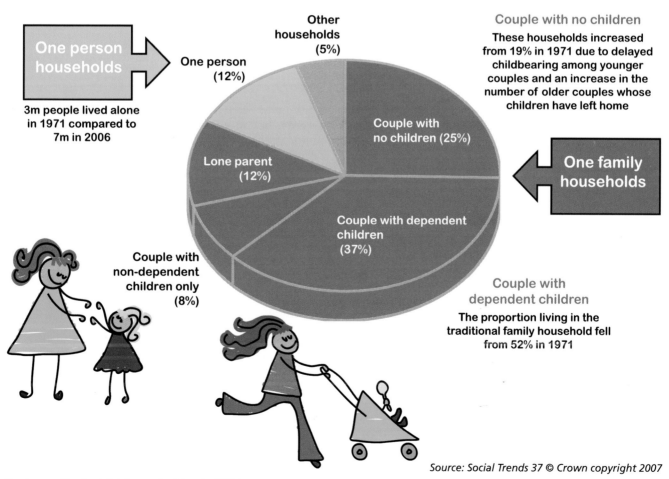

One person households

3m people lived alone in 1971 compared to 7m in 2006

One person (12%)

Other households (5%)

Lone parent (12%)

Couple with non-dependent children only (8%)

Couple with no children (25%)

Couple with dependent children (37%)

Couple with no children
These households increased from 19% in 1971 due to delayed childbearing among younger couples and an increase in the number of older couples whose children have left home

One family households

Couple with dependent children
The proportion living in the traditional family household fell from 52% in 1971

Source: Social Trends 37 © Crown copyright 2007

http://www.ons.gov.uk

Due to rounding the total does not add up to 100%

Kippers

**Kids In Parents' Pockets
Eroding Retirement Savings**

Adults living with their parents, by age group and gender, England, 2006

Males   Females

"Why waste money on rent when I don't need to?" Ruby, London

58% 39% 22% 11% 9% 3%

| 20–24 | 25–29 | 30–34 |

Age groups

The key reasons for young people living at home longer in Britain are:

- The high-priced housing market – Average house prices are 204% higher than in 1995 compared with a 92% rise in average incomes. First-time buyers are having to pay larger deposits to buy their first home resulting in them getting on the property ladder at a later age

- Mounting student debt – The number of young students who live in the family home is almost entirely related to increases in tuition fees. Students who are the first in their family to go to university and from lower socio-economic backgrounds are most worried about debt.

The comforts provided by parents could also contribute.

Eight out of ten Italian men aged 18 to 30 live with their parents. Italian parents tend to enjoy their children's companionship and other services they provide and are willing to 'bribe' them into cohabitation in exchange for some payment.

In 2006 43.5% of Canadian 20-29 year olds lived at home. Staying in school longer and difficulty finding a stable, full-time job are historical reasons behind the rising trend. Most recently the rise has been part fuelled by shifting family values – baby boomers often have a relationship with their adolescent and adult children that is more akin to friendship compared to past generations.

The same trend has been noted in France, Germany, Australia and the United States.

"Home-cooked meals, clean clothes and a fully-stocked fridge... and the crazy house prices too" Tomo, Liverpool

"It is a question of freedom versus money, and in the current market, I simply cannot afford that freedom" Ian, Preston

Source: Office for National Statistics © Crown copyright 2007, various 2007

http://www.statistics.gov.uk

Financial issues

Through the roof

Annual house price inflation, UK, (% change on a year earlier) by country, August 2005 to July 2007

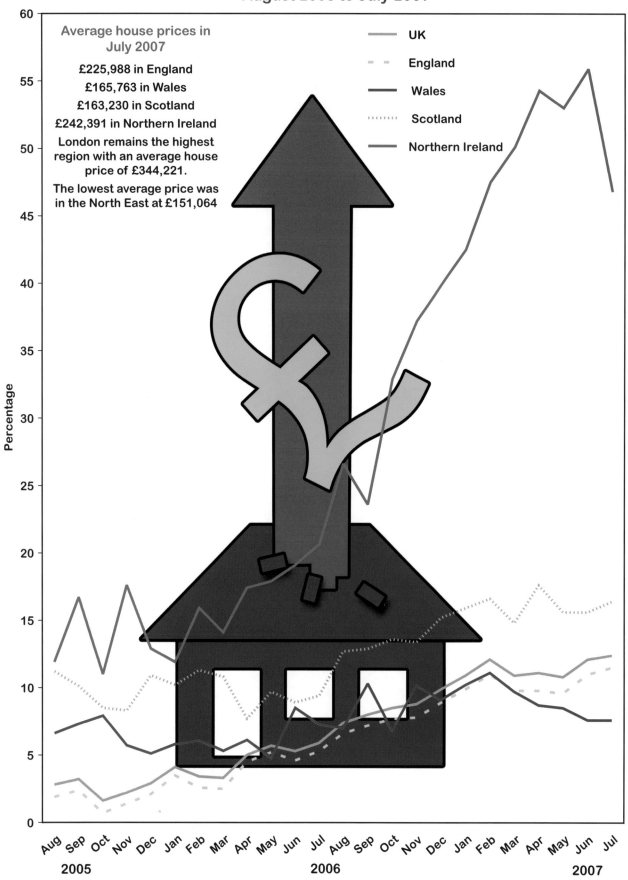

Average house prices in July 2007

£225,988 in England

£165,763 in Wales

£163,230 in Scotland

£242,391 in Northern Ireland

London remains the highest region with an average house price of £344,221.

The lowest average price was in the North East at £151,064

Legend:
- UK
- England
- Wales
- Scotland
- Northern Ireland

Y-axis: Percentage (0 to 60)

X-axis: Aug Sep Oct Nov Dec Jan Feb Mar Apr May Jun Jul Aug Sep Oct Nov Dec Jan Feb Mar Apr May Jun Jul

2005 — 2006 — 2007

Source: House Price Index July 2007, Communities and Local Government © Crown copyright

http://www.communities.gov.uk/housingstatistics

Where we live

Housing tenure, GB households, 1971-2005, %

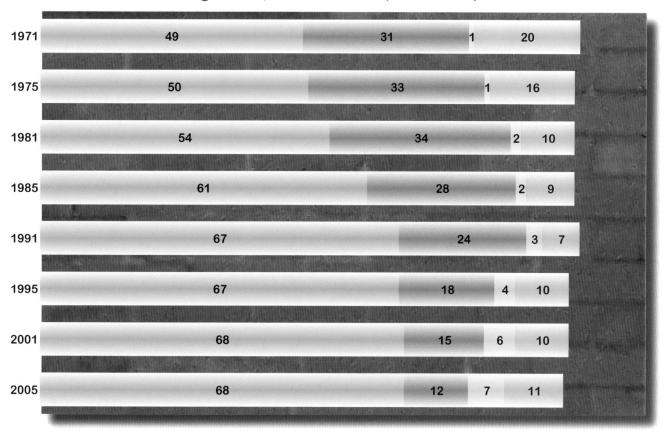

Year	Owner occupied	Rented from council	Rented from housing association	Rented privately
1971	49	31	1	20
1975	50	33	1	16
1981	54	34	2	10
1985	61	28	2	9
1991	67	24	3	7
1995	67	18	4	10
2001	68	15	6	10
2005	68	12	7	11

■ Owner occupied

■ Rented from council

■ Rented from housing association

■ Rented privately

NB Figures do not add up to 100% due to rounding

Source: General Household Survey, 2005
© Crown copyright
http://www.statistics.gov.uk

Out of reach

The situation for key workers trying to buy their own homes has worsened

Percentage of towns where key workers cannot afford to buy property, GB, 2002 and 2007

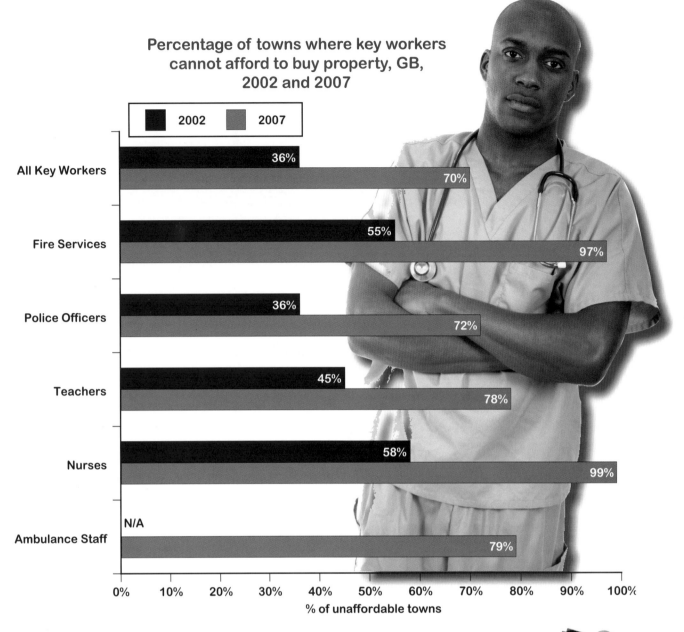

	2002	2007
All Key Workers	36%	70%
Fire Services	55%	97%
Police Officers	36%	72%
Teachers	45%	78%
Nurses	58%	99%
Ambulance Staff	N/A	79%

% of unaffordable towns

- Key workers such as teachers, nurses, police, firefighters and ambulance staff cannot afford to buy homes in many towns

- A town is classed as unaffordable if the average price of a house is more than 4.46 times the average wage of the key workers. This is also the average multiple of income a first–time buyer pays for a property

- Gerrards Cross in Buckinghamshire is the least affordable place for key workers to buy (with a house price to earnings ratio of at least 20.8 times) closely followed by Kensington and Chelsea

- Lochgelly in Fife is the most affordable town in Great Britain (house price ratio of 4.1 times salary). The most affordable in England is Nelson in the North West (ratio 4.5)

- 61 towns have moved from being affordable for all key worker occupations in 2002 to being unaffordable in 2007

- 29 of the top 30 least affordable towns are in the south of England, the other town is Altrincham in the North West

Source: Annual Halifax Key Worker Housing Review, HBOS plc 2007

http://www.hbosplc.com

Priced out

The under 30s are staying in the private rented sector longer before buying their own property

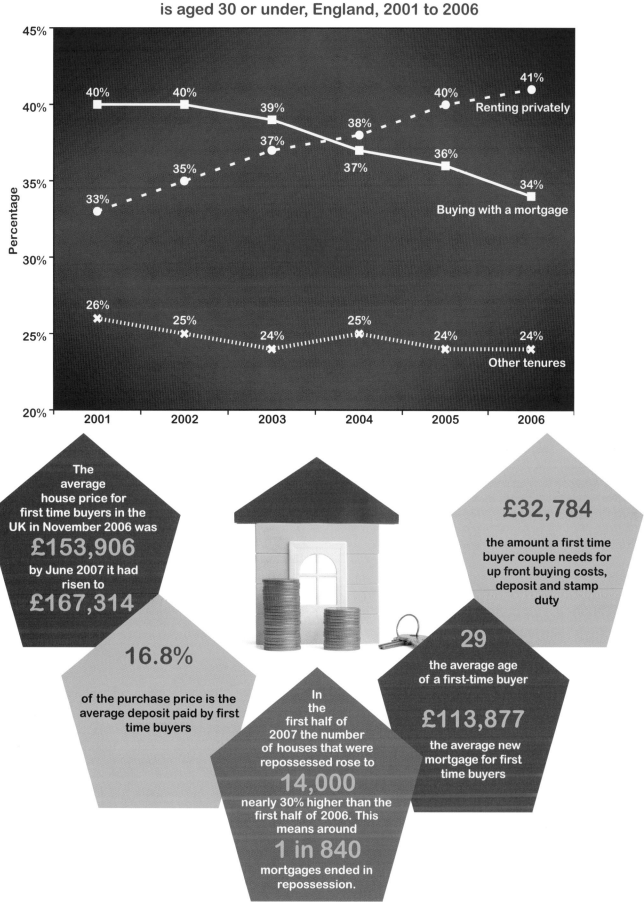

Trends in household tenure where the householder is aged 30 or under, England, 2001 to 2006

Percentage (y-axis: 20% to 45%)

Renting privately:
- 2001: 33%
- 2002: 35%
- 2003: 37%
- 2004: 38%
- 2005: 40%
- 2006: 41%

Buying with a mortgage:
- 2001: 40%
- 2002: 40%
- 2003: 39%
- 2004: 37%
- 2005: 36%
- 2006: 34%

Other tenures:
- 2001: 26%
- 2002: 25%
- 2003: 24%
- 2004: 25%
- 2005: 24%
- 2006: 24%

The average house price for first time buyers in the UK in November 2006 was **£153,906** by June 2007 it had risen to **£167,314**

£32,784 the amount a first time buyer couple needs for up front buying costs, deposit and stamp duty

16.8% of the purchase price is the average deposit paid by first time buyers

In the first half of 2007 the number of houses that were repossessed rose to **14,000** nearly 30% higher than the first half of 2006. This means around **1 in 840** mortgages ended in repossession.

29 the average age of a first-time buyer **£113,877** the average new mortgage for first time buyers

Source: Survey of English Housing Results: 2005/06, Communities and Local Government © Crown copyright 2007; Debt Facts and Figures, Credit Action 2007; Council of Mortgage Lenders

http://www.communities.gov.uk
http://www.creditaction.org.uk

Nowhere to go

Young people under 25 make up a relatively high proportion of those accepted as homeless

Homelessness is often considered to apply only to people sleeping rough – people who sleep in the open air or in buildings or other places not designed for habitation.

However, most statistics on homelessness relate to people who are accepted as eligible for assistance by the local authority.

These are usually people who cannot remain in their current accommodation through no fault of their own.

46% of those who applied to local authorities were accepted as entitled to rehousing and in priority need. Priority need means there is a compelling reason for rehousing – this might be the presence of dependent children, that the household includes a pregnant woman or that it includes members of a vulnerable group such as young people.

Applicants accepted as homeless, by age group, England, 2005–06

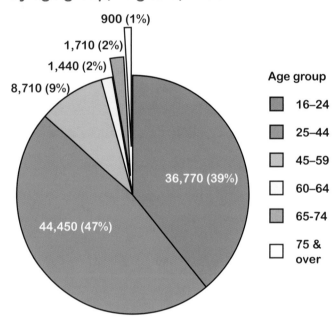

900 (1%)
1,710 (2%)
1,440 (2%)
8,710 (9%)
36,770 (39%)
44,450 (47%)

Age group

- 16–24
- 25–44
- 45–59
- 60–64
- 65-74
- 75 & over

Youth homelessness, England

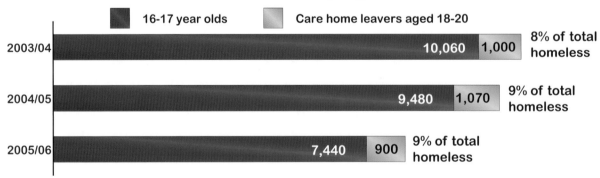

16-17 year olds   Care home leavers aged 18-20

	16-17 year olds	Care home leavers aged 18-20	
2003/04	10,060	1,000	8% of total homeless
2004/05	9,480	1,070	9% of total homeless
2005/06	7,440	900	9% of total homeless

16 and 17 year olds (with certain exceptions) and young people aged between 18 and 20 who were formerly in care have a priority need for accommodation under the homelessness legislation. This means that if they become homeless through no fault of their own, the local authority must find them suitable accommodation.

Source: Tackling Youth Homelessness 2007, Department for Communities and Local Government © Crown copyright

http://www.homeoffice.gov.uk

Spending nation

The total value of the UK includes the value of buildings, vehicles, machinery, bridges, roads, the shares we own and the money in our bank accounts at the end of 2006.

The UK is worth more than ever, yet debt is becoming a way of life

For Sale: UK

£6,525bn

Housing is the most valuable asset (60% of total net worth), with a total value of £3,915 billion, up 10% on the previous year.

Most of our country's wealth is in property and that is where much of our debt lies. The average UK house price is now £214,222, the average mortgage for first time buyers is £118,322. Homebuyers under 25 owe an average of £20,290 on unsecured credit, compared to £12,113 for tenants of the same age.

It is estimated that 11.7m people were saving less in July 2007 compared with three months earlier, with 6.8m people saving nothing at all.

Only 46% of people save regularly – the lowest level recorded in two years. Half of the population (53%) could survive financially for just 17 days, should they suffer an unexpected loss of income – one in four (25%) have less than £3,000 saved and a further one in four (27%) have no savings at all.

Over 7.5m people only save money for short-term goals and about 3m describe themselves as 'frivolous spenders' – making purchases based on desirability rather than affordability, the buy now, think later culture.

More than 8.3m (18%) holidaymakers get into debt to fund their summer break – 63% paying for it on plastic.

Over 80% of Britons regularly overspend (26% to cheer themselves up), 4m enjoy it too much to increase the amount they save.

44% of those aged 16 - 24 say their friends pressure them to spend when they have run out of money. Average consumer debt for 24-year-olds is £16,351, personal loans make up the largest part (56%), followed by credit cards (28%).

Half of England's teenagers have been, or are in debt by the age of 17. In addition, 90% worry about money and spending but think of overdrafts and credit cards as ways to buy things they couldn't normally afford.

While many readily get into debt to satisfy their spending, the people who are in the money spend more happily.

Britain's first ever Spend List shows how the financial elite spend their money. Purchases include £85m penthouses, £4.6m earrings, £72m yachts (Roman Abramovich owns four) and £30m weddings.

Leading estate agents report that the number of clients able to pay £5m and £10m cash for properties has risen sharply. Jets cost from around £13m to as much as £40m for the next generation Challenger 605, yet demand is now so high, manufacturers are turning customers away. For an exclusive £500,000 plus watch, the wait is up to three years.

The explosion in personal fortunes is also driving prices for art. In 2006, a mystery buyer paid £49.5m at Sotheby's in New York for a Picasso – roughly double what experts felt the painting was worth.

http://www.statistics.gov.uk
http://www.creditaction.org.uk
http://uk.virginmoney.com
Source: Office for National Statistics, Consumer price index & Retail price index © Crown copyright 2007, Credit Action

Debt dilemma

Today in the UK:

» Consumers will borrow an additional £322m

» The average household debt will increase by over £13

» 77 properties will be repossessed

» 317 people will be declared insolvent or bankrupt

» 2,750 County Court Judgements (CCJs) issued

» Bank and building societies will hand out £1bn in mortgages

» Citizen Advice Bureaux will deal with 5,300 debt problems

» The average car will cost £15 to run

» More than 7,716 loan repayments are going unpaid every day

» The average home will cost £30 to run

» Raising a child to the age of 21 will now set you back £23.50 a day

» The price of a typical house will increase by £44

» £500m will be withdrawn from cash machines by 7.5m people across the UK

» 24.5m transactions worth £1.4bn will be spent on plastic cards

Financial Stress: Top 10

Financial stress is a measure used by the credit agency Experian to define an individual's 'potential to become over-stretched and struggle with further payments'. Areas with the highest levels of stress are:

1	Manchester	6	Kingston upon Hull
2	Glasgow	7	Liverpool
3	Nottingham	8	Southwark
4	Knowsley	9	Tower Hamlets
5	Middlesbrough	10	Hackney

Experian uses an analysis of the number of credit cards and personal loans that people take out, as well as how regularly payments are made on their debt.
Information from Mori's Financial Services Survey was also studied, alongside publicly available information on bad debts and County Court Judgements.

Total consumer credit lending to individuals in July 2007 was £214bn.
This has increased 5.3% in the last 12 months.

Total UK personal debt at the end of July 2007 stood at £1,355bn.
Debt grew by 10.1% in the previous 12 months which equates to an increase of £117bn.

Total lending in July 2007 grew by £10.3bn.
Secured lending grew by £9.2bn in the month.
Consumer credit lending grew by £1.1bn.

Total secured lending on homes at the end of July 2007 stood at £1,140bn.
This has increased 11.0% in the last 12 months.

Source: Credit Action, Experian
http://www.creditaction.org.uk

Budget breakdown

UK households spent an average of £443 a week in 2005/06. The largest proportion, (14%) was on transport

Average weekly expenditure on main commodities and services, UK households 2005/6

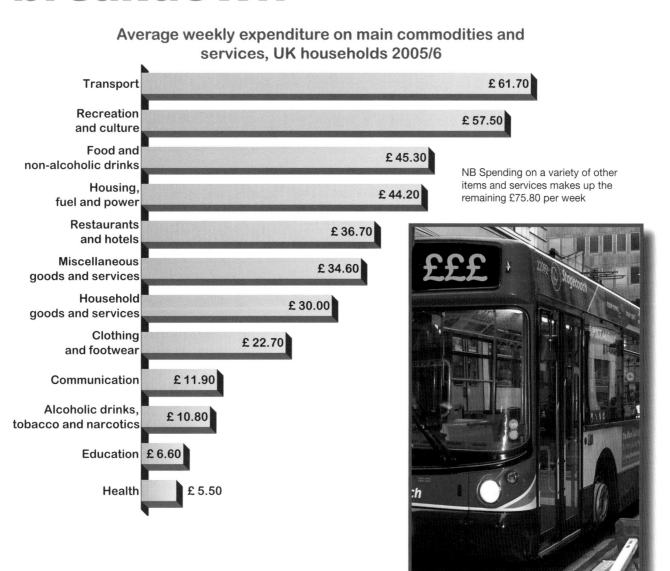

Transport	£ 61.70
Recreation and culture	£ 57.50
Food and non-alcoholic drinks	£ 45.30
Housing, fuel and power	£ 44.20
Restaurants and hotels	£ 36.70
Miscellaneous goods and services	£ 34.60
Household goods and services	£ 30.00
Clothing and footwear	£ 22.70
Communication	£ 11.90
Alcoholic drinks, tobacco and narcotics	£ 10.80
Education	£ 6.60
Health	£ 5.50

NB Spending on a variety of other items and services makes up the remaining £75.80 per week

Breakdown of average weekly transport expenditure, UK households 2005/6

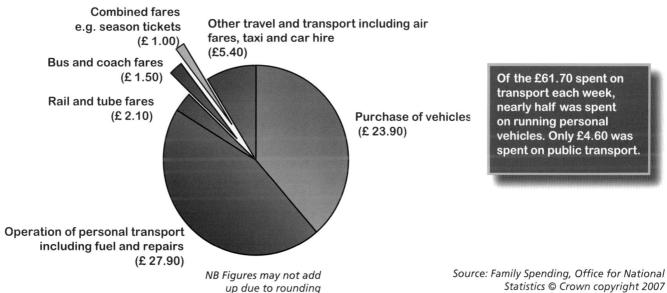

Combined fares e.g. season tickets (£ 1.00)

Other travel and transport including air fares, taxi and car hire (£5.40)

Bus and coach fares (£ 1.50)

Rail and tube fares (£ 2.10)

Purchase of vehicles (£ 23.90)

Operation of personal transport including fuel and repairs (£ 27.90)

Of the £61.70 spent on transport each week, nearly half was spent on running personal vehicles. Only £4.60 was spent on public transport.

NB Figures may not add up due to rounding

Source: Family Spending, Office for National Statistics © Crown copyright 2007
http://www.statistics.gov.uk

What we own

Households with durable goods, UK, 1998/99 and 2005/06, %

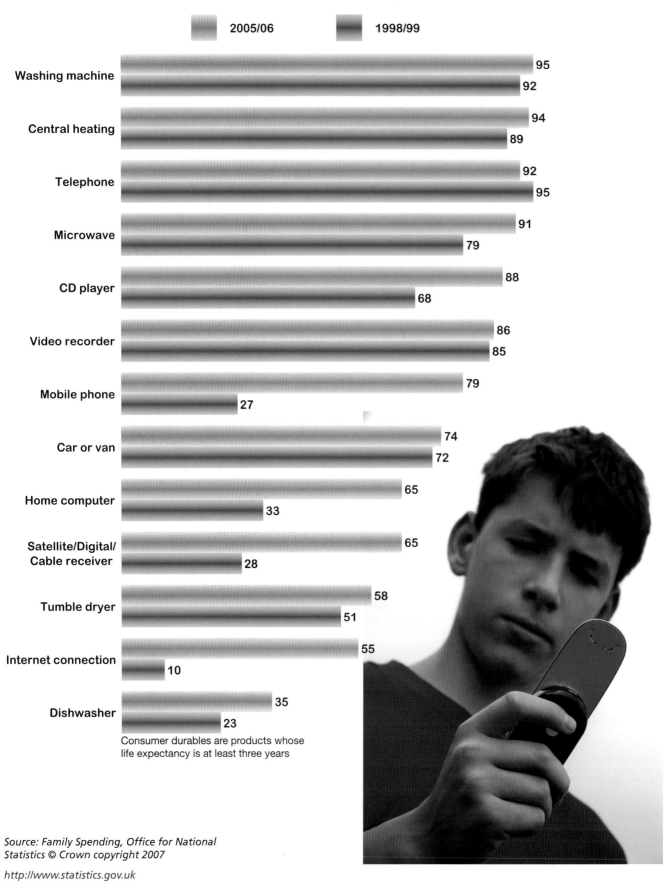

2005/06   1998/99

Item	2005/06	1998/99
Washing machine	95	92
Central heating	94	89
Telephone	92	95
Microwave	91	79
CD player	88	68
Video recorder	86	85
Mobile phone	79	27
Car or van	74	72
Home computer	65	33
Satellite/Digital/Cable receiver	65	28
Tumble dryer	58	51
Internet connection	55	10
Dishwasher	35	23

Consumer durables are products whose life expectancy is at least three years

Source: Family Spending, Office for National Statistics © Crown copyright 2007

http://www.statistics.gov.uk

Bank of mum & dad

Most children receive regular pocket money from their mums and dads

Average amount of pocket money per week, by age and gender

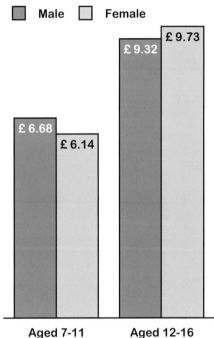

■ Male   □ Female

	Aged 7-11	Aged 12-16
Male	£6.68	£9.32
Female	£6.14	£9.73

Children in the North East and in Yorkshire & Humberside are most likely to get pocket money – 77% and 75% respectively – while those in the South West are least likely to receive it, 52%.

Average amount of pocket money per week, by region

South East	£10.43
East Midlands	£10.01
North West	£9.73
East England	£9.40
Scotland	£8.53
Northern Ireland	£8.46
London	£8.16
Wales	£7.35
West Midlands	£6.73
South West	£6.72
Yorkshire & Humberside	£5.92
North East	£5.70
UK	£8.01

Top 10 items children spend their pocket money on

Sweets/chocolate/crisps
Drinks
Going out
Food
Gifts
Clothes
Magazines
Mobile phone
Dvds/videos
Computer games/equipment

» 31% of children earn their pocket money by doing jobs around the home: 35% from tidying their bedroom and cleaning their house and 32% from washing up.

» 35% of girls get paid for doing the chores, compared with only 28% of boys.

» Older girls are also more likely to receive money for doing well at school or in exams. 22% of girls aged 12 to 16 are rewarded for academic achievement compared with 14% of boys in the same age group.

Source: Halifax Pocket Money Survey 2007

http://www.hbosplc.com

Poor pay more

An illustration of how poverty can cost more, UK 2006, £ per year

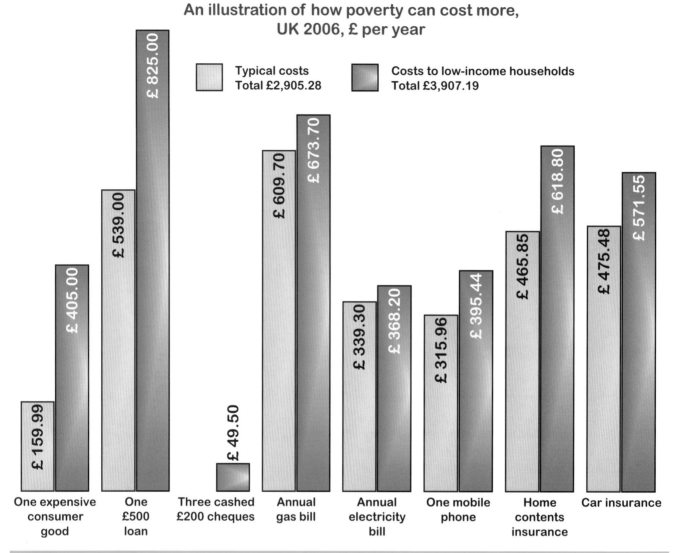

Typical costs
Total £2,905.28

Costs to low-income households
Total £3,907.19

Category	Typical costs	Costs to low-income households
One expensive consumer good	£159.99	£405.00
One £500 loan	£539.00	£825.00
Three cashed £200 cheques	£49.50	
Annual gas bill	£609.70	£673.70
Annual electricity bill	£339.30	£368.20
One mobile phone	£315.96	£395.44
Home contents insurance	£465.85	£618.80
Car insurance	£475.48	£571.55

Many low-income families use credit agreements and high-cost mail order catalogues to purchase consumer goods. This spreads the cost but is more expensive long-term.

Insurers charge higher premiums for both car and home insurance in less affluent areas.

Home credit and doorstep lenders offer loans to those with a poor credit rating, but the interest on these loans is very high.

Low-income families often opt for pre-payment energy meters, which means they miss out on the savings that can be made by paying by Direct Debit. In 2004,

25% of the fuel poor in England were pre-payment customers compared with just under 6% of all householders.

The cost of line rental for land phone lines and the disappearance of public telephones has made the mobile phone an essential. Pre-pay mobile phones do not require a credit check, but are on average 22% more expensive over a year than a monthly payment plan.

Cash machines in low-income areas are often those that charge up to £3. Cheque-cashing services typically charge a fee and a percentage of the amount to be cashed.

Source: Save the Children and the Family Welfare Association: The Poverty Premium © Save the Children, Family Welfare Association 2007

http://www.savethechildren.org.uk
http://www.fwa.org.uk

Losing out 1

In 2005/06, 11.4% of children were living in poverty in the UK

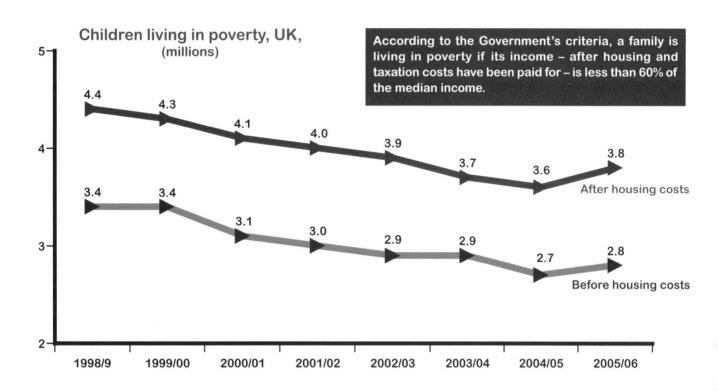

Children living in poverty, UK, (millions)

After housing costs: 4.4 (1998/9), 4.3 (1999/00), 4.1 (2000/01), 4.0 (2001/02), 3.9 (2002/03), 3.7 (2003/04), 3.6 (2004/05), 3.8 (2005/06)

Before housing costs: 3.4 (1998/9), 3.4 (1999/00), 3.1 (2000/01), 3.0 (2001/02), 2.9 (2002/03), 2.9 (2003/04), 2.7 (2004/05), 2.8 (2005/06)

According to the Government's criteria, a family is living in poverty if its income – after housing and taxation costs have been paid for – is less than 60% of the median income.

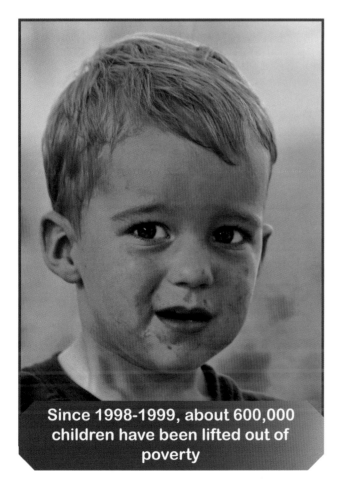

Since 1998-1999, about 600,000 children have been lifted out of poverty

What is poverty?

In 2005/06, 18% of the population lived in households with below 60% of median income before housing costs, 22% after housing costs

Income before housing costs is shown because some people choose to spend more of their income on housing costs and benefit from a better quality of life by paying more for better quality accommodation.

However, for those who don't, the increase in housing costs is leaving many people with little income to pay for life's necessities.

Income after housing costs pays for food, fuel, clothing, transport, school trips, holidays, birthdays, Christmas, all other necessities and the interest charged by home credit companies.

Certain groups of people have an above average risk of low income such as:

- children (in particular, children in unemployed lone-parent families, children of couples where the parents are unemployed or work only part-time, and those in families with four or more children)

- workless households, ethnic minorities, disabled people, Local Authority tenants, Housing Association tenants, those with no educational qualifications, people living in Inner London, older pensioners

In real terms, over the past year or so, poor families have probably been standing still. It is just that the benefits they receive are not rising as fast as median wages, so they are relatively worse off under the measurement of poverty relative to the median income.

Losing out 2

The Family Resources Survey includes questions about whether families have certain goods and services. If they do not have them they are asked whether that is by choice or because they cannot afford them. This is a useful way of measuring living standards of children and their relative deprivation.

Bottom quintile*, top quintile and all children: Extent of deprivation of items and services, UK % of children

*quintile = fifth		Bottom quintile	Top quintile	All children
Outdoor space/facilities to play safely	Have this	75	95	85
	Don't have this	25	5	15
Enough bedrooms for every child 10 years or over and of a different gender	Child/ren has/have this	72	96	80
	Want but can't afford this	26	2	18
	Don't want or need; doesn't apply	2	1	2
Celebrations on special occasions	Child/ren has/have this	88	98	95
	Want but can't afford this	10	0	4
	Don't want or need; doesn't apply	2	2	2
Leisure equipment such as sports equipment or a bicycle	Child/ren has/have this	78	95	88
	Want but can't afford this	15	1	7
	Don't want or need; doesn't apply	6	4	5
At least one week's holiday away from home with family	Child/ren has/have this	40	92	64
	Want but can't afford this	55	3	31
	Don't want or need; doesn't apply	5	4	5
Hobby or leisure activity	Child/ren does/do this	67	86	78
	Would like to but can't afford this	14	0	6
	Don't want or need; doesn't apply	19	14	16
Swimming at least once a month	Child/ren does/do this	49	72	59
	Would like to but can't afford this	22	1	11
	Don't want or need; doesn't apply	29	27	30
Have friends round for tea or a snack once a fortnight	Child/ren does/do this	62	84	71
	Would like to but can't afford this	17	1	8
	Don't want or need; doesn't apply	21	16	21
Gone on school trip at least once a term	Child/ren has/have this	83	95	89
	Would like to but can't afford this	13	0	6
	Don't want or need; doesn't apply	4	4	5
Go to a playgroup at least once a week	Child/ren does/do this	52	81	65
	Would like to but can't afford this	15	1	7
	Don't want or need; doesn't apply	33	18	28
Average income (£ per week equivalised)		181	733	443
Income growth 1994/95 to 2005/06		24%	23%	27%

Source: Households below average income statistical report, Family Resources Survey, 2005-06, Department for Work and Pensions © Crown copyright 2007

http://www.dwp.gov.uk

Below the breadline

There were 336,000 jobs which paid less than the minimum wage in 2006, that's 1.3% of jobs in the UK

% of jobs paid below the minimum wage, UK 1998-2006

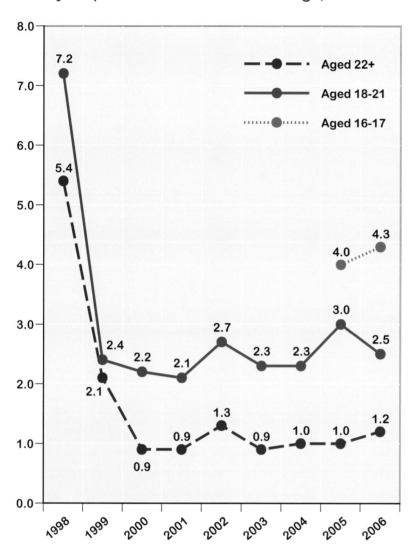

Legend:
- Aged 22+
- Aged 18-21
- Aged 16-17

Data points:
- 7.2 (1998)
- 5.4 (1998)
- 2.4 (1999)
- 2.1 (1999)
- 2.2 (2000)
- 0.9 (2000)
- 2.1 (2001)
- 0.9 (2001)
- 2.7 (2002)
- 1.3 (2002)
- 2.3 (2003)
- 0.9 (2003)
- 2.3 (2004)
- 1.0 (2004)
- 3.0 (2005)
- 1.0 (2005)
- 4.0 (2005)
- 2.5 (2006)
- 1.2 (2006)
- 4.3 (2006)

National minimum wage, hourly rates, UK, 1999-2007

	16-17	18-21	22 +
Apr 1999 - May 2000		£3.00	£3.60
Jun 2000 - Sep 2000		£3.20	£3.60
Oct 2000 - Sep 2001		£3.20	£3.70
Oct 2001 - Sep 2002		£3.50	£4.10
Oct 2002 - Sep 2003		£3.60	£4.20
Oct 2003 - Sep 2004		£3.80	£4.50
Oct 2004 - Sep 2005	£3.00	£4.10	£4.85
Oct 2005 - Sep 2006	£3.00	£4.25	£5.05
Oct 2006 - Sep 2007	£3.30	£4.45	£5.35
Oct 2007-	£3.40	£4.60	£5.52

UK legislation covering minimum wage rates for employees over the age of 18 was introduced on 1st April 1999. In October 2004, a national minimum wage was introduced for 16 to 17 year olds.

Employers who fail to pay the minimum wage can face up to a £5,000 fine.

The Government has already targeted the hairdressing and childcare sectors for enforcement. The next sector will be hotels followed by hospitality.

Source: Annual Survey of Hours and Earnings (ASHE) 2006 © Crown copyright

http://www.statistics.gov.uk/
http://www.dti.gov.uk

Mind the gap

The gender pay gap reduced only slightly from 20.7% in 1997 to 17.2% in 2006

Mean hourly earnings excluding overtime, UK 1997-2006, £
(Full-time employees on adult rates, whose pay was unaffected by absence)

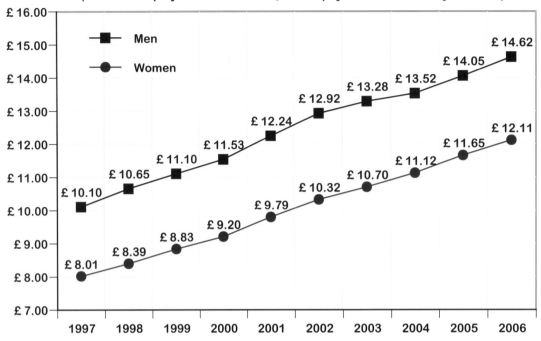

Men
Women

£ 10.10, £ 10.65, £ 11.10, £ 11.53, £ 12.24, £ 12.92, £ 13.28, £ 13.52, £ 14.05, £ 14.62
£ 8.01, £ 8.39, £ 8.83, £ 9.20, £ 9.79, £ 10.32, £ 10.70, £ 11.12, £ 11.65, £ 12.11

1997 1998 1999 2000 2001 2002 2003 2004 2005 2006

Median gross weekly earnings by age, UK 2006, £
(Full-time employees on adult rates*, whose pay was unaffected by absence)

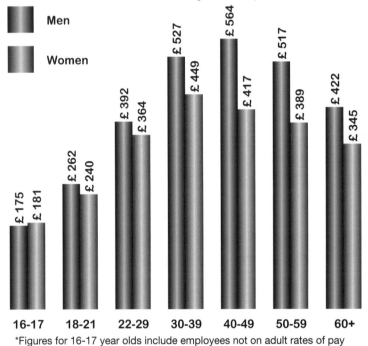

Men
Women

16-17: £ 175 / £ 181
18-21: £ 262 / £ 240
22-29: £ 392 / £ 364
30-39: £ 527 / £ 449
40-49: £ 564 / £ 417
50-59: £ 517 / £ 389
60+: £ 422 / £ 345

*Figures for 16-17 year olds include employees not on adult rates of pay

NB Mean is the average calculated by dividing the total by the number of employees.
The median is the value below which 50% of employees fall.

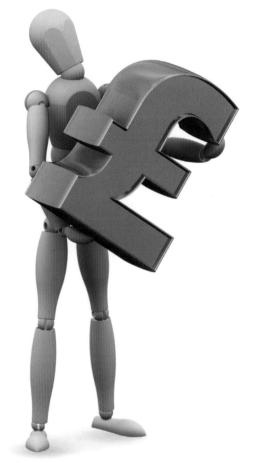

Source: Office for National Statistics, Annual Survey of Hours and Earnings (ASHE) 2006 © Crown copyright

http://www.statistics.gov.uk/

Food & drink

Meal ticket

52% of people 'always' or 'usually' check labels before buying a food product for the first time

Q: When you buy food products for the first time, what information do you usually look for?

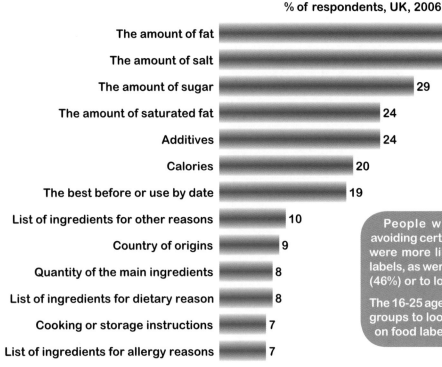

% of respondents, UK, 2006

The amount of fat	50
The amount of salt	40
The amount of sugar	29
The amount of saturated fat	24
Additives	24
Calories	20
The best before or use by date	19
List of ingredients for other reasons	10
Country of origins	9
Quantity of the main ingredients	8
List of ingredients for dietary reason	8
Cooking or storage instructions	7
List of ingredients for allergy reasons	7

NB under 5% not shown

People with allergies (54%) and those avoiding certain foods for religious reasons (51%) were more likely to say they always check food labels, as were those on a diet for medical reasons (46%) or to lose weight (44%).

The 16-25 age group were less likely than other age groups to look for information about ingredients on food labels (37%).

Q: What do you think about the amount of information provided on food labels?

% of respondents, UK, 2006

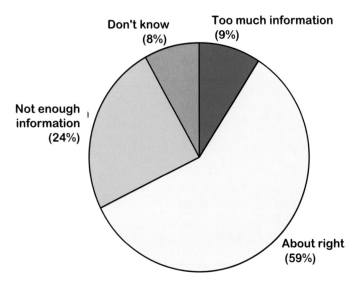

- Don't know (8%)
- Too much information (9%)
- Not enough information (24%)
- About right (59%)

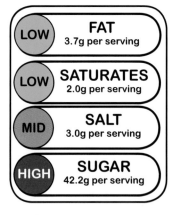

LOW	**FAT** 3.7g per serving
LOW	**SATURATES** 2.0g per serving
MID	**SALT** 3.0g per serving
HIGH	**SUGAR** 42.2g per serving

What do the traffic light colours mean?

If we want to eat a healthy diet, one of the key things we should be doing is trying to cut down on fat (especially saturated fat), salt and added sugars.

With traffic light colours, you can see at a glance if the food you're looking at has high, medium or low amounts of fat, saturated fat, sugars and salt in 100g of the food.

Red means the food is high in something we should be trying to cut down on. Amber means the food is a reasonable choice for most of the time and the more green lights, the healthier the choice.

Source: Consumer Attitudes to Food Standards, Food Standards Agency © Crown copyright, 2007

http://www.food.gov.uk
http://www.eatwell.gov.uk

Checkout

How most food shopping is done, 2006

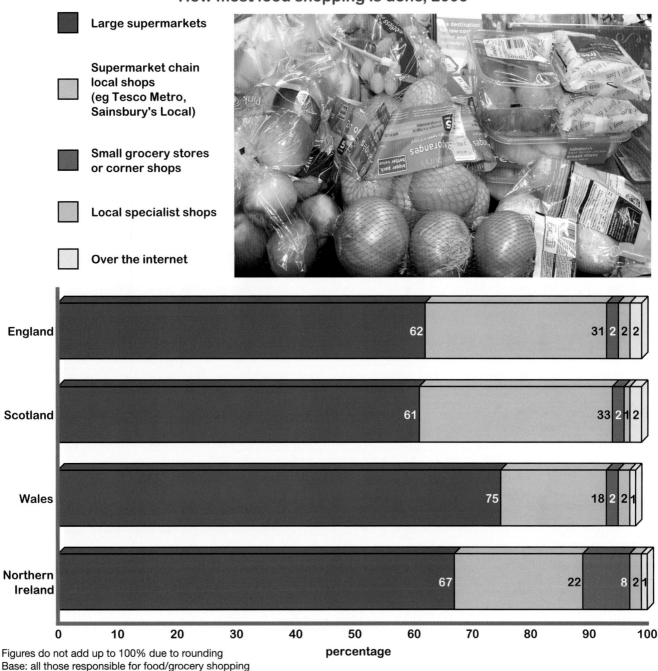

- ■ Large supermarkets
- □ Supermarket chain local shops (eg Tesco Metro, Sainsbury's Local)
- ■ Small grocery stores or corner shops
- □ Local specialist shops
- □ Over the internet

England: 62 | 31 2 2 2
Scotland: 61 | 33 2 1 2
Wales: 75 | 18 2 2 1
Northern Ireland: 67 | 22 8 2 1

percentage (0 to 100)

Figures do not add up to 100% due to rounding
Base: all those responsible for food/grocery shopping

Almost two-thirds (63%) of UK shoppers use large supermarkets for most of their shopping, a further 30% used the smaller, local shops of the supermarket chains.

However, small grocery stores and local shops play an important part in 'top-up' shopping.

Local specialist shops such as butchers and greengrocers also play a role here, with 27% of UK respondents using these outlets but for less than 5% of their shopping.

The majority of people do their main food shop once a week or more often (81%) and a top-up shop one to three times a week (70%).

While only 2% of respondents undertook most of their food shopping via the internet, 5% did some food shopping this way.

Those in semi-rural areas were more likely to use large supermarkets (68%) versus rural areas (59%) and urban areas (60%).

Where people chose to shop may simply reflect the availability of different types of shops in their area.

Consumer Attitudes to Food Standards, Food Standards Agency © Crown copyright, 2007

http://www.food.gov.uk

Healthy habits

Food purchasing habits are becoming healthier. Fruit and vegetable purchases increased by 7.7% and many people are switching from whole milk to semi-skimmed

Food purchases, UK, 2004/5 - 2005/6, grams per person per week

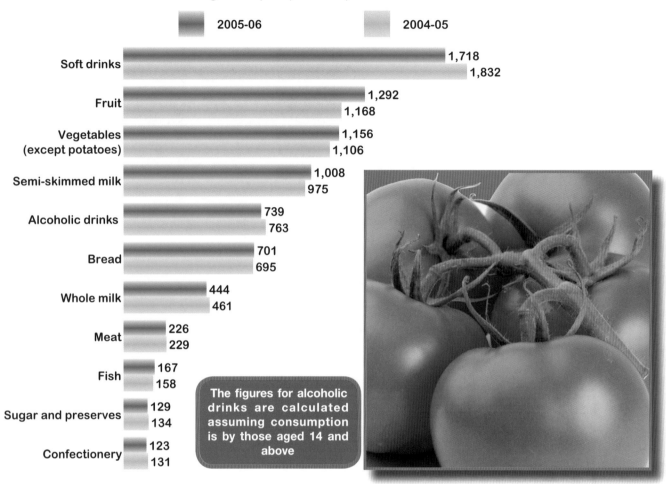

■ 2005-06   ■ 2004-05

	2005-06	2004-05
Soft drinks	1,718	1,832
Fruit	1,292	1,168
Vegetables (except potatoes)	1,156	1,106
Semi-skimmed milk	1,008	975
Alcoholic drinks	739	763
Bread	701	695
Whole milk	444	461
Meat	226	229
Fish	167	158
Sugar and preserves	129	134
Confectionery	123	131

The figures for alcoholic drinks are calculated assuming consumption is by those aged 14 and above

Food purchases, UK, percentage change 2004/5 - 2005/6

Fruit	10.6
Fish	5.7
Vegetables (except potatoes)	4.5
Semi-skimmed milk	3.3
Bread	0.8
Meat	-1.5
Alcoholic drinks	-3.1
Sugar and preserves	-3.3
Whole milk	-3.8
Confectionery	-6.1
Soft drinks	-6.2

Source: Expenditure and Food Survey 2006, Office for National Statistics © Crown copyright, 2007

http://www.defra.gov.uk
http://www.statistics.gov.uk

Five-a-day

The UK is becoming more aware of the importance of fruit and vegetables as part of a healthy diet, with 55% eating five portions or more each day

Q How many portions of fruit and vegetables do you think you should eat every day? UK, 2000-2006, %

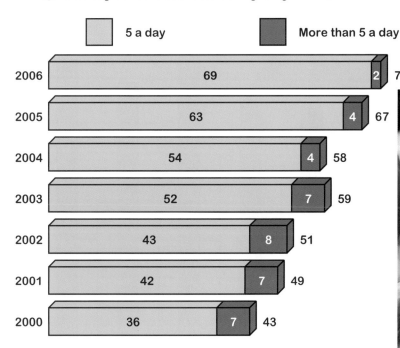

	5 a day	More than 5 a day

- 2006: 69 | 2 → 71
- 2005: 63 | 4 → 67
- 2004: 54 | 4 → 58
- 2003: 52 | 7 → 59
- 2002: 43 | 8 → 51
- 2001: 42 | 7 → 49
- 2000: 36 | 7 → 43

Q How many portions of fruit and vegetables did you eat yesterday? UK, 2006, %

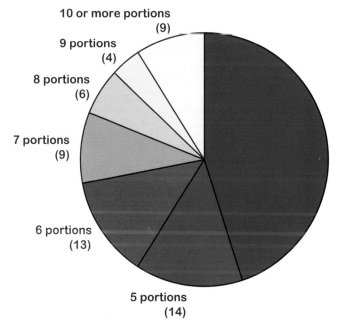

- 10 or more portions (9)
- 9 portions (4)
- 8 portions (6)
- 7 portions (9)
- 6 portions (13)
- 5 portions (14)
- Under 5 portions (45)

Base: A representative sample of 3,513 respondents were interviewed about their eating habits between August and October 2006

Source: Consumer Attitudes to Food Standards, Food Standards Agency © Crown copyright, 2007
http://www.food.gov.uk

Fun food?

A quarter of families eat out at least once a week, but what are children being offered to eat in restaurants and tourist attractions?

Average NME* sugar and saturated fat content of children's menus compared to school meal nutrition standards, %

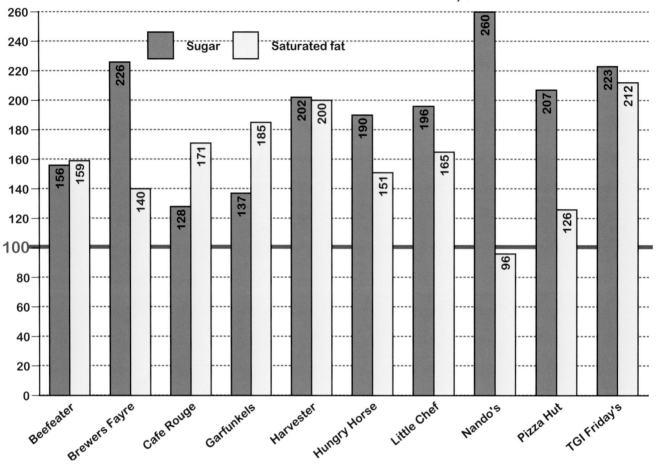

The 100% marker shows the maximum recommended content of sugar and saturated fat in a school meal.

* Non-Milk Extrinsic sugars are 'extra' or 'added' sugars that have been extracted from plants and added to food, in contrast to sugars that occur naturally.

These include table sugar, sugar in cakes, biscuits and chocolate, sugar in soft drinks and fruit juices and much more.

In order to get the average NME sugar and saturated fat content each restaurant's children's menu was analysed.

❝ Given the frequency with which families now eat out, popular restaurants need to start taking responsibility for what they are feeding the nation's children, and stop peddling junk that risks undermining the good work now being done on school meals. Hiding behind the excuse that unhealthy food is okay as a one-off treat is no longer acceptable, because we are eating out so frequently, and reinforces in children's minds that fatty, sugary processed food is a treat and that naturally sweet fruit and vegetables are to be resisted. ❞

The Real Meal Deal

LITTLE CHEF

Tourist attraction healthy eating rankings, score out of 25

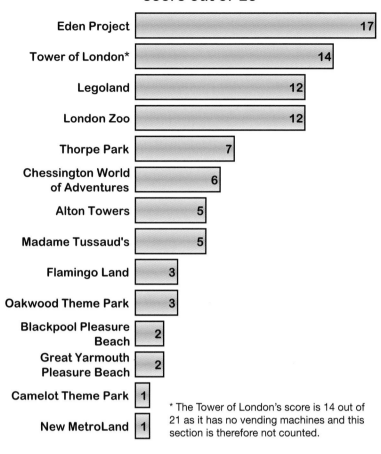

Attraction	Score
Eden Project	17
Tower of London*	14
Legoland	12
London Zoo	12
Thorpe Park	7
Chessington World of Adventures	6
Alton Towers	5
Madame Tussaud's	5
Flamingo Land	3
Oakwood Theme Park	3
Blackpool Pleasure Beach	2
Great Yarmouth Pleasure Beach	2
Camelot Theme Park	1
New MetroLand	1

* The Tower of London's score is 14 out of 21 as it has no vending machines and this section is therefore not counted.

Tourist attractions were given scores based on the availability of free drinking water, healthy drinks in vending machines, the availability of fresh fruit, and the quality of children's meals. The categories and scores can be seen in the table. The number in brackets shows the potential score for each category.

Venue	Free fresh drinking water (/3)	Healthy drinks in vending machines (/4)	Healthy cold drinks ex. water (/5)	Fresh fruit on site (/4)	Children's meals (/4)	Food promotion (/5)	Time taken to find fruit
Eden Project	1	0	5	4	2	5	2mins
Tower of London	1	n/a	3	4	3	3	1hr
Legoland	3	0	2	2	2	3	35mins
London Zoo	1	0	3	2	3	3	1hr 15mins
Thorpe Park	3	1	1	1	1	0	1hr 20mins
Chessington World of Adventures	1	1	2	1	1	0	1hr
Alton Towers	0	1	2	1	1	0	1hr 5mins
Madame Tussaud's	0	2	2	1	0	0	1hr 5mins
Flamingo Land	0	1	1	0	1	0	none
Oakwood Theme Park	0	1	1	1	0	0	1hr 10mins
Blackpool Pleasure Beach	0	0	1	0	1	0	3hrs 45mins
Great Yarmouth Pleasure Beach	0	0	1	0	1	0	none
Camelot Theme Park	0	1	0	0	0	0	none
New Metroland	0	0	1	0	0	0	none

Source: The real meal deal, The Soil Association in partnership with Organix. © The Soil Association 2006
http://www.soilassociation.org

Snack attack

11% of people in the UK avoid certain food types to lose weight, yet 40% of people snack between meals, and not always on the right foods

Q. What foods do you avoid to lose weight?

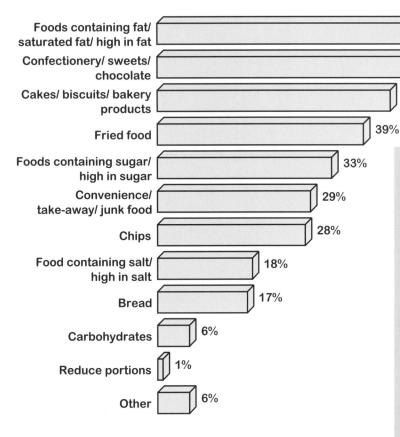

- Foods containing fat/ saturated fat/ high in fat — 62%
- Confectionery/ sweets/ chocolate — 47%
- Cakes/ biscuits/ bakery products — 44%
- Fried food — 39%
- Foods containing sugar/ high in sugar — 33%
- Convenience/ take-away/ junk food — 29%
- Chips — 28%
- Food containing salt/ high in salt — 18%
- Bread — 17%
- Carbohydrates — 6%
- Reduce portions — 1%
- Other — 6%

A total of 39% of people in the UK avoid certain types of foods. Reasons for avoiding food include: medical reasons (16%), because they are vegetarian (9%), due to food allergies (7%) and for religious reasons (3%), as well as dieting.

As well as avoiding certain food types, 45% of people are making a special effort to eat more fruit and 38% to eat more vegetables. When it comes to snacking, two fifths of snackers reach for the fruit, fewer snack on vegetables.

While cakes, biscuits and bakery product are the third most avoided item for dieters, they are eaten by almost a third of snackers.

The time when we snack seems to affect our choice. Fresh fruit is more likely to be snacked on during week days (40%) compared with weekends (34%). While crisps and savoury snacks are slightly more likely to be eaten at the weekend (23%) compared with week days (19%).

Q. What foods do you snack on?

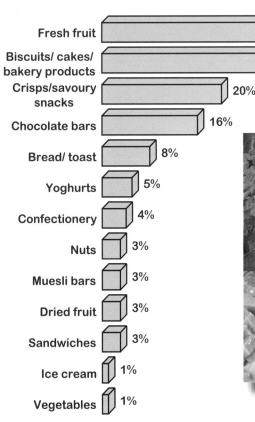

- Fresh fruit — 40%
- Biscuits/ cakes/ bakery products — 28%
- Crisps/savoury snacks — 20%
- Chocolate bars — 16%
- Bread/ toast — 8%
- Yoghurts — 5%
- Confectionery — 4%
- Nuts — 3%
- Muesli bars — 3%
- Dried fruit — 3%
- Sandwiches — 3%
- Ice cream — 1%
- Vegetables — 1%

Source: Consumer Attitudes to Food Standards, Food Standards Agency © Crown copyright, 2007
http://www.fsa.gov.uk

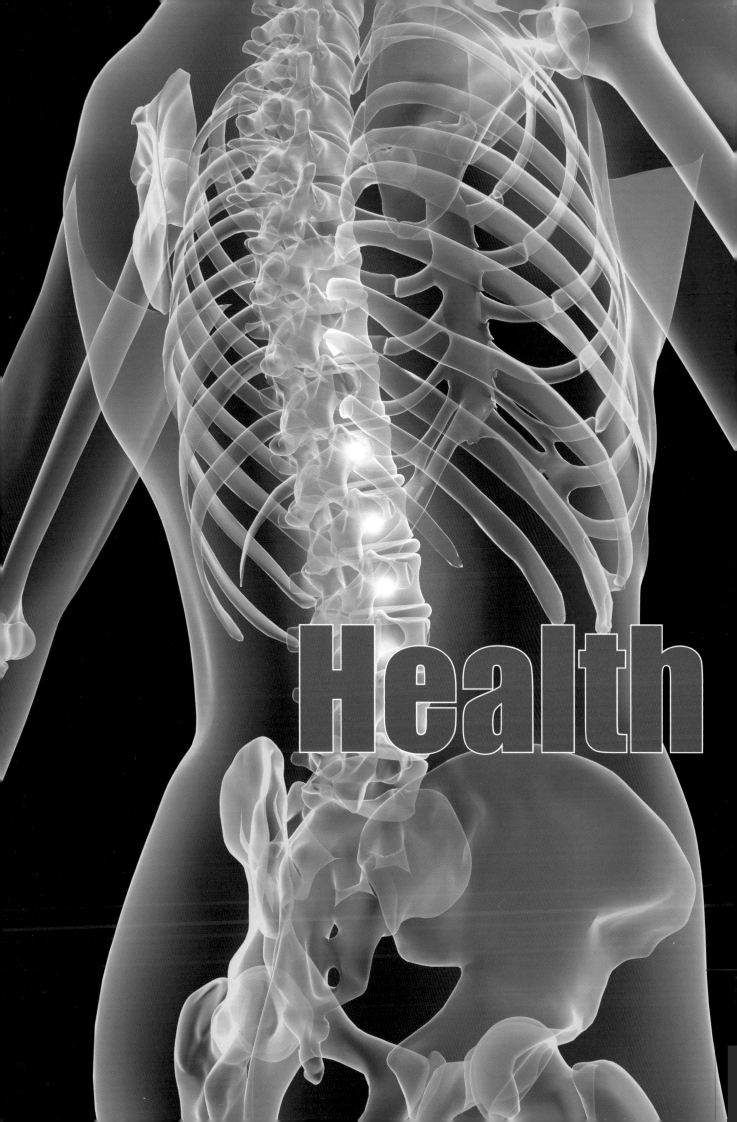

Health

Be patient

Inpatients waiting by time band as at 31st January, England 2004-2007, %

- 0 to 13 weeks
- 13 to 26 weeks
- More than 26 weeks

2004: 57.9 / 27.3 / 14.8
2005: 65.5 / 26.3 / 8.2
2006: 74.8 / 25.2 / 0.0
2007: 75.7 / 24.2 / 0.0

Figures do not add up to 100% due to rounding

Median waiting time as of 31st January, England 2004-2007, no. of weeks

Inpatients: 11.2 (2004), 9.3 (2005), 7.9 (2006), 7.6 (2007)
Outpatients: 4.8 (2005), 3.7 (2006), 3.2 (2007)

Outpatients waiting for first appointment with consultant, by time band as of 31st January, England 2005-2007, %

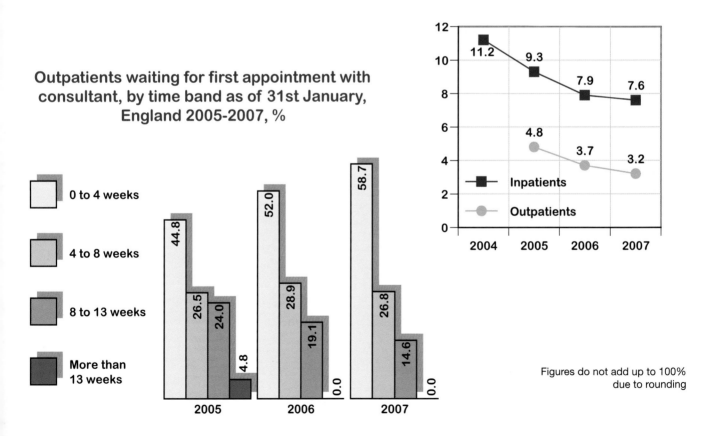

- 0 to 4 weeks
- 4 to 8 weeks
- 8 to 13 weeks
- More than 13 weeks

2005: 44.8 / 26.5 / 24.0 / 4.8
2006: 52.0 / 28.9 / 19.1 / 0.0
2007: 58.7 / 26.8 / 14.6 / 0.0

Figures do not add up to 100% due to rounding

Source: Department of Health: NHS Inpatient and Outpatient waiting times figures, January 2007 © Crown copyright 2007

http://www.gnn.gov.uk
http://www.dh.gov.uk

Wait for life

483 patients died in 2005-06 while waiting for their transplant. Is an opt out system the answer?

Number of donors and transplants in the UK, and patients on the active transplants lists at 31 March, 2006

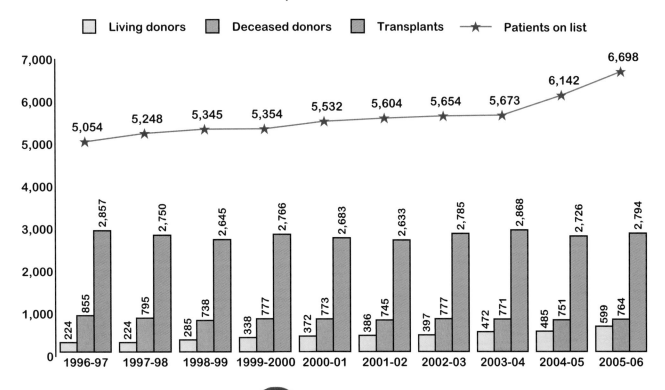

Legend: Living donors | Deceased donors | Transplants | Patients on list

Year	Living donors	Deceased donors	Transplants	Patients on list
1996-97	224	855	2,857	5,054
1997-98	224	795	2,750	5,248
1998-99	285	738	2,645	5,345
1999-2000	338	777	2,766	5,354
2000-01	372	773	2,683	5,532
2001-02	386	745	2,633	5,604
2002-03	397	777	2,785	5,654
2003-04	472	771	2,868	5,673
2004-05	485	751	2,726	6,142
2005-06	599	764	2,794	6,698

The facts

Deceased donors can give a heart, lungs, two kidneys, pancreas, liver and small bowel and can restore the sight of two people by donating their corneas. Bone and tissue such as skin, heart valves and tendons can also be donated. Skin grafts have helped people with severe burns, and bone is used in orthopaedic surgery.

Traditionally deceased organ donors have come from two groups: road accident and brain haemorrhage patients. Improved road safety and medical intervention mean that fewer in both groups are dying.

The need for transplants is expected to rise steeply over the next decade due to an ageing population, an increase in kidney failure and scientific advances resulting in more people being suitable for a transplant.

All the major religions support organ donation and many actively promote it.

NHS Organ Donor Register Tel: 0845 60 60 400

www.uktransplant.org.uk

The future?

While nearly 90% of the UK population say they're willing to donate their organs after death, only 20% have put their names on the NHS organ donor register. This is one way of opting in to the organ donation system. Other ways are telling the family your wishes or carrying a donor card.

However, there's been a lot of discussion about whether the UK should have an opt-out system, whereby everyone is considered to be a potential donor unless they've specifically said they don't want to donate.

European countries with opt-out policies showed a 16.2% increase in the number of donors.

Public opinion in the UK is shifting and this could result in a change in the law governing organ donation. A BBC poll in May 2005 found that 61% of those questioned supported a change to an opt-out system.

Source: Transplant Activity in the UK 2005-06, NHS Blood & Transplant, BBC Health

http://www.uktransplant.org.uk
http://www.bbc.co.uk/health

Safety screen

Cervical cancer kills 1,120 women a year in the UK, but many cases could be prevented

Women are invited for their first routine screening at 25, then at 3-yearly intervals until the age of 49, then at 5-yearly intervals until the age of 65.

Women under 25 are not usually tested because cancer is rare in this age group. Also natural changes in the body may lead to inaccurate results.

A recent medical development has caused controversy. A vaccination intended for all 12-year-old girls to protect against *human papillomavirus* (HPV) which causes most cervical cancers could cut deaths from the disease by 75%.

This could mean 262 deaths each year, compared with the current level of around 1,000. The number of annual cases of the disease would also drop from 2,841 to 682.

Since HPV is a common sexually transmitted infection, some have expressed concerns that providing a jab to children at a young age might encourage promiscuity. However, most parents support the vaccine.

The programme would cost more than all other childhood injections put together, but the benefit would be reaped decades later.

Numbers of women invited for screening and numbers of women tested, by age group, England 2005/6

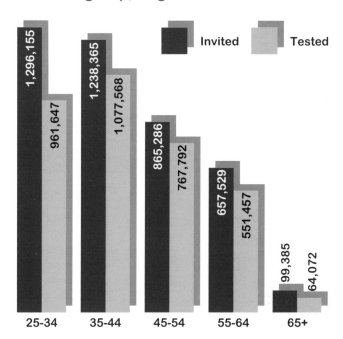

Invited — Tested

Age group	Invited	Tested
25-34	1,296,155	961,647
35-44	1,238,365	1,077,568
45-54	865,286	767,792
55-64	657,529	551,457
65+	99,385	64,072

Reasons for not attending screening, England, 2006, %

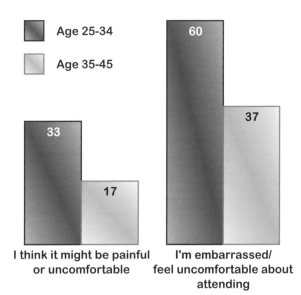

Age 25-34
Age 35-45

	I think it might be painful or uncomfortable	I'm embarrassed/ feel uncomfortable about attending
Age 25-34	33	60
Age 35-45	17	37

Base: Women who had not previously attended for screening

A survey was conducted to find out why women chose not to attend:

• 90% understood the purpose of cervical screening
• Women who had previously attended screening appointments were more likely to cite lack of time or forgotten appointments as reasons why they didn't attend

Sources: NHS Cervical Screening Programme annual review 2006 © NHSCSP 2007, Office for National Statistics: Cervical Screening programme England 2005-6 © The Information Centre, 2006

http://www.ic.nhs.uk
http://www.cancerscreening.nhs.uk

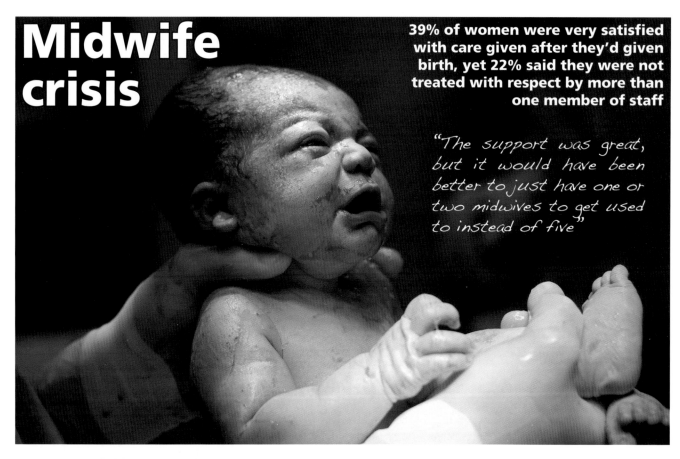

Midwife crisis

39% of women were very satisfied with care given after they'd given birth, yet 22% said they were not treated with respect by more than one member of staff

"The support was great, but it would have been better to just have one or two midwives to get used to instead of five"

More than four out of five women (83%) selected the term 'supportive' to describe the staff who looked after them during labour and birth, 'kind' (79%), 'sensitive' and 'warm' were selected less often (56% and 60%).

The more negative descriptors of care were chosen less often altogether, with 'rushed' being the most common (16% of women), followed by 'bossy' (12%). Much smaller numbers of women perceived staff as 'off-hand' (7%), 'inconsiderate' (5%) or 'unhelpful' (6%).

"...would have liked less midwives, as I felt I had to keep repeating myself. Couldn't build a bond..."

"the midwife was completely understanding and she let me do what I wanted to do"

England's NHS needs 22,000 full-time midwives to deliver their ideal standard of maternity care.

Currently there is a shortfall of over 3,000. Not only are 45% of midwives set to retire over the next decade, the number of places for student midwives is falling too.

While women were appreciative of the care they received, they would have preferred care from a small number.

	Midwife headcount	Full-time equivalents	Number of live births
1996	22,595	18,262	614,184
2006	24,469	18,862	635,679
Increase	8.3%	3.3%	3.5%

Source: National Perinatal Epidemiology Unit Recorded Delivery survey 2006; NHS Hospital and Community Health Services, Non-Medical staff, England, 1996-2006

Women were asked how they felt about the care provided from midwives during labour and birth:

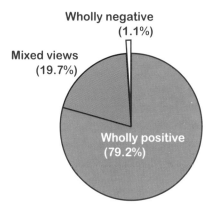

Wholly negative (1.1%)
Mixed views (19.7%)
Wholly positive (79.2%)

Women were asked how many midwives were involved during labour and birth:

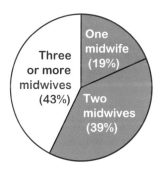

Three or more midwives (43%)
One midwife (19%)
Two midwives (39%)

http://www.npeu.ox.ac.uk/maternitysurveys/
http://www.ic.nhs.uk

Silent infection

Chlamydia is the most common bacterial sexually transmitted infection. One in ten 16-24 year olds have it

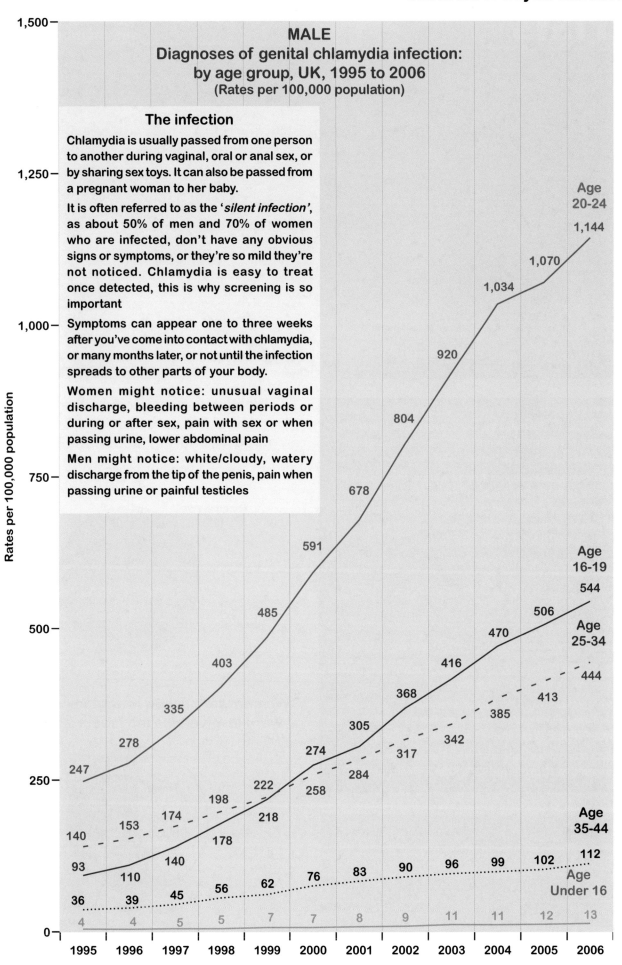

MALE
Diagnoses of genital chlamydia infection: by age group, UK, 1995 to 2006
(Rates per 100,000 population)

Rates per 100,000 population

The infection

Chlamydia is usually passed from one person to another during vaginal, oral or anal sex, or by sharing sex toys. It can also be passed from a pregnant woman to her baby.

It is often referred to as the '*silent infection*', as about 50% of men and 70% of women who are infected, don't have any obvious signs or symptoms, or they're so mild they're not noticed. Chlamydia is easy to treat once detected, this is why screening is so important

Symptoms can appear one to three weeks after you've come into contact with chlamydia, or many months later, or not until the infection spreads to other parts of your body.

Women might notice: unusual vaginal discharge, bleeding between periods or during or after sex, pain with sex or when passing urine, lower abdominal pain

Men might notice: white/cloudy, watery discharge from the tip of the penis, pain when passing urine or painful testicles

Age 20-24

1,144
1,070
1,034
920
804
678
591
485
403
335
278
247

Age 16-19
544
506
470
416
368
305
274
222
198
178
140
110
93

Age 25-34
444
413
385
342
317
284
258
218
174
153
140

Age 35-44
112
102
99
96
90
83
76
62
56
45
39
36

Age Under 16
13
12
11
11
9
8
7
7
5
5
4
4

1995 1996 1997 1998 1999 2000 2001 2002 2003 2004 2005 2006

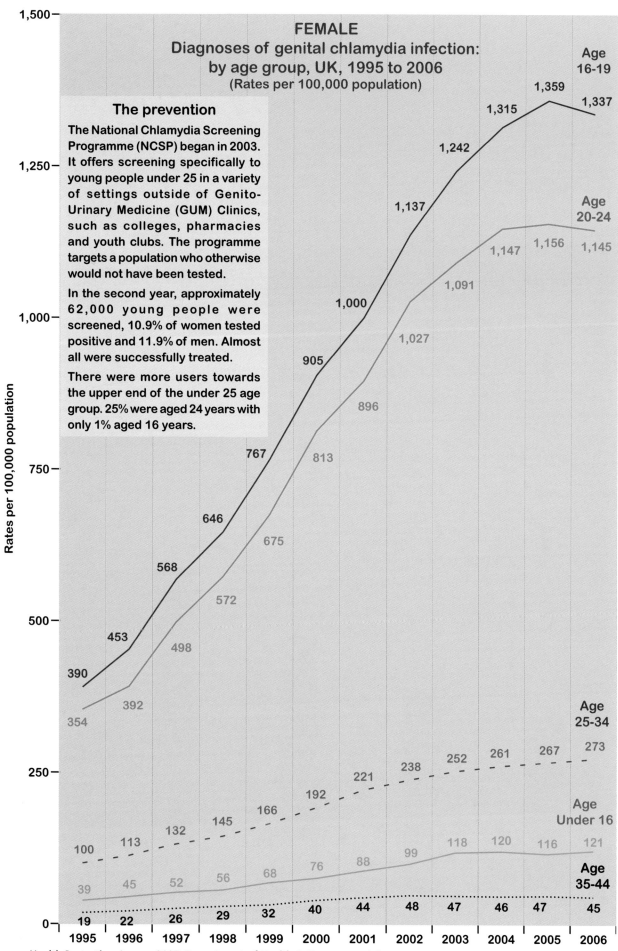

FEMALE
Diagnoses of genital chlamydia infection: by age group, UK, 1995 to 2006
(Rates per 100,000 population)

Age 16-19
Age 20-24
Age 25-34
Age Under 16
Age 35-44

The prevention

The National Chlamydia Screening Programme (NCSP) began in 2003. It offers screening specifically to young people under 25 in a variety of settings outside of Genito-Urinary Medicine (GUM) Clinics, such as colleges, pharmacies and youth clubs. The programme targets a population who otherwise would not have been tested.

In the second year, approximately 62,000 young people were screened, 10.9% of women tested positive and 11.9% of men. Almost all were successfully treated.

There were more users towards the upper end of the under 25 age group. 25% were aged 24 years with only 1% aged 16 years.

Rates per 100,000 population

Age 16-19: 390, 453, 568, 646, 767, 905, 1,000, 1,137, 1,242, 1,315, 1,359, 1,337

Age 20-24: 354, 392, 498, 572, 675, 813, 896, 1,027, 1,091, 1,147, 1,156, 1,145

Age 25-34: 100, 113, 132, 145, 166, 192, 221, 238, 252, 261, 267, 273

Age Under 16: 39, 45, 52, 56, 68, 76, 88, 99, 118, 120, 116, 121

Age 35-44: 19, 22, 26, 29, 32, 40, 44, 48, 47, 46, 47, 45

1995 1996 1997 1998 1999 2000 2001 2002 2003 2004 2005 2006

Source: Health Protection Agency 2007, Department of Health © Crown copyright; The Department of Health, Chlamydia Screening Evaluation – Interim Report, 2006

http://www.hpa.org.uk
http://www.dh.gov.uk

Superbugs

MRSA stands for *Methicillin resistant Staphylococus aureus*. It is often known as the Superbug because it is hard to eliminate.

Clostridium difficile is a bacterium found in the gut of up to 3% of healthy adults and 66% of infants, where it rarely causes problems but it can cause illness when its growth goes unchecked.

Efforts to combat MRSA, such as alcohol hand-rubs, have had no impact on C. difficile.

It forms spores which can survive for long periods in places such as on floors, around toilets and spread in the air.

Rigorous cleaning with warm water and detergent is the most effective means of removing spores from the contaminated environment and the hands of staff.

C. difficile and MRSA are known as superbugs because they are so resistant to treatment and so difficult to control.

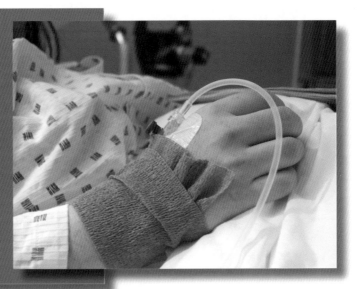

Number of death certificates mentioning MRSA or Clostridium difficile, and whether it was the underlying cause of deaths, England and Wales, 2001-2005

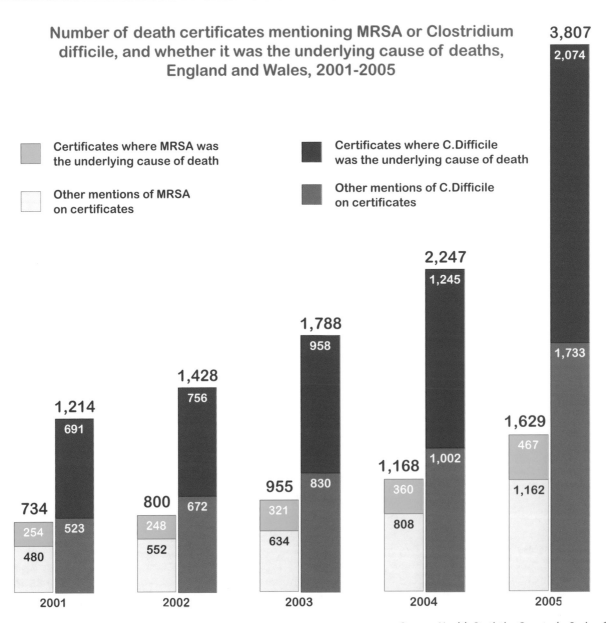

Certificates where MRSA was the underlying cause of death

Other mentions of MRSA on certificates

Certificates where C.Difficile was the underlying cause of death

Other mentions of C.Difficile on certificates

2001 — 734 (254, 480); 1,214 (691, 523)

2002 — 800 (248, 552); 1,428 (756, 672)

2003 — 955 (321, 634); 1,788 (958, 830)

2004 — 1,168 (360, 808); 2,247 (1,245, 1,002)

2005 — 1,629 (467, 1,162); 3,807 (2,074, 1,733)

Source: Health Statistics Quarterly, Spring 2007, ONS © Crown copyright 2007

http://www.statistics.gov.uk

Memories matter

> Dementia describes a collection of symptoms, including a decline in memory, communication and reasoning skills, and the gradual loss of ability to carry out daily activities. It can start at any age, but is most common amongst older people, and is progressive, ie the symptoms get worse over time. There are a number of different types and causes

Types of dementia, UK 2005

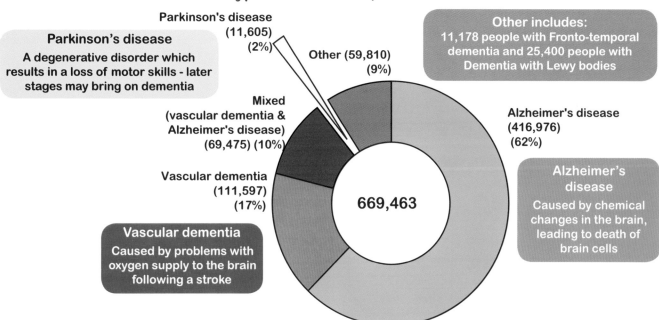

Parkinson's disease (11,605) (2%)

Parkinson's disease
A degenerative disorder which results in a loss of motor skills - later stages may bring on dementia

Other (59,810) (9%)

Other includes:
11,178 people with Fronto-temporal dementia and 25,400 people with Dementia with Lewy bodies

Mixed (vascular dementia & Alzheimer's disease) (69,475) (10%)

Alzheimer's disease (416,976) (62%)

Vascular dementia (111,597) (17%)

669,463

Alzheimer's disease
Caused by chemical changes in the brain, leading to death of brain cells

Vascular dementia
Caused by problems with oxygen supply to the brain following a stroke

- In less than 20 years nearly a million people will be living with dementia. This will soar to 1.7 million people by 2050.

- There are 15,000 people under 65 years of age with dementia in the UK. This figure could be an underestimate due to a lack of referral to services. The real figure could be as much as three times higher.

- For every five years you live past 30, your chance of developing dementia doubles.

- There are nearly double the number of women with dementia over the age of 65 than men (222,925 men and 445,641 women).

- Families bear the biggest burden of dementia. 63.5% of people with late onset dementia live at home.

- Individuals caring for people with dementia save the public purse more than £6 billion per year.

- Dementia is one of the main causes of disability later in life, ahead of some forms of cancer, cardiovascular disease and stroke. Yet, as a country we spend much less on dementia than on these other conditions.

- Dementia costs the UK £17 billion each year. This equates to £539 per second or £46.6 million per day.

Source: Dementia UK; Alzheimer's Society, Kings College London and LSE © Alzheimer's Society 2007

http://www.alzheimers.org.uk

Dying for a drink

Alcohol-related death rates, by gender, UK, 1991–2005

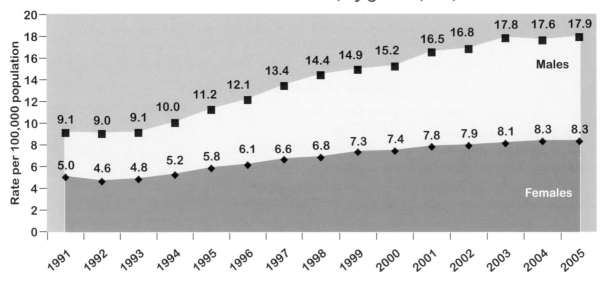

Number of alcohol related deaths, by gender and age group, UK 1991-2005

	1-14		15-34		35-54		55-74		75+	
	M	F	M	F	M	F	M	F	M	F
1991	0	2	116	63	954	512	1,205	764	257	271
1992	4	1	104	52	951	465	1,185	724	279	258
1993	3	4	134	60	979	507	1,188	746	256	232
1994	3	3	150	52	1,121	598	1,314	776	261	247
1995	3	1	153	61	1,257	681	1,461	832	306	272
1996	3	2	154	57	1,520	774	1,491	835	289	281
1997	4	4	160	66	1,760	834	1,615	911	317	305
1998	1	4	199	61	1,922	854	1,696	988	354	290
1999	1	1	206	85	1,950	1,000	1,839	961	365	313
2000	1	1	185	103	2,006	990	1,934	1,019	357	288
2001	0	1	222	86	2,244	1,098	2,051	1,043	421	333
2002	0	0	215	81	2,235	1,103	2,201	1,115	418	333
2003	2	0	188	98	2,408	1,082	2,417	1,188	428	353
2004	1	1	198	89	2,364	1,166	2,436	1,186	432	348
2005	1	0	192	93	2,403	1,173	2,521	1,189	449	365

Alcohol-related deaths only includes those directly due to alcohol consumption. This includes all deaths from chronic liver disease and cirrhosis even where alcohol was not specifically mentioned. Alcohol can be linked to other diseases such as cancers of the mouth, oesophagus and liver, but these are not included. Nor are deaths due to traffic accidents and other accidents, suicides and homicides where alcohol may have played a role.

It is estimated that annually there are between 15,000 and 22,000 deaths in which alcohol played a part.

Source: Office for National Statistics © Crown copyright 2006

http://www.statistics.gov.uk

Cost of care

Working age Incapacity Benefit* caseload, by medical condition, UK, 1995 and 2006

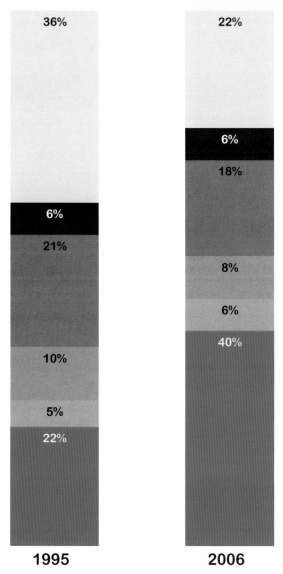

1995 — 36%, 6%, 21%, 10%, 5%, 22%

2006 — 22%, 6%, 18%, 8%, 6%, 40%

Legend:
- Other
- Injury and poisoning
- Musculoskeletal
- Circulatory and respiratory
- Diseases of the nervous systems
- Mental and behavioural

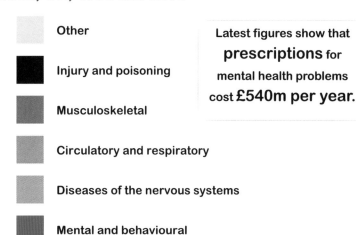

Latest figures show that **prescriptions** for mental health problems cost **£540m per year.**

* Incapacity Benefit is paid to people who are incapable of work and who have paid sufficient National Insurance contributions throughout their working life

Mental health problems are estimated to cost the country more than £77 billion a year through the costs of care, economic losses and premature death.

Only 24% of adults with mental health problems are in work – the lowest employment rate for any of the main groups of disabled people.

Fewer than four in ten employers say they would recruit someone with a mental health problem.

Around 300 people out of 1,000 will experience mental health problems every year:
- 230 of these will visit a GP
- 102 of these will be diagnosed as having a mental health disorder

- 24 of these will be referred to a specialist psychiatric service
- 6 will become inpatients in psychiatric hospitals.

The number of people claiming benefits because of eating disorders had gone up by 130% from 800 in 1997 to 1,830.

The number of people out of work because of drug and alcohol-related problems rose by 80% from 76,200 to 136,700.

Source: Reducing dependency, increasing opportunity: options for the future of welfare to work © Crown copyright 2007, Key facts and figures, Social Exclusion Task Force © Crown copyright 2007, Mental Health information 2007, Communitycare.co.uk, BBC

http://www.dwp.gov.uk
http://www.cabinetoffice.gov.uk
http://communitycare.co.uk
http://www.bbc.co.uk

Plastic perfection?

A survey in 2007 found that more than 50% of females would consider having plastic surgery, compared with less than a quarter of men

25,000 people, mostly aged 17 to 34, were asked how they felt about their bodies

31% of size 12 women describe their body as either overweight or fat, rising to 66% amongst size 14 women

53% of girls, aged 12 to 16, feel that their body image either stops them from getting a boyfriend or means that they cannot relax in a relationship

The most popular cosmetic surgery procedures, UK, 2006

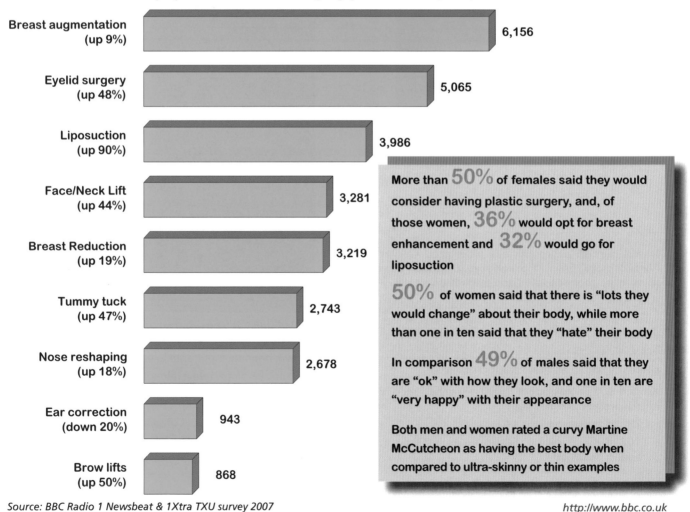

Breast augmentation (up 9%)	6,156
Eyelid surgery (up 48%)	5,065
Liposuction (up 90%)	3,986
Face/Neck Lift (up 44%)	3,281
Breast Reduction (up 19%)	3,219
Tummy tuck (up 47%)	2,743
Nose reshaping (up 18%)	2,678
Ear correction (down 20%)	943
Brow lifts (up 50%)	868

More than **50%** of females said they would consider having plastic surgery, and, of those women, **36%** would opt for breast enhancement and **32%** would go for liposuction

50% of women said that there is "lots they would change" about their body, while more than one in ten said that they "hate" their body

In comparison **49%** of males said that they are "ok" with how they look, and one in ten are "very happy" with their appearance

Both men and women rated a curvy Martine McCutcheon as having the best body when compared to ultra-skinny or thin examples

Source: BBC Radio 1 Newsbeat & 1Xtra TXU survey 2007
The British Association of Aesthetic Plastic Surgeons, 2007

http://www.bbc.co.uk
http://www.baaps.org.uk

Silent struggle

1.1 million people in the UK suffer with an eating disorder and young people aged 14-25 are most at risk

People still see eating disorders as trivial and self inflicted, instead of serious and life threatening mental illnesses.

Eating disorders include Anorexia Nervosa, Bulimia Nervosa, binge eating disorder and Orthorexia.

Someone with an eating disorder will often find it extremely difficult to tell anyone about it, even once they recognise the problem. This can lead to a dangerous delay in treatment.

The facts:

90% of parents said they felt confident about discussing eating disorders with their children. Yet only 1% of those suffering from an eating disorder said they could talk to their parents about it.

"My dad thinks that I only have anorexia to get attention."
"My mum treated me like it was my fault..."

20% of those who become seriously ill with an eating disorder can die prematurely.

Early treatment is crucial for recovery and to avoid the long term consequences to physical health and mental wellbeing. Yet 62% of young people waited more than 6 months before seeking help.

40% of parents said they would recognise the early signs, but only 21% of young people said their parents had noticed the eating disorder first. 92% couldn't tell anyone that they had a problem.

"I was worried what people would think of me and whether they would think I was a bad person."
"I did feel a lot of shame, grief, anger and embarrassment because I am male and thought eating disorders were only for women."

The actress Keira Knightley recently won a law suit against a national newspaper for claiming she had an eating disorder and that people like her contributed towards eating disorders. She donated the compensation along with some of her own money to eating disorder charity BEAT.

Only 9% felt they might be able to talk to someone at school. Just 17% felt they might be able to talk to a doctor or nurse.

"One teacher noticed, but she didn't confront me. It would have helped if somebody had acknowledged it."

"My first GP put me off. I was told that lots of women have this problem. I felt I had no right to help."

The solution?

42% said the media showing more 'real' bodies could help prevent eating disorders. This compared to parents understanding and doctors knowing more at 20% each.

Source: Time to Tell, Eating disorder association, 2006, Somethings got to change, BEAT, 2007
http://www.edauk.com

Survivors

Five year survival rates for all cancers, selected European countries, 2007

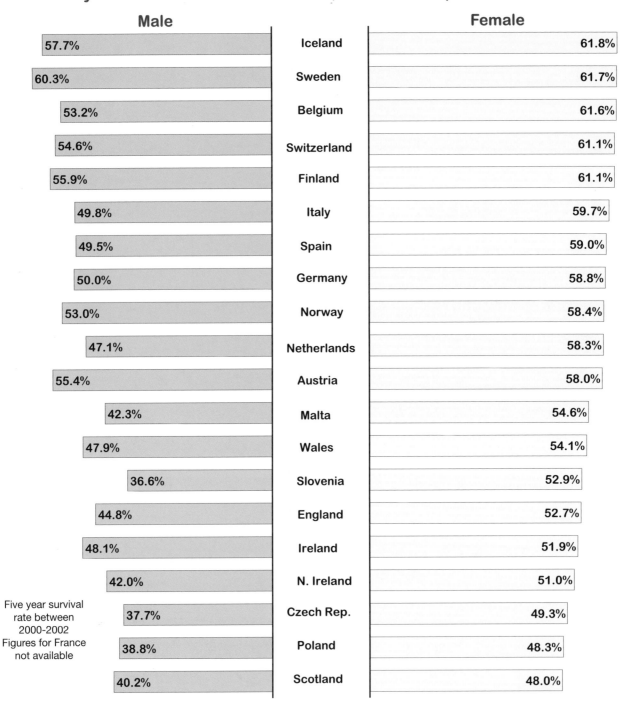

Male		Female
57.7%	Iceland	61.8%
60.3%	Sweden	61.7%
53.2%	Belgium	61.6%
54.6%	Switzerland	61.1%
55.9%	Finland	61.1%
49.8%	Italy	59.7%
49.5%	Spain	59.0%
50.0%	Germany	58.8%
53.0%	Norway	58.4%
47.1%	Netherlands	58.3%
55.4%	Austria	58.0%
42.3%	Malta	54.6%
47.9%	Wales	54.1%
36.6%	Slovenia	52.9%
44.8%	England	52.7%
48.1%	Ireland	51.9%
42.0%	N. Ireland	51.0%
37.7%	Czech Rep.	49.3%
38.8%	Poland	48.3%
40.2%	Scotland	48.0%

Five year survival rate between 2000-2002 Figures for France not available

Comparison between Europe and USA survival rates

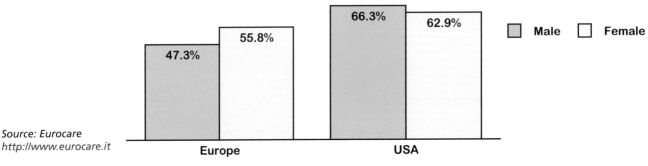

Europe: Male 47.3%, Female 55.8%
USA: Male 66.3%, Female 62.9%

■ Male □ Female

Source: Eurocare
http://www.eurocare.it

Internet & media

Media age

Over the 40 years since the first email was sent, communications technology has become more available, sophisticated and user-driven than ever

Converging communications

The drive for companies to combine various devices and services affects what we buy and how we listen and view.

More than half of UK households now have broadband.

90% of UK singles sales by volume now come from digital downloads to the computer or a mobile handset.

Increasing numbers of channels such as Channel 4, ITV and the BBC are launching internet-based on-demand and/or live access to their content.

Millions of consumers worldwide now share online gaming experiences.

Combined devices such as sophisticated mobile phones have affected sales of alarms, cameras and, increasingly, mp3 players and games consoles.

Children have increasing access to communications devices and services – three-quarters of eleven year olds own a TV set, a games console and a mobile phone.

Television

Digital television penetration broke through the 80% barrier in 2007 with 20.4m multichannel homes.

More households now have Freeview devices (8.4m) than pay set top boxes (8.0m). 1.7% of households subscribe to high-definition television services (450,000).

The main networks have offset their loss of audience share with their spin-off channels such as Film4, More4, E4, ITV3 and ITV4.

Telecoms

There were more households with a mobile connection (93%) than with a fixed connection (90%) for the first time in 2006.

At the end of 2006 there were nearly 70m active mobile phone subscriptions in the UK, with people now owning multiple handsets.

3G moved into the mainstream in 2006 with connections growing by 70% to reach 7.8m.

Radio

Over the last five year listening hours have fallen most among 25-34 year olds (17.3%) and children (8.7%) but have increased among the over-55s by 5.5%.

58% of listeners have accessed radio through one of the digital platforms - 41% via DTV, 24% over the internet, and 8% via mobile phone.

In 2008 there will be ten new national digital radio services as well as text and data services.

Cumulative DAB digital radio set sales passed 5m during the first quarter of 2007, while 27% of UK adults now own an MP3 player, with 5% using them to listen to radio podcasts.

Life online

More time was spent on eBay than on any other web site, and social networking sites Bebo, MySpace, Facebook and YouTube are all in the top ten sites by time spent.

In the seven months to May 2007, the UK user base of YouTube increased by nearly a half to 6.5m users, while Wikipedia's increased by 30% to 6.4m. MySpace's audience increased by 25% since November 2006, and FaceBook's user base has quadrupled since October 2006. We can expect these increases to continue.

User-generated content: the volume of material being uploaded to Web 2.0 sites is substantial. Every day 1,845 new articles appear on Wikipedia, 3,744,000 new photos are uploaded to Flickr and 65,000 new video clips are loaded onto YouTube. Assuming an average YouTube clip is 30 seconds long, 542 hours worth are uploaded every day – that's a year's worth of new video appearing on the site every 16 days.

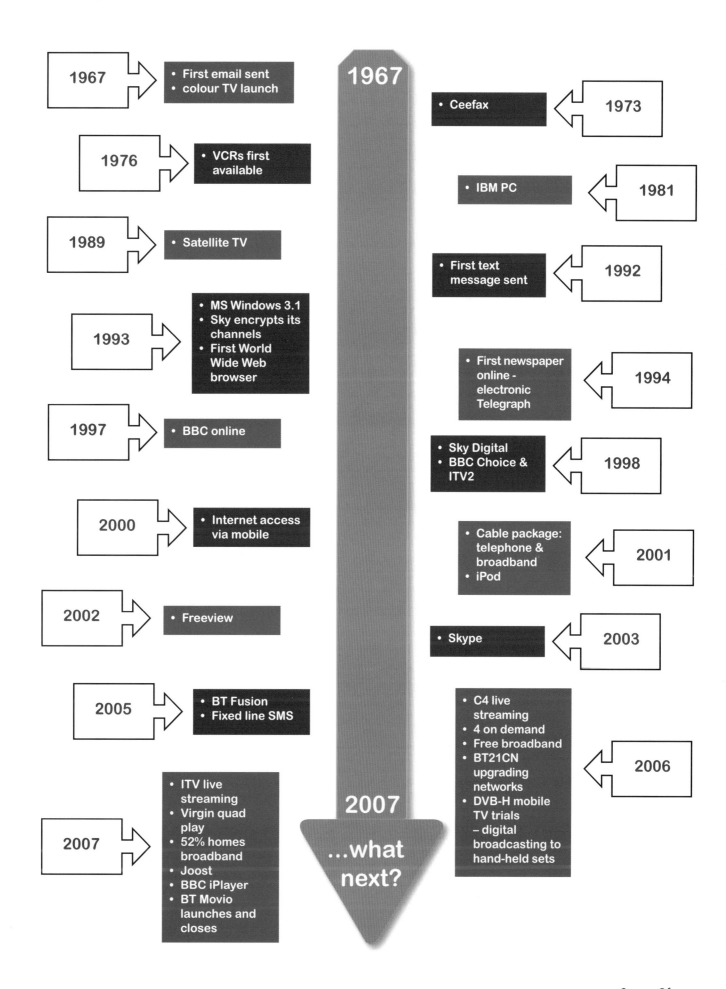

1967

1967	• First email sent • colour TV launch
1976	• VCRs first available
1989	• Satellite TV
1993	• MS Windows 3.1 • Sky encrypts its channels • First World Wide Web browser
1997	• BBC online
2000	• Internet access via mobile
2002	• Freeview
2005	• BT Fusion • Fixed line SMS
2007	• ITV live streaming • Virgin quad play • 52% homes broadband • Joost • BBC iPlayer • BT Movio launches and closes

1973	• Ceefax
1981	• IBM PC
1992	• First text message sent
1994	• First newspaper online - electronic Telegraph
1998	• Sky Digital • BBC Choice & ITV2
2001	• Cable package: telephone & broadband • iPod
2003	• Skype
2006	• C4 live streaming • 4 on demand • Free broadband • BT21CN upgrading networks • DVB-H mobile TV trials – digital broadcasting to hand-held sets

2007

...what next?

Source: Ofcom
http://www.ofcom.org.uk

Through the net

Households with access to the internet, GB
percentages and numbers (millions)

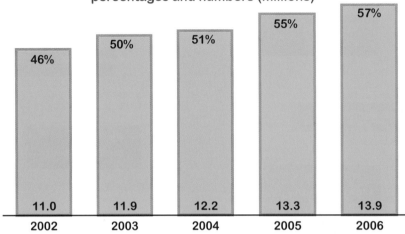

46%	50%	51%	55%	57%
11.0	11.9	12.2	13.3	13.9
2002	2003	2004	2005	2006

Of the 43% of households that did not have internet access:

24% said that they didn't need the internet

24% said that they lacked the necessary skills

14% said the equipment costs were too high

11% said that access costs were too high (telephone etc)

The higher an individual's income, the more likely he or she is to have accessed the internet:

51% of adults with an income of £10,400 or less had never used the internet.

93% with an income of £36,400 or more had used the internet in the three months prior to interview.

Households with internet connections subscribing to dial up or broadband service providers, UK, 2004–2007

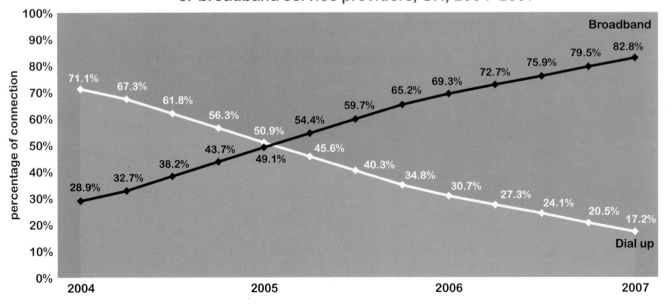

Broadband: 28.9%, 32.7%, 38.2%, 43.7%, 50.9%, 54.4%, 59.7%, 65.2%, 69.3%, 72.7%, 75.9%, 79.5%, 82.8%

Dial up: 71.1%, 67.3%, 61.8%, 56.3%, 49.1%, 45.6%, 40.3%, 34.8%, 30.7%, 27.3%, 24.1%, 20.5%, 17.2%

percentage of connection — 0% to 100%

2004   2005   2006   2007

When adults last used the internet, by gender and age-group, 2006 (percentages)

There is still a large divide between the young and the old, with 83% of the 16 to 24 age group accessing the internet within 3 months prior to interview, compared with 15% of the 65+ age group.

Men: 30, 2, 3, 65

Women: 40, 2, 3, 55

16-24: 10, 3, 4, 83

25-44: 17, 2, 3, 79

45-54: 26, 2, 4, 68

55-64: 43, 2, 3, 52

65+: 82, 2, 1, 15

Legend:
- Never used it
- More than 1 year ago
- Between 3 months and 1 year ago
- Within the last 3 months

28 million adults (60% of the UK adult population) accessed the internet in the three months prior to interview with men more likely to do so than women.

Internet activities of adults who have accessed the internet in the last three months, 2006	UK %	Male %	Female %
Searching for information about goods or services	84	88	79
Using email	80	81	80
General browsing or surfing	72	75	68
Searching for information about travel and accommodation	71	72	69
Playing or downloading games, images or music	45	51	40
Internet banking	42	47	37
Reading or downloading on-line news (inc. newspapers or news magazines)	35	43	27
Activities related specifically to employment (current or future job)	32	35	28
Seeking health related information	27	26	28
Activities related to a school, college or university course	27	24	30
Looking for a job or sending a job application	24	26	23
Listening to web radios/watching web television	23	30	16
Downloading software other than games	23	33	13
Other communication eg chat rooms, message boards	20	23	18
Post educational activities (eg leisure activities)	18	20	16
Selling goods or services	17	22	13
Telephoning over the internet/video conferencing	10	13	7

Source: Office for National Statistics © Crown copyright 2006

http://www.statistics.gov.uk

iBuy

Q: Have you ever researched or bought any of these products or services online? % of respondents

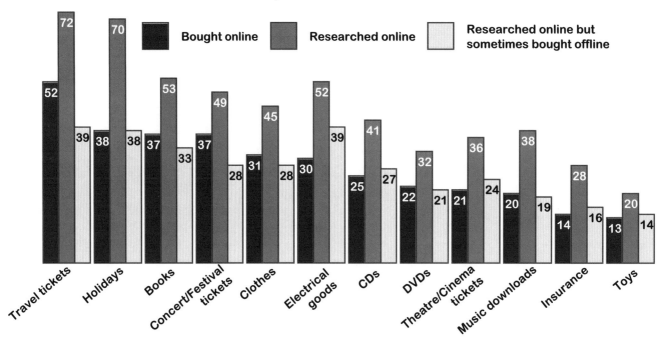

- ■ Bought online
- ■ Researched online
- □ Researched online but sometimes bought offline

Travel tickets: 52, 72, 39
Holidays: 38, 70, 38
Books: 37, 53, 33
Concert/Festival tickets: 37, 49, 28
Clothes: 31, 45, 28
Electrical goods: 30, 52, 39
CDs: 25, 41, 27
DVDs: 22, 32, 21
Theatre/Cinema tickets: 21, 36, 24
Music downloads: 20, 38, 19
Insurance: 14, 28, 16
Toys: 13, 20, 14

Amount spent (Euros) and number of items bought in previous six months, Europe 2006

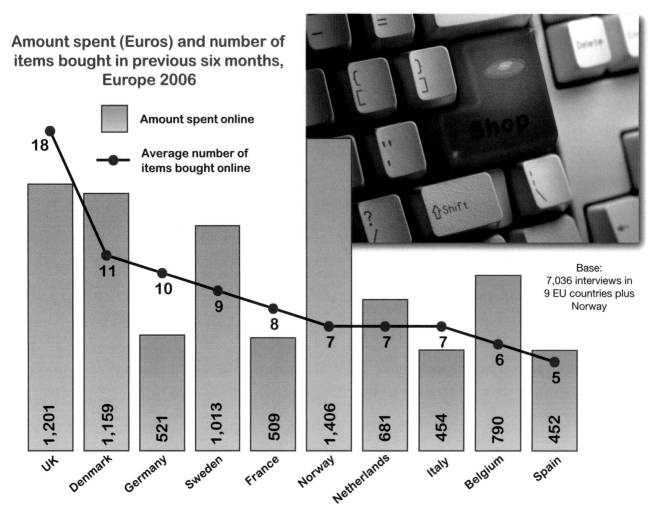

- Amount spent online
- ●— Average number of items bought online

Country	Amount spent	Items
UK	1,201	18
Denmark	1,159	11
Germany	521	10
Sweden	1,013	9
France	509	8
Norway	1,406	7
Netherlands	681	7
Italy	454	7
Belgium	790	6
Spain	452	5

Base:
7,036 interviews in
9 EU countries plus
Norway

Source: Mediascope Europe Media Consumption Study, EIAA, 2006

http://www.eiaa.net/

PC world

World population, internet usage and penetration
(usage growth 2000-2007 in brackets)

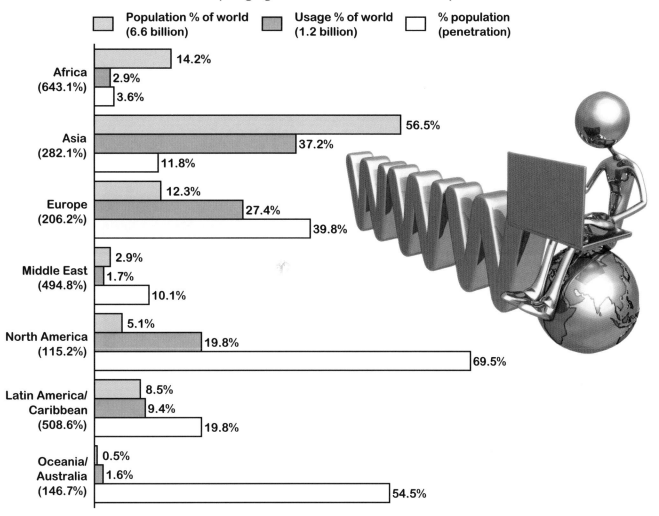

Population % of world (6.6 billion) | Usage % of world (1.2 billion) | % population (penetration)

Africa (643.1%)
- 14.2%
- 2.9%
- 3.6%

Asia (282.1%)
- 56.5%
- 37.2%
- 11.8%

Europe (206.2%)
- 12.3%
- 27.4%
- 39.8%

Middle East (494.8%)
- 2.9%
- 1.7%
- 10.1%

North America (115.2%)
- 5.1%
- 19.8%
- 69.5%

Latin America/ Caribbean (508.6%)
- 8.5%
- 9.4%
- 19.8%

Oceania/ Australia (146.7%)
- 0.5%
- 1.6%
- 54.5%

Percentage of internet users by language

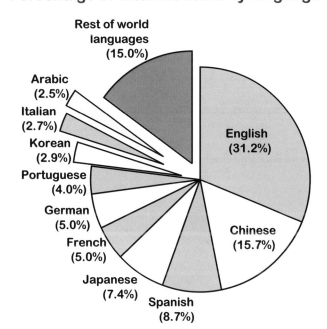

- Rest of world languages (15.0%)
- Arabic (2.5%)
- Italian (2.7%)
- Korean (2.9%)
- Portuguese (4.0%)
- German (5.0%)
- French (5.0%)
- Japanese (7.4%)
- Spanish (8.7%)
- Chinese (15.7%)
- English (31.2%)

The population of each region has to be taken into account when considering their percentage of world internet usage. For example, while Asia accounts for 37.2% of global internet use only 11.8% of Asia's 3.7 billion population uses the internet.

Distribution within regions is also very unequal. China and Japan account for 37.1% & 19.8% of internet usage within Asia with countries like Afghanistan, Cambodia and Singapore accounting for less than 1% of that region's usage.

On the other hand, North America's population of 335 million accounts for only 5.1% of the world. Yet 69% of their population use the internet accounting for 19.8% of global internet users. This explains why usage growth is smallest in this region compared to somewhere like Africa whose growth has increased by 643.1% yet only 3.6% of the population have used the internet.

Source: Internet World Stats

http://www.internetworldstats.com

Download nation

In a survey, 57% of respondents had downloaded music from the internet, but over half of downloaders buy the same number or more CDs than they used to

Q: How often do you...

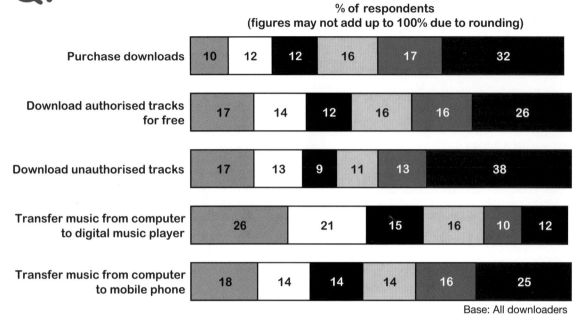

% of respondents
(figures may not add up to 100% due to rounding)

	More than once per week	About weekly	About fortnightly	About monthly	Less than monthly	Rarely
Purchase downloads	10	12	12	16	17	32
Download authorised tracks for free	17	14	12	16	16	26
Download unauthorised tracks	17	13	9	11	13	38
Transfer music from computer to digital music player	26	21	15	16	10	12
Transfer music from computer to mobile phone	18	14	14	14	16	25

Base: All downloaders

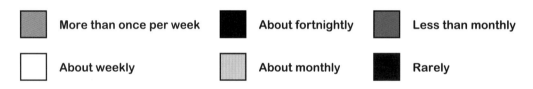

- More than once per week
- About fortnightly
- Less than monthly
- About weekly
- About monthly
- Rarely

Base: All downloaders

Q: What effect does downloading have on the number of CDs you buy?

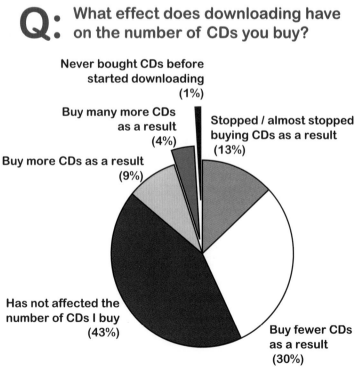

Never bought CDs before started downloading (1%)

Buy many more CDs as a result (4%)

Stopped / almost stopped buying CDs as a result (13%)

Buy more CDs as a result (9%)

Has not affected the number of CDs I buy (43%)

Buy fewer CDs as a result (30%)

Q: Why do you purchase legal downloads?

% of respondents
(respondents could choose more than one response)

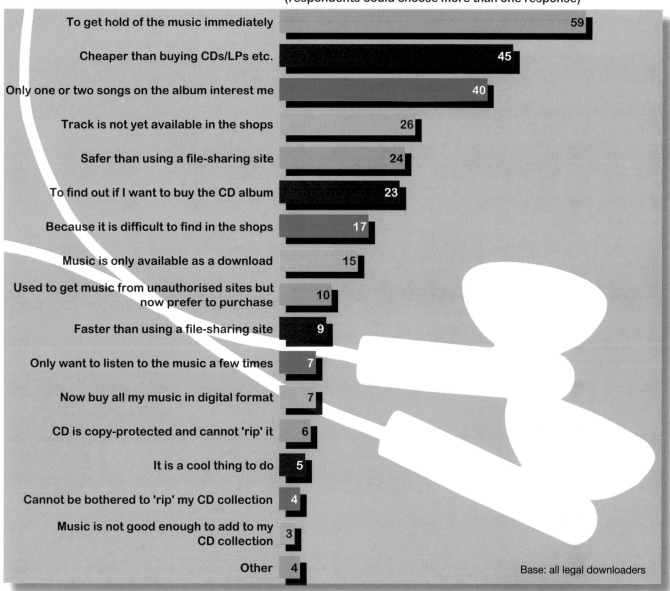

To get hold of the music immediately	59
Cheaper than buying CDs/LPs etc.	45
Only one or two songs on the album interest me	40
Track is not yet available in the shops	26
Safer than using a file-sharing site	24
To find out if I want to buy the CD album	23
Because it is difficult to find in the shops	17
Music is only available as a download	15
Used to get music from unauthorised sites but now prefer to purchase	10
Faster than using a file-sharing site	9
Only want to listen to the music a few times	7
Now buy all my music in digital format	7
CD is copy-protected and cannot 'rip' it	6
It is a cool thing to do	5
Cannot be bothered to 'rip' my CD collection	4
Music is not good enough to add to my CD collection	3
Other	4

Base: all legal downloaders

Q: How extensive is your understanding of the law about what you are legally allowed to download?
(Base: all respondents)

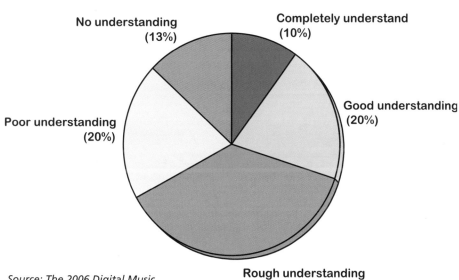

- No understanding (13%)
- Completely understand (10%)
- Good understanding (20%)
- Poor understanding (20%)
- Rough understanding (37%)

iPod Touch courtesy of Apple

Source: The 2006 Digital Music Survey, Entertaining Media Research sponsored by OLSWANG

http://www.olswang.com/dms

Digital universe

We create new digital bits every time we take a picture with our digital cameras. Then we email them to friends and family and create even more digital bits

A guide to bits and bytes	
Bit (b)	1 or 0
Byte (B)	8 bits
Kilobyte (KB)	1,000 bytes
Megabyte (MB)	1,000 KB
Gigabyte (GB)	1,000 MB
Terabyte (TB)	1,000 GB
Petabyte (PB)	1,000 TB
Exabyte (EB)	1,000 PB
Zettabyte (ZB)	1,000 EB

Digital information is everywhere; in our DVDs, mobile phones, digital cameras and MP3 files as well as on the Internet. The amount of digital information created in 2006 was 161 exabytes, which is about 3 million times the information in all the books ever written.

Size of the digital universe, worldwide 2006 and projected for 2010, exabytes

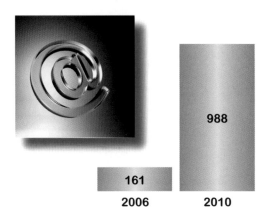

161 — 2006
988 — 2010

Regional share of digital data, worldwide 2006

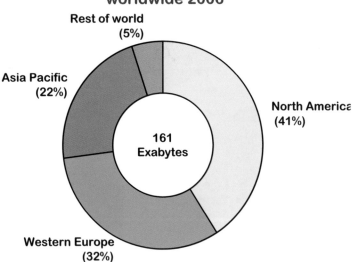

161 Exabytes

- Rest of world (5%)
- Asia Pacific (22%)
- North America (41%)
- Western Europe (32%)

Population, Internet users and IT spending, distribution by region, worldwide 2006, %

☐ IT spending   ☐ Internet users   ☐ Population

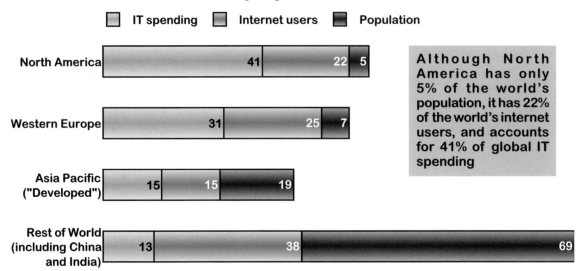

Region	IT spending	Internet users	Population
North America	41	22	5
Western Europe	31	25	7
Asia Pacific ("Developed")	15	15	19
Rest of World (including China and India)	13	38	69

Although North America has only 5% of the world's population, it has 22% of the world's internet users, and accounts for 41% of global IT spending

Source: IDC, The Expanding Digital Universe sponsored by EMC, March 2007   *http://www.emc.com/about/destination/digital_universe/*

Digital switch

The first TV region will switch from analogue to digital in 2008, but fewer than a fifth of adults know when their region's changeover is due

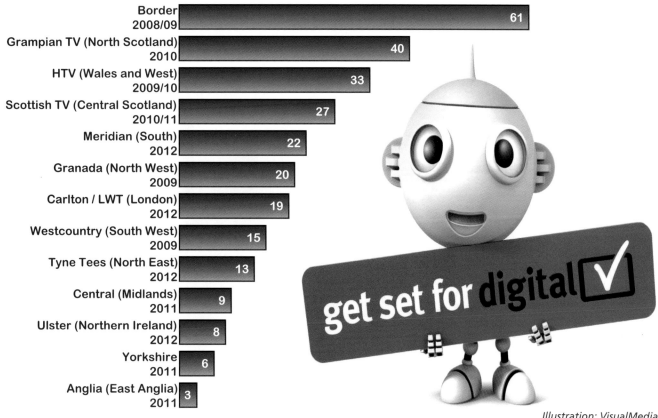

Respondents who correctly identified the year their region would switch to digital TV, UK 2007, %
(The actual changeover year for each region is shown)

Region	%
Border 2008/09	61
Grampian TV (North Scotland) 2010	40
HTV (Wales and West) 2009/10	33
Scottish TV (Central Scotland) 2010/11	27
Meridian (South) 2012	22
Granada (North West) 2009	20
Carlton / LWT (London) 2012	19
Westcountry (South West) 2009	15
Tyne Tees (North East) 2012	13
Central (Midlands) 2011	9
Ulster (Northern Ireland) 2012	8
Yorkshire 2011	6
Anglia (East Anglia) 2011	3

get set for digital ✓

Illustration: VisualMedia

Has the Government provided you with enough information about the changeover to digital TV? UK, 2007, %

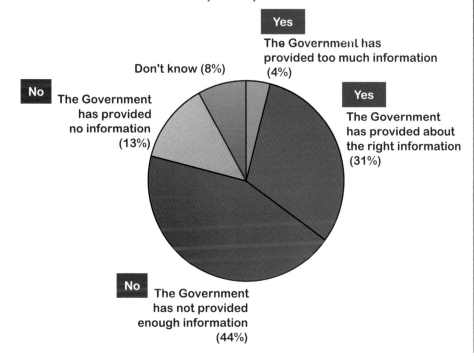

Yes The Government has provided too much information (4%)

Yes The Government has provided about the right information (31%)

Don't know (8%)

No The Government has provided no information (13%)

No The Government has not provided enough information (44%)

Switching off the existing analogue broadcasting system will allow a boost to the digital TV signal and provide people with a greater choice of digital viewing options.

83% of respondents didn't know or guessed incorrectly when their region would be switching to digital TV.

Generally, people believe that their region is being switched over earlier than it actually will be; the greatest information gap was in Ulster, where the most popular guess was 2008 – four years before it is actually due.

12 million adults thought they would need a new TV to receive digital.

Only one in six adults knew all four ways of receiving digital television (cable, digital box, satellite dish and telephone line). This figure was even lower (11%) amongst 18-24 year olds.

Source: USwitch and YouGov: Digital TV Survey 2007

http://www.yougov.com

News views

Importance of terrestrial TV, by genre, UK 2006, %
(Respondents could choose five genres)

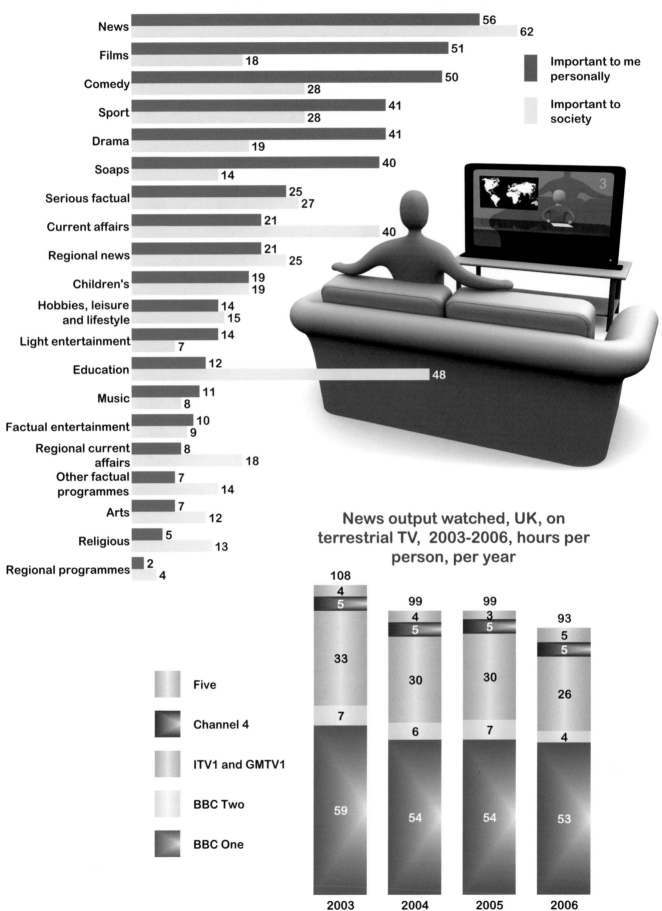

Genre	Important to me personally	Important to society
News	56	62
Films	51	18
Comedy	50	28
Sport	41	28
Drama	41	19
Soaps	40	14
Serious factual	25	27
Current affairs	21	40
Regional news	21	25
Children's	19	19
Hobbies, leisure and lifestyle	14	15
Light entertainment	14	7
Education	12	48
Music	11	8
Factual entertainment	10	9
Regional current affairs	8	18
Other factual programmes	7	14
Arts	7	12
Religious	5	13
Regional programmes	2	4

Important to me personally
Important to society

News output watched, UK, on terrestrial TV, 2003-2006, hours per person, per year

Legend:
- Five
- Channel 4
- ITV1 and GMTV1
- BBC Two
- BBC One

	2003	2004	2005	2006
Total	108	99	99	93
Five	4	4	3	5
Channel 4	5	5	5	5
ITV1 and GMTV1	33	30	30	26
BBC Two	7	6	7	4
BBC One	59	54	54	53

How well are the five terrestrial channels meeting the objectives of public service broadcasting?

Regular viewers of each channel were asked to give their opinion in answer to these statements, on a scale of 1-10
(where 10 means the statement applies completely, and 1 means it does not apply at all)

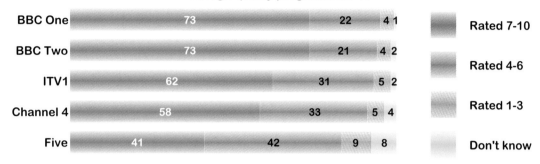

"Shows well-made, high-quality programmes." %

Channel	Rated 7-10	Rated 4-6	Rated 1-3	Don't know
BBC One	73	22	4	1
BBC Two	73	21	4	2
ITV1	62	31	5	2
Channel 4	58	33	5	4
Five	41	42	9	8

Legend: Rated 7-10 / Rated 4-6 / Rated 1-3 / Don't know

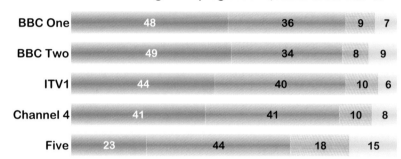

"Shows enough new programmes, made in the UK." %

Channel	Rated 7-10	Rated 4-6	Rated 1-3	Don't know
BBC One	48	36	9	7
BBC Two	49	34	8	9
ITV1	44	40	10	6
Channel 4	41	41	10	8
Five	23	44	18	15

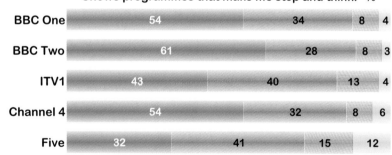

"Shows programmes that make me stop and think." %

Channel	Rated 7-10	Rated 4-6	Rated 1-3	Don't know
BBC One	54	34	8	4
BBC Two	61	28	8	3
ITV1	43	40	13	4
Channel 4	54	32	8	6
Five	32	41	15	12

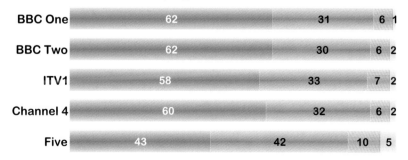

"Shows programmes I want to watch." %

Channel	Rated 7-10	Rated 4-6	Rated 1-3	Don't know
BBC One	62	31	6	1
BBC Two	62	30	6	2
ITV1	58	33	7	2
Channel 4	60	32	6	2
Five	43	42	10	5

Source: Public Service Broadcasting: Annual Report 2007, Ofcom

http://www.ofcom.org.uk

What to watch

Annual % share of viewing (individuals), UK 1986-2006

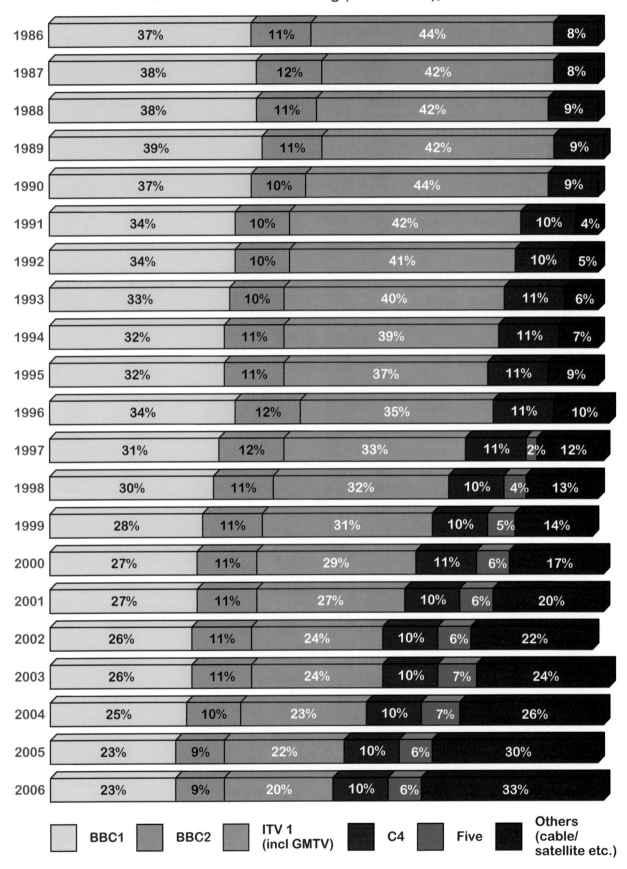

Year	BBC1	BBC2	ITV 1 (incl GMTV)	C4	Five	Others (cable/satellite etc.)
1986	37%	11%	44%	8%		
1987	38%	12%	42%	8%		
1988	38%	11%	42%	9%		
1989	39%	11%	42%	9%		
1990	37%	10%	44%	9%		
1991	34%	10%	42%	10%		4%
1992	34%	10%	41%	10%		5%
1993	33%	10%	40%	11%		6%
1994	32%	11%	39%	11%		7%
1995	32%	11%	37%	11%		9%
1996	34%	12%	35%	11%		10%
1997	31%	12%	33%	11%	2%	12%
1998	30%	11%	32%	10%	4%	13%
1999	28%	11%	31%	10%	5%	14%
2000	27%	11%	29%	11%	6%	17%
2001	27%	11%	27%	10%	6%	20%
2002	26%	11%	24%	10%	6%	22%
2003	26%	11%	24%	10%	7%	24%
2004	25%	10%	23%	10%	7%	26%
2005	23%	9%	22%	10%	6%	30%
2006	23%	9%	20%	10%	6%	33%

Figures may not add up to 100% due to rounding

Source: BARB 2007
http://www.barb.co.uk

Commercial appeal

UK companies spent nearly £3.7 billion on advertising in 2006

Who are they and what do they produce?

Procter & Gamble: cleaning and personal care brands, eg Oral B, Gillette, Ariel, Braun

Unilever: foods and household product brands, eg Flora, Wall's, Dove, Comfort

COI Communications: the UK Government's marketing and communications company

Reckitt Benckiser: cleaning and personal care brands, eg Dettol, Calgon, Lemsip, Bonjela

Masterfoods: Confectionery, food and pet food brands, eg Mars, Maltesers, Dolmio, Uncle Ben's, Whiskas

new
Dove Dove
Body Lotion with
Self-Tanning Agents

Expenditure on advertising and % spent on TV advertising, top 20 companies, UK, 2006

■ % spent on TV advertising   ■ Expenditure on advertising

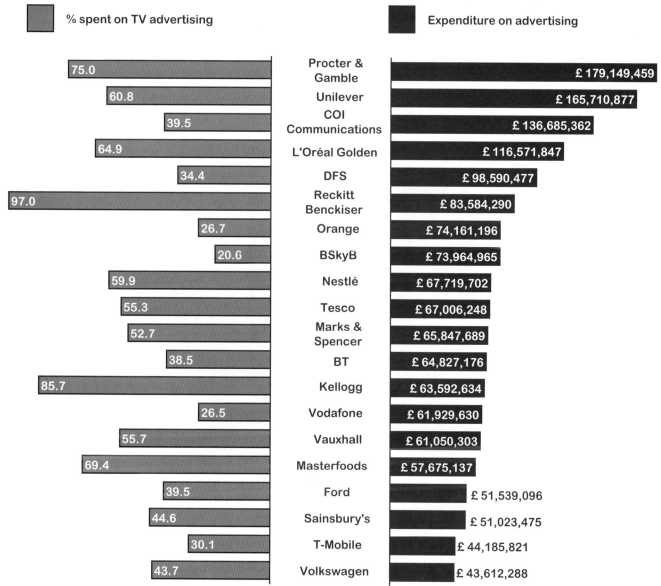

Company	% spent on TV advertising	Expenditure on advertising
Procter & Gamble	75.0	£ 179,149,459
Unilever	60.8	£ 165,710,877
COI Communications	39.5	£ 136,685,362
L'Oréal Golden	64.9	£ 116,571,847
DFS	34.4	£ 98,590,477
Reckitt Benckiser	97.0	£ 83,584,290
Orange	26.7	£ 74,161,196
BSkyB	20.6	£ 73,964,965
Nestlé	59.9	£ 67,719,702
Tesco	55.3	£ 67,006,248
Marks & Spencer	52.7	£ 65,847,689
BT	38.5	£ 64,827,176
Kellogg	85.7	£ 63,592,634
Vodafone	26.5	£ 61,929,630
Vauxhall	55.7	£ 61,050,303
Masterfoods	69.4	£ 57,675,137
Ford	39.5	£ 51,539,096
Sainsbury's	44.6	£ 51,023,475
T-Mobile	30.1	£ 44,185,821
Volkswagen	43.7	£ 43,612,288

Source: Neilsen Media Research/Marketing magazine, February 2007

Competent callers

While 82% of all UK adults own a mobile phone, only 49% of people aged 65+ own one

- Reasons for owning a mobile phone change with age. The majority (82%) of older people with a mobile phone had got it 'for emergencies', compared to 56% of all adults.

- Among those aged 65+ who own a mobile phone almost two in five claim to make no use of it in a typical week.

- Older people make on average five calls and send two texts per week, whilst the average UK adult makes 20 calls and sends 28 texts.

- Consequently, older people spend far less on their mobile phone, just £8 per month compared to the £22 UK adult average.

- When it comes to the dangers of mobile phones, adults of all ages show similar concern. Two-fifths of all adults (42%) and of older people (40%) are concerned about mobile phones.

- The two main areas of worry for older people relate to health risk (16%) and risk to society standards and values (15%).

Top 5 weekly uses for mobile phone	Aged 65+	All UK
Making personal/ business calls	58%	85%
Sending personal/ business text messages	17%	70%
Looking back at stored text messages	4%	28%
Taking photos using the phone	2%	24%
Getting sports/ team news/score alerts	1%	5%

How competent mobile phone owners over 65 years old feel at certain tasks (UK 'Can do with confidence' average in brackets)

- Can do with confidence
- Interested, can't do with confidence
- Not interested/ no need

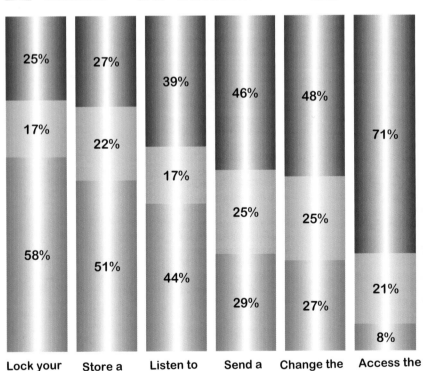

Lock your phone (88%)	Store a new contact (88%)	Listen to voicemail (83%)	Send a text (81%)	Change the ringtone (79%)	Access the internet (38%)
25%	27%	39%	46%	48%	71%
17%	22%	17%	25%	25%	21%
58%	51%	44% / 29%	29%	27%	8%

Source: Media Literacy Audit, Report on media literacy amongst older people, Ofcom, 2006

http://www.ofcom.org.uk

Law & order

Knife culture

Knives are the most common type of weapon used in violent crime

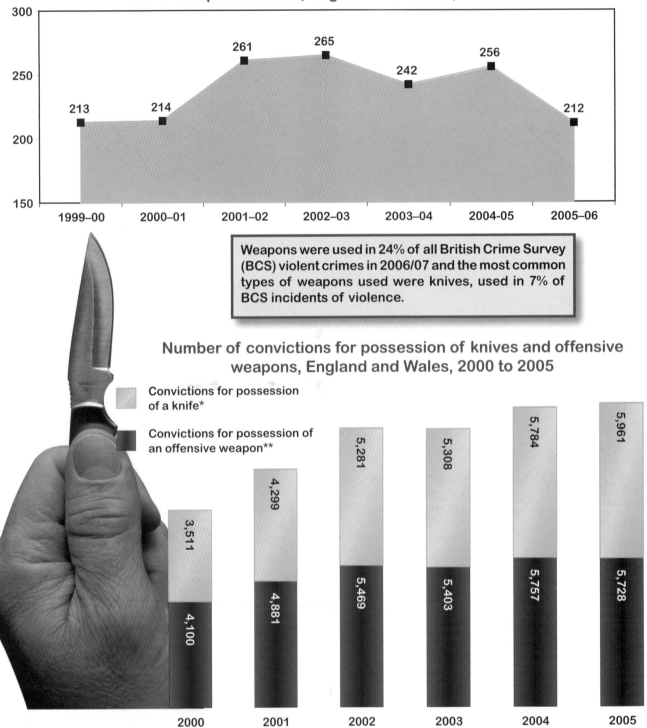

Offences recorded as homicide where the method of killing was a sharp instrument, England and Wales, 1999-2006

- 1999–00: 213
- 2000–01: 214
- 2001–02: 261
- 2002–03: 265
- 2003–04: 242
- 2004–05: 256
- 2005–06: 212

> Weapons were used in 24% of all British Crime Survey (BCS) violent crimes in 2006/07 and the most common types of weapons used were knives, used in 7% of BCS incidents of violence.

Number of convictions for possession of knives and offensive weapons, England and Wales, 2000 to 2005

Convictions for possession of a knife*

Convictions for possession of an offensive weapon**

Year	Convictions for possession of a knife*	Convictions for possession of an offensive weapon**
2000	3,511	4,100
2001	4,299	4,881
2002	5,281	5,469
2003	5,308	5,403
2004	5,784	5,757
2005	5,961	5,728

* It is an offence to have an article with a blade or a sharp point in a public place. (An exemption applies to folding pocket knives with a blade of less than three inches.)

** It is an offence to have any offensive weapon in a public place (without lawful authority or reasonable excuse). An offensive weapon is "any article made or adapted for use for causing injury to the person." Offensive weapons include: knuckle-dusters, sword-sticks, hand-claws, foot-claws, belt buckle knives, push daggers, butterfly knives, blow-pipes, guns, truncheons etc.

Source: Banning Offensive Weapons, Home Office
© Crown copyright 2007

http://www.homeoffice.gov.uk

Gun culture

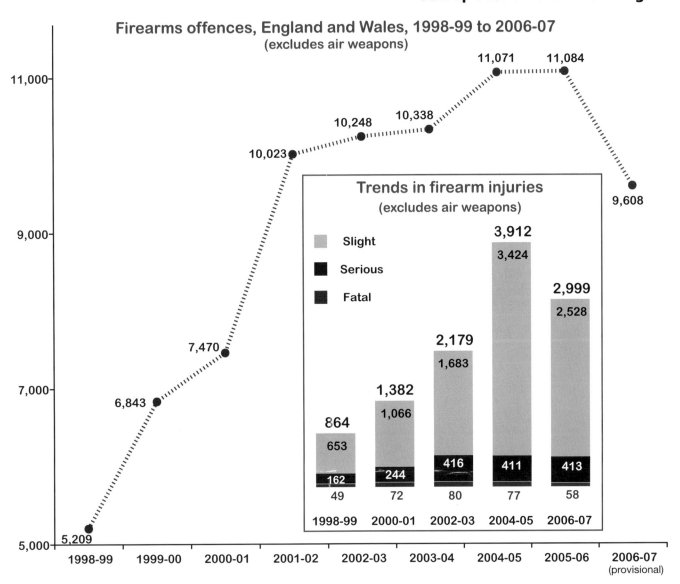

Firearms offences, England and Wales, 1998-99 to 2006-07
(excludes air weapons)

11,000 —
9,000 —
7,000 —
5,000 —

5,209 • 6,843 • 7,470 • 10,023 • 10,248 • 10,338 • 11,071 • 11,084 • 9,608

1998-99 · 1999-00 · 2000-01 · 2001-02 · 2002-03 · 2003-04 · 2004-05 · 2005-06 · 2006-07 (provisional)

Trends in firearm injuries
(excludes air weapons)

- Slight
- Serious
- Fatal

Year	Total	Slight	Serious	Fatal
1998-99	864	653	162	49
2000-01	1,382	1,066	244	72
2002-03	2,179	1,683	416	80
2004-05	3,912	3,424	411	77
2006-07	2,999	2,528	413	58

Over 2,100 British adults were surveyed in September 2007

45% believe that their area is not as safe as it was five years ago as a result of gun and knife crime (56% in London)

29% feel that they or their immediate family are at threat (42% London; 32% urban areas v 23% rural areas)

12% (1 in 8) men know someone who has or has had an illegal firearm

18% of men would able to acquire an illegal firearm

88% support an increase in the penalty for possessing an illegal firearm

72% support an increase in the number of armed police patrols to combat gun and knife crime

Source: Gun and knife crime in Great Britain, Policy Exchange 2007, Homicides, Firearm Offences and Intimate Violence 2005/06, Crime in England and Wales 2006/07 © Crown copyright 2007

http://www.policyexchange.org.uk
http://www.homeoffice.gov.uk

Phone alone

**An estimated 800,000 owners a
year have their mobiles stolen**

Where victims of mobile phone theft had them stolen, England and Wales, 2005/06

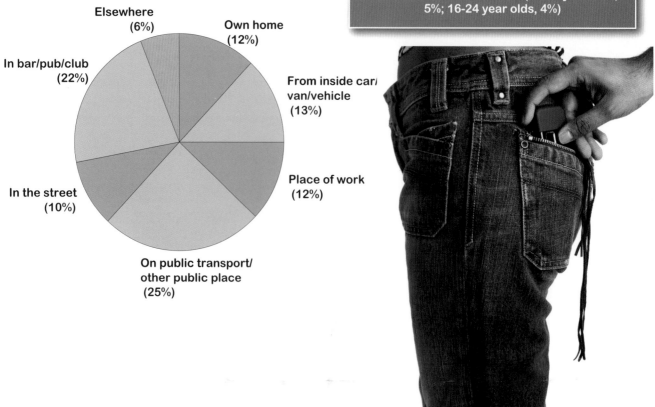

- Elsewhere (6%)
- Own home (12%)
- In bar/pub/club (22%)
- From inside car/van/vehicle (13%)
- In the street (10%)
- Place of work (12%)
- On public transport/other public place (25%)

Individuals aged 12 to 24 were more likely than any other age group to have had their phone stolen in the last 12 months (12-15 year olds, 5%; 16-24 year olds, 4%)

Circumstances of how the phone was stolen, England and Wales, 2005/06

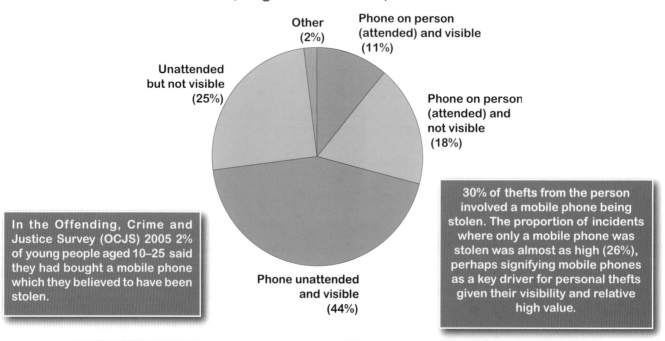

- Other (2%)
- Phone on person (attended) and visible (11%)
- Unattended but not visible (25%)
- Phone on person (attended) and not visible (18%)
- Phone unattended and visible (44%)

In the Offending, Crime and Justice Survey (OCJS) 2005 2% of young people aged 10–25 said they had bought a mobile phone which they believed to have been stolen.

30% of thefts from the person involved a mobile phone being stolen. The proportion of incidents where only a mobile phone was stolen was almost as high (26%), perhaps signifying mobile phones as a key driver for personal thefts given their visibility and relative high value.

With a sample size of 48,000 interviews, the British Crime Survey measures the amount of crime by asking people aged 16 and over, living in private households, about crimes they have experienced in the last year

Source: Mobile phone theft, plastic card and identity fraud: Findings from the 2005/06 British Crime Survey, Home Office © Crown copyright 2007

http://www.homeoffice.gov.uk

Fear factor

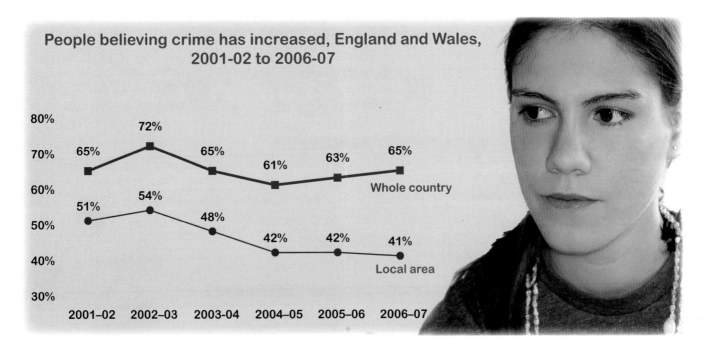

People believing crime has increased, England and Wales, 2001-02 to 2006-07

(Whole country line) 65%, 72%, 65%, 61%, 63%, 65%

(Local area line) 51%, 54%, 48%, 42%, 42%, 41%

Years: 2001–02, 2002–03, 2003-04, 2004–05, 2005–06, 2006–07

Respondents were asked their perception of how crime levels have changed in the country as a whole and in their local area over the past two years.

Those who had experienced crime in the previous 12 months were far more likely to think that local crime had risen 'a lot', 27% compared with 10% who had not.

Experiences of crime did not appear to affect perceptions of changes in crime in the country as a whole. Certain groups were more likely to perceive a rise in crime, eg
- women more than men,
- older people rather than younger
- readers of national 'tabloids' rather then readers of 'broadsheets'

% with high levels of worry about violent crime and actual victims of violence, by gender and age, 2006-07

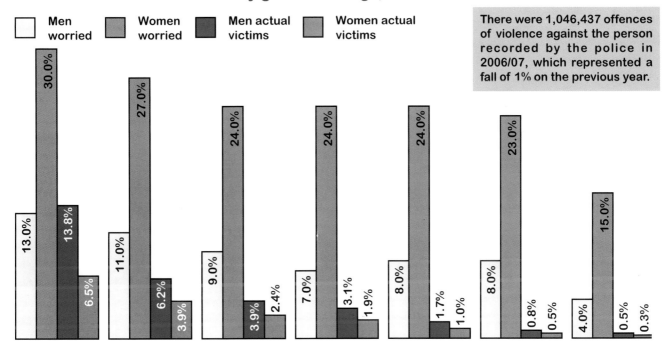

Legend: Men worried / Women worried / Men actual victims / Women actual victims

Values: 13.0%, 30.0%, 13.8%, 6.5%; 11.0%, 27.0%, 6.2%, 3.9%; 9.0%, 24.0%, 3.9%, 2.4%; 7.0%, 24.0%, 3.1%, 1.9%; 8.0%, 24.0%, 1.7%, 1.0%; 8.0%, 23.0%, 0.8%, 0.5%; 4.0%, 15.0%, 0.5%, 0.3%

There were 1,046,437 offences of violence against the person recorded by the police in 2006/07, which represented a fall of 1% on the previous year.

The BCS is a victimisation survey in which 47,000+ adults are asked about their experiences of crime

Source: Crime in England and Wales 2006-07, Home Office © Crown copyright 2007

http://www.homeoffice.gov.uk

Cause for alarm?

The fear of burglary in the EU was greater than the actual incidence

Experience of and attitudes to burglary,
selected EU countries 2005, %

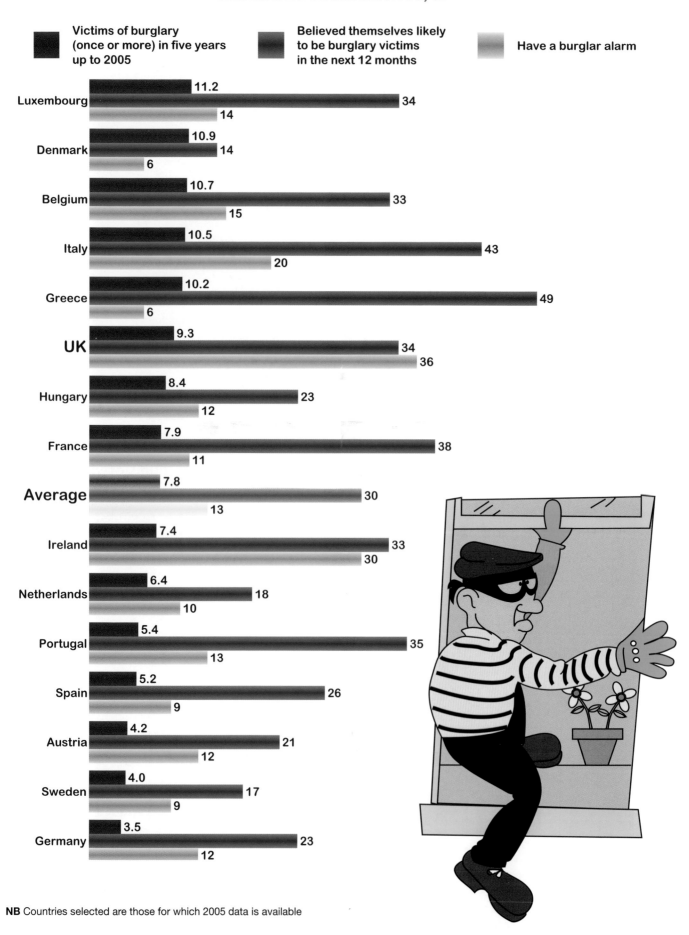

■ Victims of burglary (once or more) in five years up to 2005
■ Believed themselves likely to be burglary victims in the next 12 months
■ Have a burglar alarm

Luxembourg
11.2
34
14

Denmark
10.9
14
6

Belgium
10.7
33
15

Italy
10.5
43
20

Greece
10.2
49
6

UK
9.3
34
36

Hungary
8.4
23
12

France
7.9
38
11

Average
7.8
30
13

Ireland
7.4
33
30

Netherlands
6.4
18
10

Portugal
5.4
35
13

Spain
5.2
26
9

Austria
4.2
21
12

Sweden
4.0
17
9

Germany
3.5
23
12

NB Countries selected are those for which 2005 data is available

Q How should burglars be punished for repeat offences?

Selected EU countries 2005, %

Prison sentence | Community service

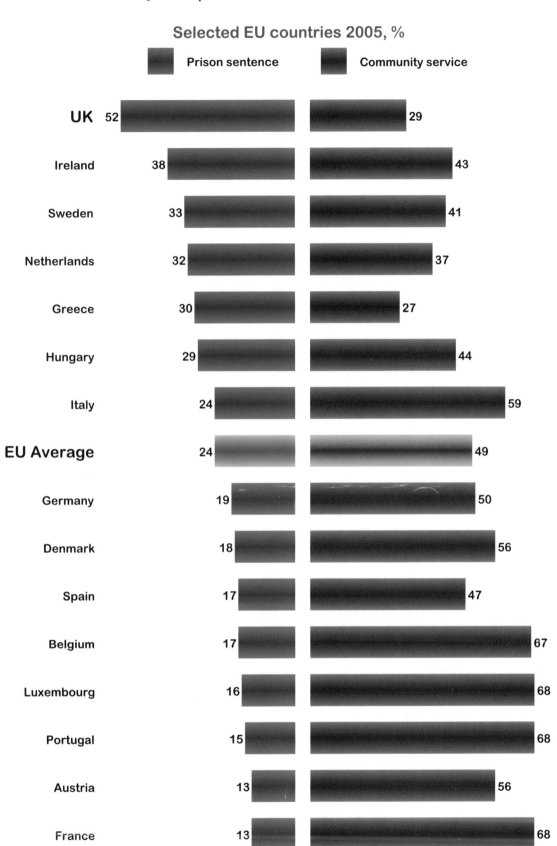

Country	Prison sentence	Community service
UK	52	29
Ireland	38	43
Sweden	33	41
Netherlands	32	37
Greece	30	27
Hungary	29	44
Italy	24	59
EU Average	24	49
Germany	19	50
Denmark	18	56
Spain	17	47
Belgium	17	67
Luxembourg	16	68
Portugal	15	68
Austria	13	56
France	13	68

NB Only these two options were offered in the survey

Source: The burden of crime in the EU: a comparative analysis of the European crime and safety survey 2005 © EUICS 2007

http://www.crimereduction.gov.uk/statistics/
http://www.europeansafetyobservatory.eu/

London law

The Metropolitan Police has made significant progress against criminality in London

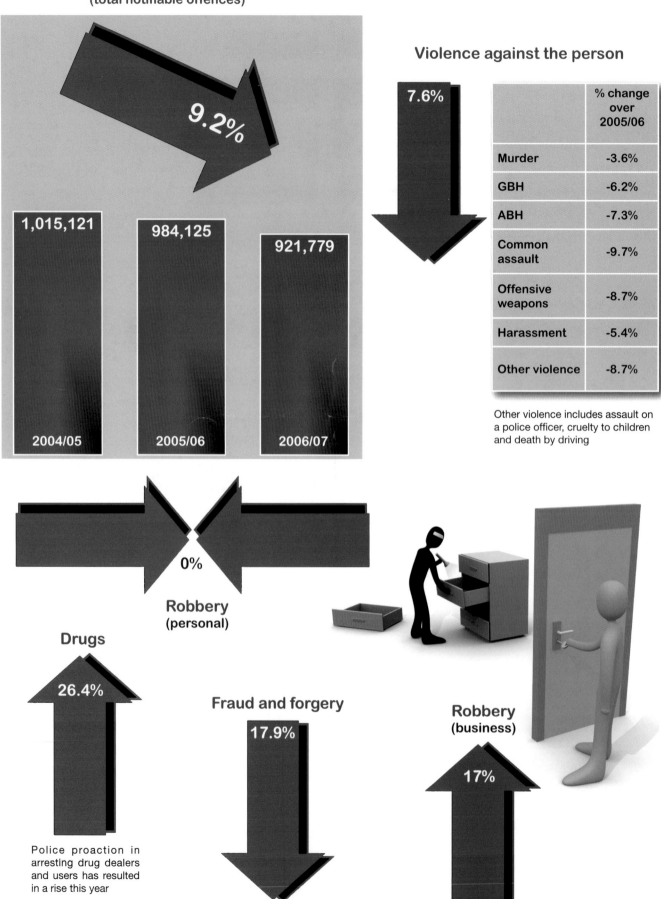

Crime continues to fall
(total notifiable offences)

9.2%

1,015,121	984,125	921,779
2004/05	2005/06	2006/07

Violence against the person

7.6%

	% change over 2005/06
Murder	-3.6%
GBH	-6.2%
ABH	-7.3%
Common assault	-9.7%
Offensive weapons	-8.7%
Harassment	-5.4%
Other violence	-8.7%

Other violence includes assault on a police officer, cruelty to children and death by driving

0%

Robbery
(personal)

Drugs

26.4%

Police proaction in arresting drug dealers and users has resulted in a rise this year

Fraud and forgery

17.9%

Robbery
(business)

17%

Motor vehicle crime

5.8%

	% change over 2005/06
Theft of vehicles	-13.5%
Theft from vehicles	-2.3%

Trident* gun crime

15.0%

2005/06	266
2006/07	226

*A special Metropolitan Police initiative set up in 1998 to tackle gun crime amongst London's black communities

Gun-enabled crime

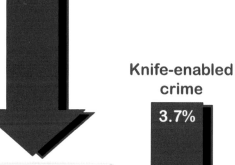

11.3%

2005/06	3,807
2006/07	3,375

Knife-enabled crime

3.7%

2005/06	12,589
2006/07	12,124

Hate crime

	% change over 2005/06
Homophobic crime	-8.5%
Domestic violence	-9.4%
Racist crime	-11.9%

Sexual offences

9.6%

	% change over 2005/06
Rape	-3.9%
Others	-11.3%

Other includes abuse of children through prostitution or pornography and trafficking for sexual exploitation

Burglary

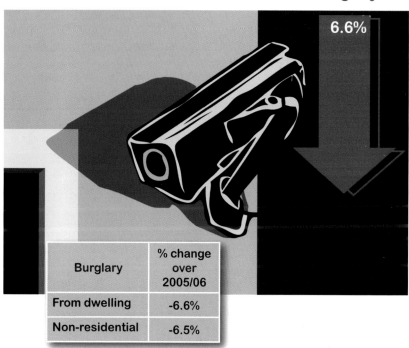

6.6%

Burglary	% change over 2005/06
From dwelling	-6.6%
Non-residential	-6.5%

Source: Metropolitan Police Authority

http://www.mpa.gov.uk
http://www.stoptheguns.org

Seasonal crime

Many types of violent crime peak in the summer months and drop in the winter, whereas theft of motor vehicles typically falls in the summer

Crimes showing peaks in summer and troughs in winter, England and Wales
(Based on monthly data collected 2000–2005)

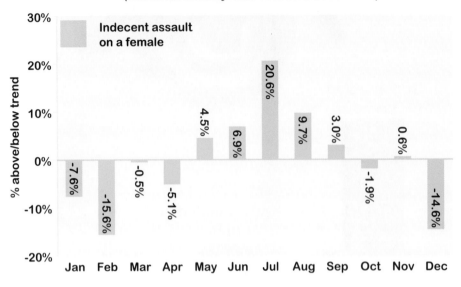

Indecent assault on a female

% above/below trend

- Jan: -7.6%
- Feb: -15.6%
- Mar: -0.5%
- Apr: -5.1%
- May: 4.5%
- Jun: 6.9%
- Jul: 20.6%
- Aug: 9.7%
- Sep: 3.0%
- Oct: -1.9%
- Nov: 0.6%
- Dec: -14.6%

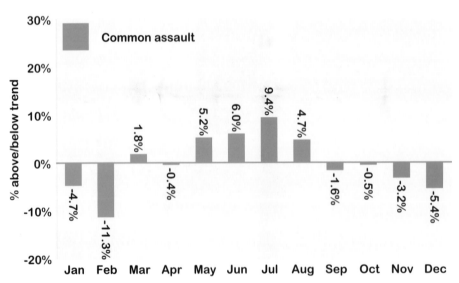

Common assault

% above/below trend

- Jan: -4.7%
- Feb: -11.3%
- Mar: 1.8%
- Apr: -0.4%
- May: 5.2%
- Jun: 6.0%
- Jul: 9.4%
- Aug: 4.7%
- Sep: -1.6%
- Oct: -0.5%
- Nov: -3.2%
- Dec: -5.4%

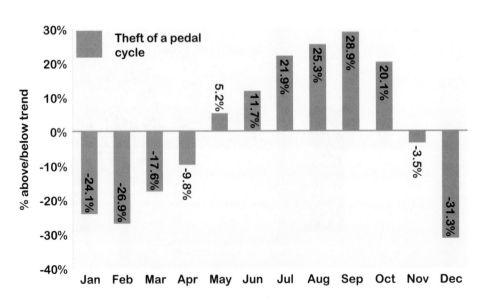

Theft of a pedal cycle

% above/below trend

- Jan: -24.1%
- Feb: -26.9%
- Mar: -17.6%
- Apr: -9.8%
- May: 5.2%
- Jun: 11.7%
- Jul: 21.9%
- Aug: 25.3%
- Sep: 28.9%
- Oct: 20.1%
- Nov: -3.5%
- Dec: -31.3%

Crimes showing **peaks** in **winter** and **troughs** in **summer**, England and Wales

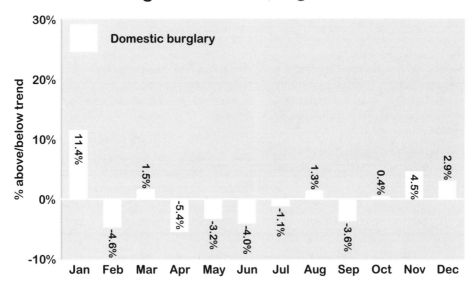

Domestic burglary

% above/below trend

Jan	Feb	Mar	Apr	May	Jun	Jul	Aug	Sep	Oct	Nov	Dec
11.4%	-4.6%	1.5%	-5.4%	-3.2%	-4.0%	-1.1%	1.3%	-3.6%	0.4%	4.5%	2.9%

The January peak of 11.4% in domestic burglary may be due to burglars resting over Christmas, then catching up in January when there are also more new goods in homes to steal, or perhaps there is more need to burgle in January following the excesses of Christmas

Arson, unlike other criminal damage offences shows rises in summer, peaking at 14% in August

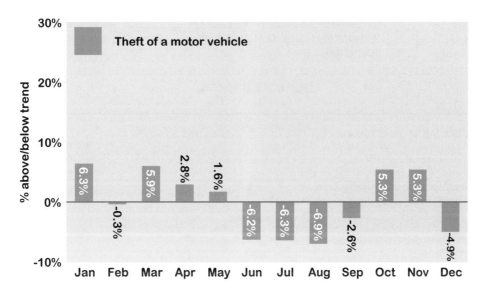

Theft of a motor vehicle

% above/below trend

Jan	Feb	Mar	Apr	May	Jun	Jul	Aug	Sep	Oct	Nov	Dec
6.3%	-0.3%	5.9%	2.8%	1.6%	-6.2%	-6.3%	-6.9%	-2.6%	5.3%	5.3%	-4.9%

Source: Seasonality in recorded crime: preliminary findings, Home Office © Crown copyright 2007

http://www.homeoffice.gov.uk

Evasion

Uninsured motorists are six times as likely to be driving an unroadworthy vehicle and three times as likely to have been convicted of dangerous driving

Tax Facts

Before a vehicle can legally go on the road it must be registered with the Driver and Vehicle Licensing Agency (DVLA), have a valid vehicle tax disc, have a current test certificate (if it is over three years old) and the driver must have a minimum of Third Party insurance.

The tax disc shows that the owner has paid Vehicle Excise Duty, commonly known as road tax. This is an annual payment for any vehicle using public roads.

The DVLA now has the power to clamp untaxed vehicles, to tow them away and to sell or crush them if they remain unclaimed. Nevertheless, evasion of road tax is on the increase.

Why does road tax matter?

The Treasury lost about £217 million of revenue due to unpaid road tax – money which could have been spent not just on roads but on many other services. Untaxed drivers may also be driving unroadworthy vehicles and be uninsured.

Estimated unlicensed stock by tax class, Great Britain, 2004-2006
(in thousands)

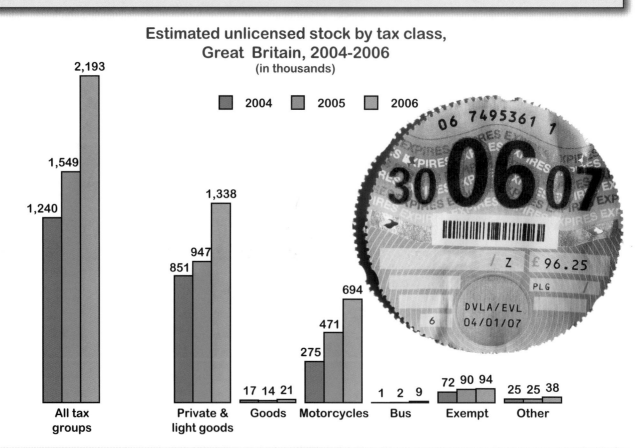

Legend: 2004, 2005, 2006

- All tax groups: 1,240 / 1,549 / 2,193
- Private & light goods: 851 / 947 / 1,338
- Goods: 17 / 14 / 21
- Motorcycles: 275 / 471 / 694
- Bus: 1 / 2 / 9
- Exempt: 72 / 90 / 94
- Other: 25 / 25 / 38

Uninsured facts

» 1 in 15 vehicles on the road were untaxed and a million motorists may be driving without insurance – one in twenty.

» Evasion rates are higher for older vehicles - the ones which are likely to have more problems passing the MoT test of roadworthiness.

» Accidents involving uninsured motorists add an extra £30 a year to motor insurance premiums.

» Uninsured motorists are 10 times more likely to have been convicted of drink driving and 4 times more likely to have a conviction for driving without due care and attention.

» 15% of uninsured drivers are aged 17 to 21 and 33% are aged 21 to 29.

» In 2006 78,000 vehicles were seized by the police for no insurance, 40% of which were crushed or sold.

» West Gorton, Manchester is the place where you are most likely to be hit by an uninsured driver – 6 times the national average.

» There are more uninsured vehicles on the road in London than anywhere else, about 450,000.

Source: Vehicle Excise Duty Evasion 2006 Department for Transport © Crown copyright 2007
Association of British Insurers press release Feb 2007

http://www.dft.gov.uk
http://www.abi.org.uk

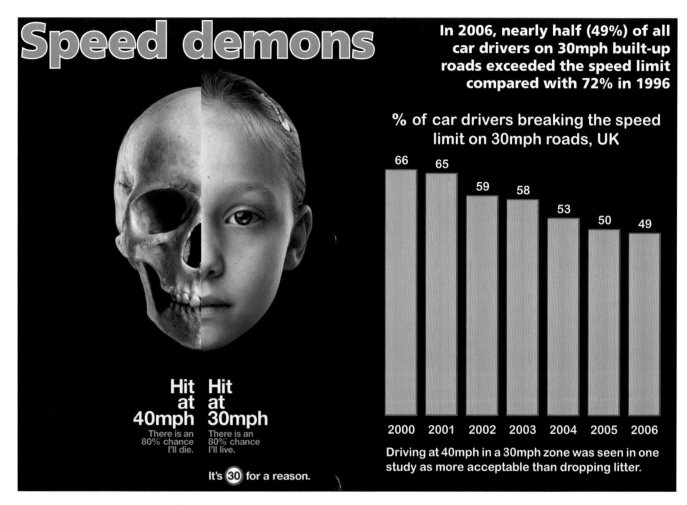

Speed demons

In 2006, nearly half (49%) of all car drivers on 30mph built-up roads exceeded the speed limit compared with 72% in 1996

% of car drivers breaking the speed limit on 30mph roads, UK

2000	2001	2002	2003	2004	2005	2006
66	65	59	58	53	50	49

Hit at 40mph
There is an 80% chance I'll die.

Hit at 30mph
There is an 80% chance I'll live.

It's **30** for a reason.

Driving at 40mph in a 30mph zone was seen in one study as more acceptable than dropping litter.

Car drivers at or above the speed limit on roads in **built-up** areas, UK 2006, %

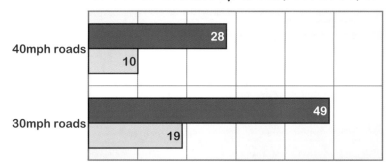

- 40mph roads: 28 (Over the speed limit), 10 (More than 5mph over)
- 30mph roads: 49 (Over the speed limit), 19 (More than 5mph over)

■ Over the speed limit
□ More than 5mph over the speed limit

Car drivers at or above the speed limit on roads in **non built-up** areas, UK 2006, %

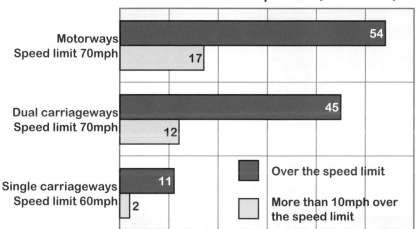

- Motorways Speed limit 70mph: 54 (Over the speed limit), 17 (More than 10mph over)
- Dual carriageways Speed limit 70mph: 45 (Over the speed limit), 12 (More than 10mph over)
- Single carriageways Speed limit 60mph: 11 (Over the speed limit), 2 (More than 10mph over)

■ Over the speed limit
□ More than 10mph over the speed limit

More motorcyclists travelled at more than 10mph above the speed limit, on all road types than car drivers.

76% of articulated heavy goods vehicles exceeded their 40mph limit.

There is a high incidence of speeding by HGVs on 30mph roads: 44% of 2-axle HGVs exceeded the speed limit, 15% by more than 5mph.

The speeds are recorded as vehicles pass over an automatic counter and do not represent speeds over a longer distance. They do however provide an indication of compliance with speed limits.

Source: Department for Transport: Road statistics 2006: Traffic, speeds and congestion © Crown copyright 2007

http://www.dft.gov.uk
http://www.thinkroadsafety.gov.uk/campaigns/slowdown/slowdown.htm

Young crime...

7% of 10-25 year olds have committed six or more offences. They are responsible for 83% of all offences committed by this age group

The Offending, Crime and Justice Survey is a self-report survey which collects longitudinal data (ie information from the same individuals over time) to allow researchers to examine the pathways into and out of delinquency. Almost 5,000 young people aged 10 to 25 were surveyed.

Causes of Youth Crime
(crime committed by the under 18s)

Some key risk factors identified for youth offending are:

» being male
» having a parent or parents who are offenders
» not living with parents/ being in care
» suffering bereavement or family breakdown
» drug or alcohol misuse
» experiencing neglect, physical, sexual or emotional abuse
» witnessing violence against a family member
» playing truant or being excluded from school
» associating with delinquent friends
» having siblings or other family members who offend

Young people committing an offence in last 12 months, England and Wales, 2005

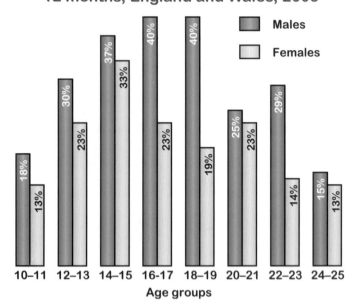

Males
Females

Age group	Males	Females
10–11	18%	13%
12–13	30%	23%
14–15	37%	33%
16–17	40%	23%
18–19	40%	19%
20–21	25%	23%
22–23	29%	14%
24–25	15%	13%

Age groups

Motivation for the offence

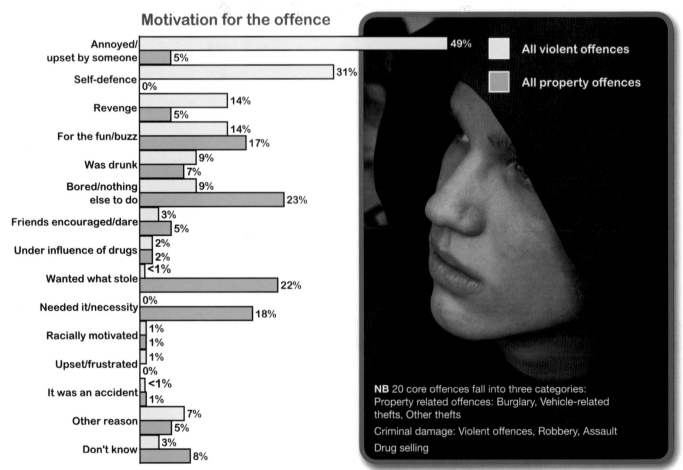

Motivation	All violent offences	All property offences
Annoyed/upset by someone	49%	5%
Self-defence	31%	0%
Revenge	14%	5%
For the fun/buzz	14%	17%
Was drunk	9%	7%
Bored/nothing else to do	9%	23%
Friends encouraged/dare	3%	5%
Under influence of drugs	2%	2%
Wanted what stole	<1%	22%
Needed it/necessity	0%	18%
Racially motivated	1%	1%
Upset/frustrated	1%	0%
It was an accident	<1%	1%
Other reason	7%	5%
Don't know	3%	8%

All violent offences
All property offences

NB 20 core offences fall into three categories:
Property related offences: Burglary, Vehicle-related thefts, Other thefts
Criminal damage: Violent offences, Robbery, Assault
Drug selling

Source: Young People and Crime: Findings from the 2005 Offending, Crime and Justice Survey, Home Office © Crown copyright 2006, Crime Info website

http://www.homeoffice.gov.uk
http://www.crimeinfo.org.uk

...and punishment

Young people who have committed a serious criminal offence can find themselves facing some time in custody. This can take place in three types of secure accommodation: Young Offender Institutions, Secure Training Centres, and Secure Children's Homes.

Places available and young people accommodated in secure children's homes, England 1996-2007

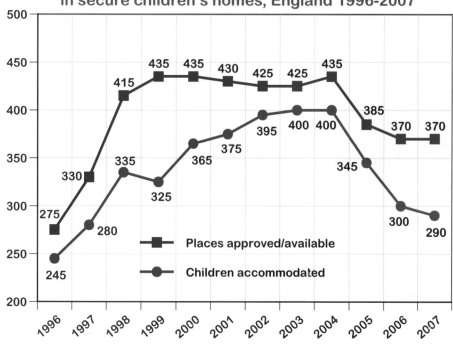

Places approved/available
Children accommodated

Secure Children's Homes, run by local authorities, accommodate the most vulnerable young offenders whose problems have contributed to their criminal behaviour. They may have been in care or have mental health problems.

People in secure children's homes tend to be younger than those in training centres or young offender institutions.

Under 18s in prison, England and Wales, 31st July 2007

362
133
51
226
603
1,096

Aged 15
Aged 16
Aged 17

Prisoners on remand
Prisoners under sentence

The total number of under 18s in prison is
2,471
82 of the prisoners under 18 were female

Source: Department for Education and Skills; Children accommodated in secure children's homes, year ending 31 March 2006 © Crown copyright 2007

http://www.dfes.gov.uk
http://www.direct.gov.uk

Detained

People who have committed crimes but who have also been diagnosed as having some sort of mental disorder can be compulsorily admitted to hospital under the Mental Health Act or the Criminal Procedure (Insanity) Act.

They are held in psychiatric hospitals. In some cases only part of a hospital may be designated for the provision of psychiatric care. High security hospitals, such as Broadmoor, Rampton and Ashworth, hold patients who require treatment under conditions of high security because of their dangerous, violent or criminal tendencies.

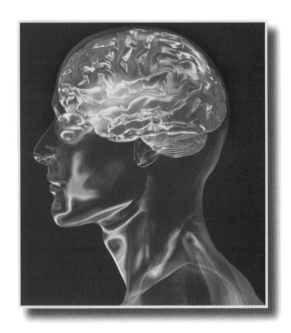

Restricted patients detained in hospital, by gender, England and Wales, 1995 to 2005

Males line: 2,214 (1995), 2,259 (1996), 2,358 (1997), 2,430 (1998), 2,515 (1999), 2,536 (2000), 2,636 (2001), 2,631 (2002), 2,720 (2003), 2,886 (2004), 2,984 (2005)

Females line: 264 (1995), 290 (1996), 292 (1997), 319 (1998), 327 (1999), 322 (2000), 333 (2001), 358 (2002), 398 (2003), 396 (2004), 411 (2005)

Y-axis: Number of patients

Restricted patients detained in hospital, by age group and gender, England and Wales, 2005 (all mental disorders)

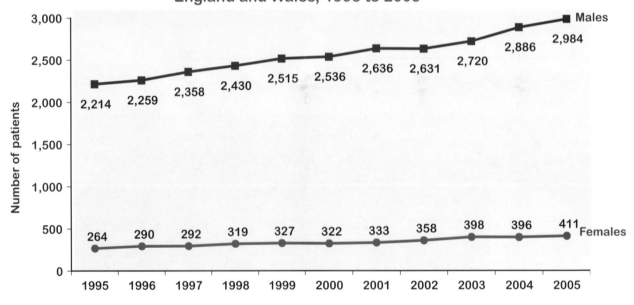

Age on 31 December 2005										
20 & under		21-39		40-59		60+		All ages		Total
M	F	M	F	M	F	M	F	M	F	
79	6	1,468	218	1,209	164	228	23	2,984	411	3,395

Source: Statistics of Mentally Disordered Offenders 2005,
Home Office © Crown copyright 2007

http://www.homeoffice.gov.uk

Security & suspicion

UK police terrorism arrests, 11 September 2001 to 31 March 2007

Key convictions in 2007
(to 31/07/07)

30 April:	5 men in fertiliser bomb plot
15 June:	7 men in Al-Qaeda linked plot
4 July:	3 men involved in inciting terrorism via the web
9 July:	21/7 suicide bombers

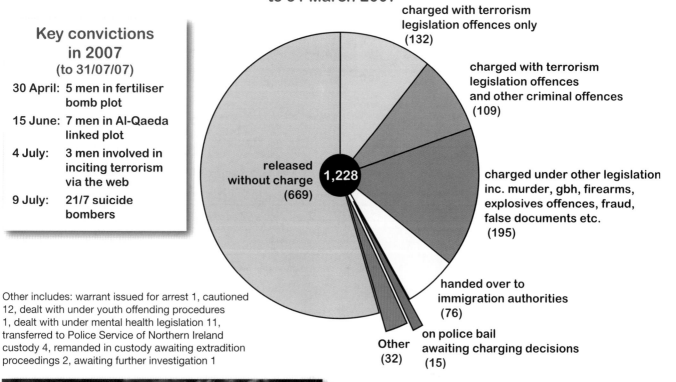

- charged with terrorism legislation offences only (132)
- charged with terrorism legislation offences and other criminal offences (109)
- charged under other legislation inc. murder, gbh, firearms, explosives offences, fraud, false documents etc. (195)
- handed over to immigration authorities (76)
- on police bail awaiting charging decisions (15)
- Other (32)
- released without charge (669)

1,228

Other includes: warrant issued for arrest 1, cautioned 12, dealt with under youth offending procedures 1, dealt with under mental health legislation 11, transferred to Police Service of Northern Ireland custody 4, remanded in custody awaiting extradition proceedings 2, awaiting further investigation 1

Since 9/11 the UK government has:

- Tightened port, airport and border security
- Speeded up extradition processes
- Frozen assets of international terrorist organisations
- Increased joint-working and intelligence sharing internationally
- Increased the size of the Security Service to analyse and act on information
- Continued the exercise programme to deal with terrorism scenarios
- Established chemical, biological, radiological and nuclear (CBRN) resilience programmes
- Increased funding:
  £85.5m to the NHS to counter bio-terrorism
  £56m to the Fire Service for decontamination programmes
  £132m to the Fire Service for search and rescue equipment
  £49m to the Metropolitan Police
  £12m to national police forces

Source: Home Office © Crown copyright 2007
http://www.homeoffice.gov.uk

Scams

3.2 million adults fall victim to scams every year, losing £3.5 billion annually

Estimated number and percentage of UK adults falling victim to scams per year

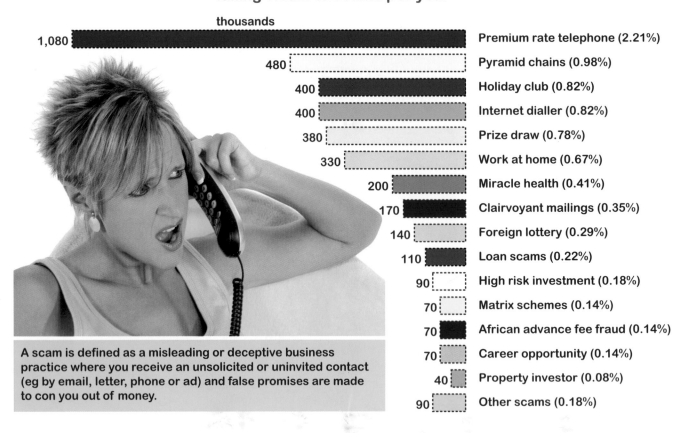

thousands

1,080	Premium rate telephone (2.21%)
480	Pyramid chains (0.98%)
400	Holiday club (0.82%)
400	Internet dialler (0.82%)
380	Prize draw (0.78%)
330	Work at home (0.67%)
200	Miracle health (0.41%)
170	Clairvoyant mailings (0.35%)
140	Foreign lottery (0.29%)
110	Loan scams (0.22%)
90	High risk investment (0.18%)
70	Matrix schemes (0.14%)
70	African advance fee fraud (0.14%)
70	Career opportunity (0.14%)
40	Property investor (0.08%)
90	Other scams (0.18%)

A scam is defined as a misleading or deceptive business practice where you receive an unsolicited or uninvited contact (eg by email, letter, phone or ad) and false promises are made to con you out of money.

Estimated annual cost of scams, by type (£million)

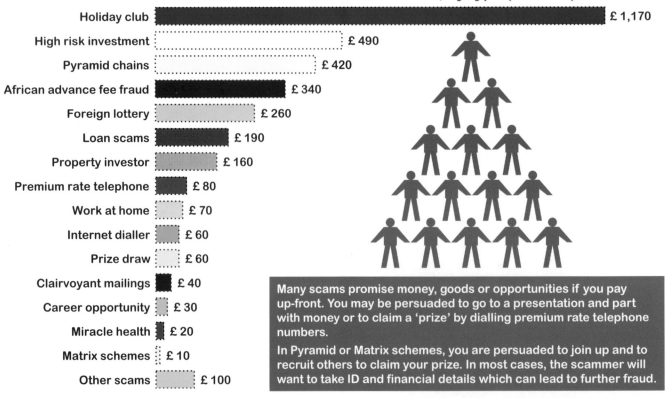

Holiday club	£ 1,170
High risk investment	£ 490
Pyramid chains	£ 420
African advance fee fraud	£ 340
Foreign lottery	£ 260
Loan scams	£ 190
Property investor	£ 160
Premium rate telephone	£ 80
Work at home	£ 70
Internet dialler	£ 60
Prize draw	£ 60
Clairvoyant mailings	£ 40
Career opportunity	£ 30
Miracle health	£ 20
Matrix schemes	£ 10
Other scams	£ 100

Many scams promise money, goods or opportunities if you pay up-front. You may be persuaded to go to a presentation and part with money or to claim a 'prize' by dialling premium rate telephone numbers.

In Pyramid or Matrix schemes, you are persuaded to join up and to recruit others to claim your prize. In most cases, the scammer will want to take ID and financial details which can lead to further fraud.

Source: Research on impact of Mass Marketed Scams, Office of Fair Trading © Crown copyright 2007

http://www.oft.gov.uk

Sport & leisure

Active adults

28.4% of adults in England have built some exercise into their lives

The Active People Survey is the largest sport and recreation survey ever undertaken with over 360,000 adults aged 16+ being interviewed

Top ten sports or activities where adults took part at least once a month*, England, 2006

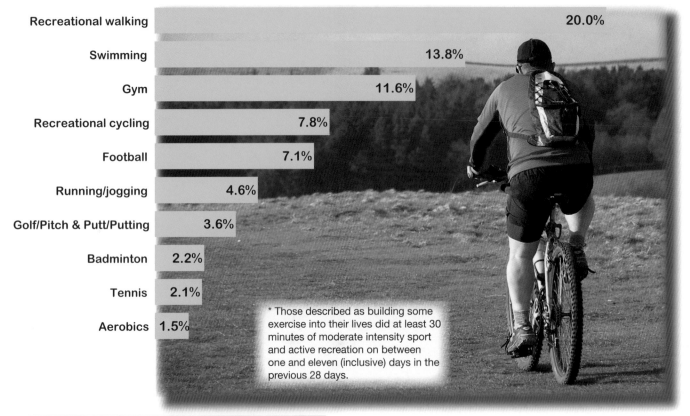

Recreational walking	20.0%
Swimming	13.8%
Gym	11.6%
Recreational cycling	7.8%
Football	7.1%
Running/jogging	4.6%
Golf/Pitch & Putt/Putting	3.6%
Badminton	2.2%
Tennis	2.1%
Aerobics	1.5%

* Those described as building some exercise into their lives did at least 30 minutes of moderate intensity sport and active recreation on between one and eleven (inclusive) days in the previous 28 days.

	Number of adults taking part at least once a month
Recreational walking	8,142,693
Swimming	5,625,539
Gym	4,722,762
Recreational cycling	3,175,650
Football	2,910,684
Running/jogging	1,872,819
Golf/Pitch & Putt/Putting	1,457,347
Badminton	900,332
Tennis	874,040
Aerobics	608,671

» Over 230 sports were identified in the survey ranging from the traditional to the unusual and the extreme (for example fencing, paintballing and surfing)

» Most sports featured in the top ten tend to have a wide appeal across men and women and people of different ages, for example swimming and badminton

» Sports such as cricket, rugby union and netball have a narrower participant base – but still rank in the top 25

Regular participation in sport and active recreation
(30 minutes continuously in any one session at least 3 days a week)

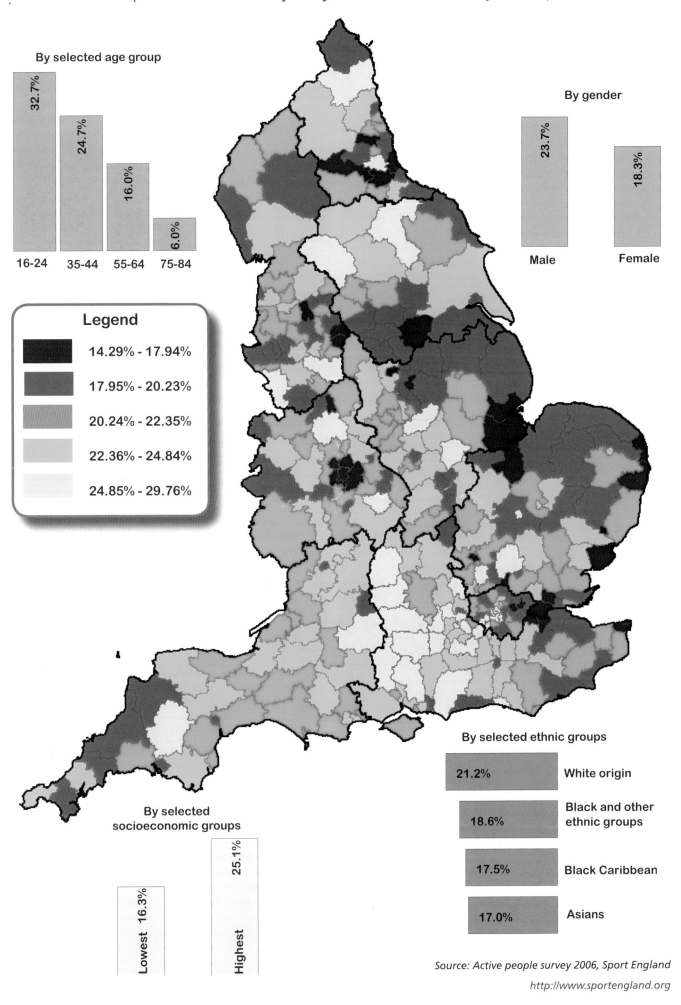

By selected age group

- 32.7% — 16-24
- 24.7% — 35-44
- 16.0% — 55-64
- 6.0% — 75-84

By gender

- 23.7% — Male
- 18.3% — Female

Legend

	14.29% - 17.94%
	17.95% - 20.23%
	20.24% - 22.35%
	22.36% - 24.84%
	24.85% - 29.76%

By selected socioeconomic groups

- Lowest 16.3%
- Highest 25.1%

By selected ethnic groups

- 21.2% — White origin
- 18.6% — Black and other ethnic groups
- 17.5% — Black Caribbean
- 17.0% — Asians

Source: Active people survey 2006, Sport England

http://www.sportengland.org

Wimbledon

Game:

The Wimbledon Tennis Championships are a unique event. This is the only one of the four prestigious 'Grand Slam' championships to be played on grass. This and other traditions such as the rule that the players must wear predominantly white and using titles (Mrs, Miss) when referring to players, mark it out as special. The sheer scale of the tournament as a public event is also impressive.

Set:

Grass and Ground Care

- Court grass is composed of 100% rye grass (chosen for its durability). All courts re-lined, rolled and mown daily during Championships. The Championships playing grass is 8mm in height.
- 1 tonne of grass seed is used each year. Maximum of 3,000 gallons of water used during the Fortnight – weather permitting.
- Centre Court's cover weighs 1 ton (wet and dry) and takes 17 people approx 22-28 seconds to cover the Court.

Catering

About 1,600 catering staff are required to serve:

- 300,000 cups of tea and coffee
- 250,000 bottles of water
- 190,000 sandwiches
- 150,000 bath buns, scones, pasties and doughnuts
- 150,000 glasses of Pimm's
- 135,000 ice creams
- 130,000 lunches
- 100,000 pints of draught beer and lager
- 60,000 Dutchees (hot dogs)
- 40,000 char-grilled meals

- 30,000 staff meals
- 30,000 portions of fish and chips
- 30,000 litres of milk
- 28,000 kilos of English strawberries
- 23,000 bananas
- 22,000 slices of pizza
- 20,000 portions of frozen yoghurt
- 17,000 bottles of champagne
- 12,000 kilos of poached salmon and smoked salmon
- 7,000 litres of dairy cream

Tickets and Finances

Wimbledon remains virtually the only major UK sporting event for which one can still buy premium tickets on the day. Queuing for day tickets has become almost an event in itself. Most tickets are bought in advance by the public via a ballot system.

Prices range from £5 for a ground ticket after 5pm on day 13 of the championship to £87 for a seat on Centre Court for the afternoon of the Men's Final.

Funds are used by the Lawn Tennis Association to develop tennis in Great Britain.

In 1879 (first year of surplus) earnings were £116, in 2006 £25,544,765.

Match:

In April 2007, the prize money for the female champion was made equal to that for the men: £700,000. Total prize money was £11,282,710,

In modern tennis, Pete Sampras has won the Men's singles a record 7 times (equalling W C Renshaw's 19th century record). Martina Navratilova has won the Women's singles an astonishing 9 times with wins stretching from 1978 to 1990.

Sources: All England Lawn Tennis Club

http://www.aeltc.com

Olympic ambition

To make Olympic champions, strong interest and ambition is required and this is where UK teenagers are failing.

This index shows some of the critical factors for the development of young athletes.

Likely winners

Top 5 countries on the index of the development of young athletes worldwide, 2007

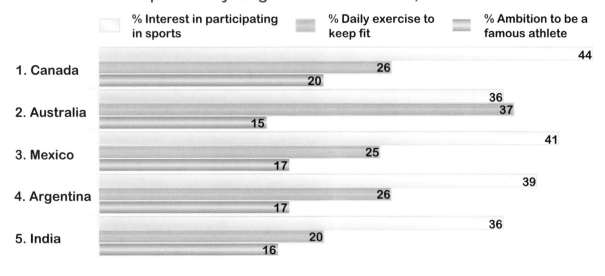

	% Interest in participating in sports	% Daily exercise to keep fit	% Ambition to be a famous athlete
1. Canada	44	26	20
2. Australia	36	37	15
3. Mexico	41	25	17
4. Argentina	39	26	17
5. India	36	20	16

Last time's winners

In the last Olympics the US topped the medal table winning a total of 36 gold medals. The People's Republic of China won 32 and Russian Federation won 27. Although these countries aren't high ranking on the index, they are likely to produce more top rate athletes because they have large populations

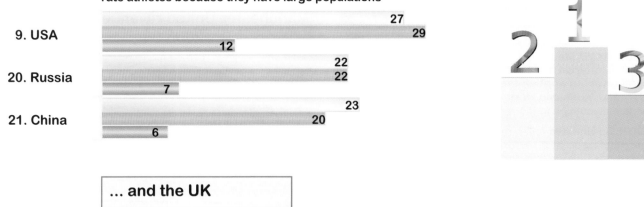

	% Interest	% Daily exercise	% Ambition
9. USA	27	29	12
20. Russia	22	22	7
21. China	23	20	6

... and the UK

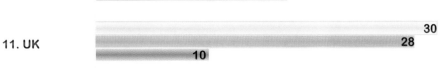

	% Interest	% Daily exercise	% Ambition
11. UK	30	28	10

The UK is likely to produce fewer top rate athletes because it has a small population. UK teenagers top the charts in terms of alcohol consumption, with 51% of teenagers over 18 regularly consuming beer, equalled only by Spain. British teenagers also consume a worrying amount of carbonated soft drinks, with 38% admitting to drinking highly-calorific drinks every day

Source: 'UK lags behind in race to produce Olympic stars', GfK NOP 2007

http://www.gfknop.com

Man U Ltd

Manchester United is the fourth richest football club in the world, and remains the most profitable footballing business

Manchester United five year revenue totals, 2002-2006 € millions

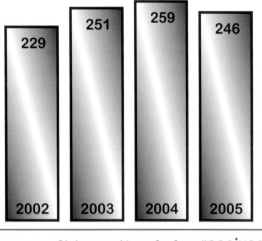

229	251	259	246	243
2002	2003	2004	2005	2006

Club record transfer fees **received:**
£17.25m for David Beckham
(from Real Madrid in 2003)
Club record transfer fees **paid:**
£29.1m for Rio Ferdinand (from Leeds United in 2002)

In 2005 American billionaire Malcolm Glazer took over Manchester United in a **£790m** buyout. Mr Glazer, via his Red Football bid vehicle, has borrowed **£265m** – secured against Man U's assets – and has a further **£275m** in other loans.

Manchester United is one of the strongest commercial brands in football and the most profitable football club operation in the world. If the gross revenues from Nike, MUTV and MUMobile were taken into account, overall revenues would be in the region of €300m (£200m).

In 2005/06 United's fall in revenue was due in part to a disappointing on pitch performance – a group stage UEFA Champions League exit and a third successive season without winning the Premier League trophy mitigated only to a small degree by a League Cup victory.

United retain the largest support of any UK club and average Premier League attendances in 2005/06 were 68,800. During the season the club expanded Old Trafford's capacity to 76,000.

Manchester United revenue sources 2005-06

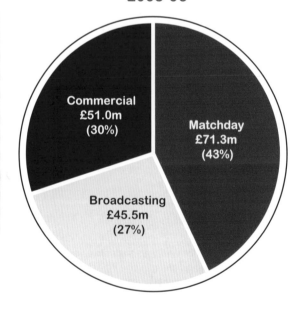

Commercial £51.0m (30%)
Matchday £71.3m (43%)
Broadcasting £45.5m (27%)

Source: Football Money League 2007, Deloitte

http://www.deloitte.co.uk

Home or away

Premier League clubs spend a fortune to buy the best players – but does this affect opportunities for young English players and the national team?

Overseas clubs benefited most from Premier League clubs' transfer spending in summer 2007, with around £250m, half of disclosed transfer spending, going to clubs outside England.

Europe has also seen high levels of transfer spending, particularly in Spain.

Real Madrid was Europe's top spender with around £80m, Thierry Henry's transfer from Arsenal helped push Barcelona's transfer spending up towards £50m, with Athletico Madrid also spending around £50m.

Clubs in the Big 5 European Leagues spent around £1bn on transfers in summer 2007.

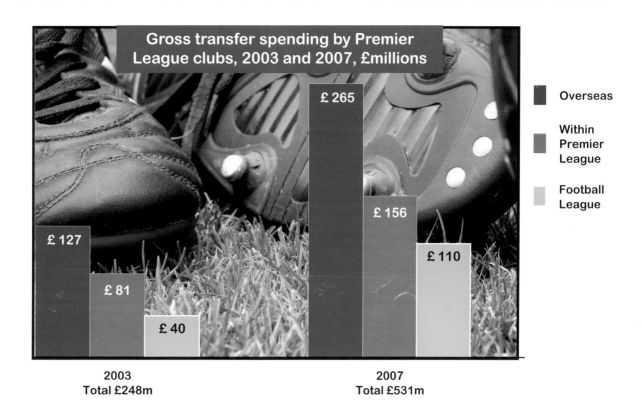

Gross transfer spending by Premier League clubs, 2003 and 2007, £millions

- Overseas
- Within Premier League
- Football League

£ 265
£ 156
£ 127
£ 110
£ 81
£ 40

2003
Total £248m

2007
Total £531m

Total appearances during 2006-07 season, by selected European leagues

76% of the starting teams that played on the first weekend of the first Premier League season in 1992 were English, only 37% were English on the first weekend of 2007.

Non-English players had scored 69% of Premier League goals (up to 3/9/07) – they had even scored two of the three own goals.

Of the 118 goals scored up to 3/9/07, only 9 have been scored by 7 English strikers.

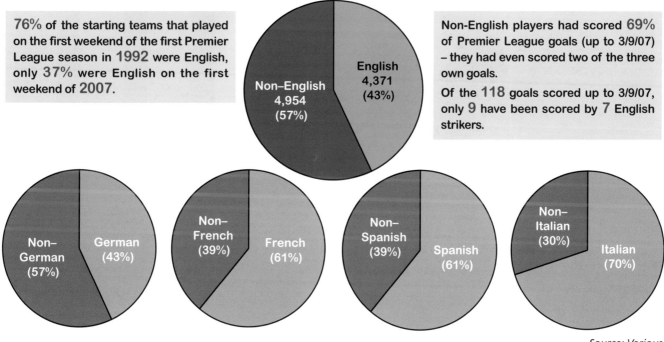

Non–English 4,954 (57%)
English 4,371 (43%)

Non–German (57%)
German (43%)

Non–French (39%)
French (61%)

Non–Spanish (39%)
Spanish (61%)

Non–Italian (30%)
Italian (70%)

Source: Various

Fanatics

How many times fans of Premiership clubs think of their teams per day 2007

(Fans were asked to estimate how much in an average day – assuming eight hours sleep)

Sheffield United	110
Charlton	104
Chelsea	90
Liverpool	81
West Ham	79
Man Utd	71
Newcastle	70
Arsenal	69
Reading	67
Portsmouth	63
Aston Villa	62
Tottenham	61
Middlesbrough	59
Blackburn	58
Man City	57
Fulham	57
Bolton	57
Wigan	57
Watford	51
Everton	43

A poll of more than 2,000 Premiership fans shows that the average fan thinks of football 80 times a day – 7% of avid fans thought about football every minute.

The research also shows that if their team is battling for honours or to avoid relegation the thinking time goes up, eg both Sheffield United and Charlton were relegated at the end of the 2007 season.

It is more than just a game for the average fan. There are all the extra hours racked up travelling to and from the match, watching TV, searching the internet and talking about the game with friends. That all adds up to 15.8 hours a week on average or 821.6 hours a year.

Top 5 travelling supporters in the Premiership 2006

■ % of fans that travelled over 1,000 miles last year
■ % of fans that travelled over 5,000 miles last year

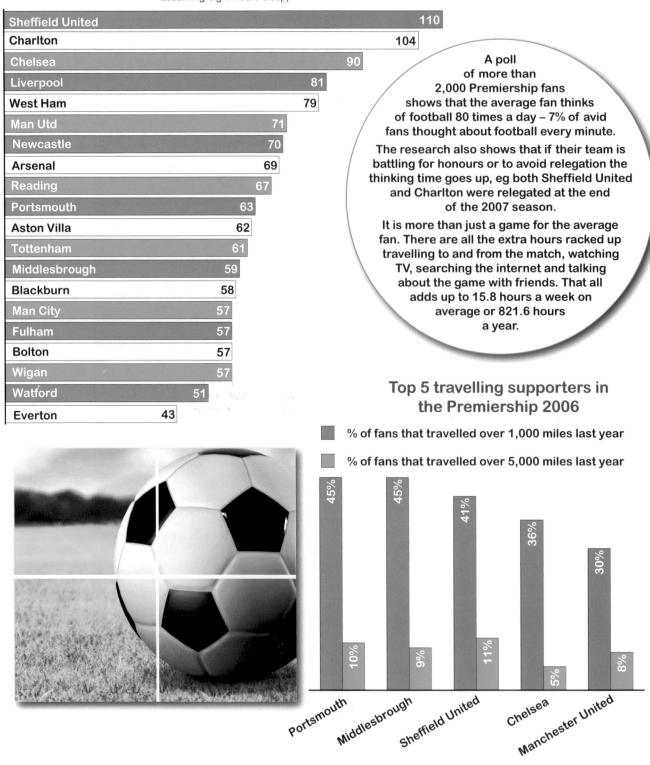

Club	Over 1,000 miles	Over 5,000 miles
Portsmouth	45%	10%
Middlesbrough	45%	9%
Sheffield United	41%	11%
Chelsea	36%	5%
Manchester United	30%	8%

Supporters travel over nine billion miles each year following their teams. That is far enough for one lucky fan to travel to Jupiter and back twelve times

The total average mileage of a travelling fan in 2006 was 1,264 miles – around 63 miles per game assuming they took in 20 games over 12 months

Most reluctant to travel far to follow their team were supporters of Everton (10%), Blackburn (11%) and Charlton (13%) who said they travelled around 1,000 miles

Reasons for fans not renewing Premiership season tickets 2007-08

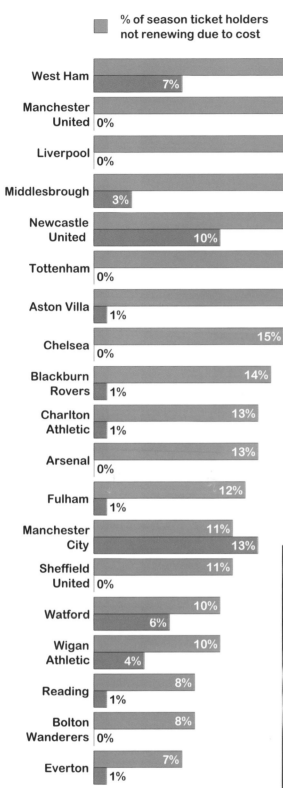

Legend:
- % of season ticket holders not renewing due to cost
- % of season ticket holders not renewing due to poor quality football

Club	Cost	Poor quality football
West Ham	28%	7%
Manchester United	24%	0%
Liverpool	22%	0%
Middlesbrough	21%	3%
Newcastle United	19%	10%
Tottenham	19%	0%
Aston Villa	17%	1%
Chelsea	15%	0%
Blackburn Rovers	14%	1%
Charlton Athletic	13%	1%
Arsenal	13%	0%
Fulham	12%	1%
Manchester City	11%	13%
Sheffield United	11%	0%
Watford	10%	6%
Wigan Athletic	10%	4%
Reading	8%	1%
Bolton Wanderers	8%	0%
Everton	7%	1%

One in eight season ticket holders may not renew due to cost.

Manchester United, Middlesbrough and Liverpool have increased their season ticket prices by 14%.

Portsmouth and Bolton fans are among the least likely to complain as costs have either been frozen or reduced.

Virgin Money's Football Fans' Price Index shows that in the past year the cost of attending games has risen by 17.84%. Increases in the cost of match tickets and replica shirts are the main reasons behind this increase.

The index is aimed at helping supporters keep track of the rises and falls in the costs of supporting their team. The company identified the match-day essentials fans buy and keeps tabs on increases and decreases.

The matchday basket of goods includes a gallon of petrol, a pint of lager, a bacon roll, a train fare, a match ticket, a replica shirt, pay-per-view cost and a match programme:

Cost in 2005-06 Season £77.95

Cost in 2006-07 Season £91.87

Source: Virgin Money's Football Fans' Prices Index 2007
http://uk.virginmoney.com

Youth clubs

The Scout movement celebrated its centenary in 2007. It has a combined membership of 360,000, but it is not the largest youth organisation in the UK

Membership of selected organisations for young people, UK
(thousands)

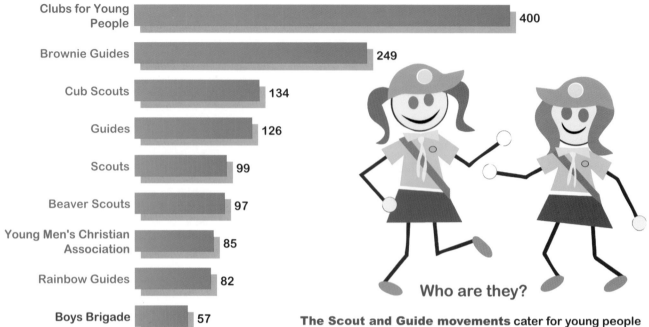

Clubs for Young People	400
Brownie Guides	249
Cub Scouts	134
Guides	126
Scouts	99
Beaver Scouts	97
Young Men's Christian Association	85
Rainbow Guides	82
Boys Brigade	57
Army Cadets	45
Combined Cadet Force	42
Air Cadets	33
Girls Brigade	26
Explorer Scouts	26
National Federation of Young Farmers	21
Guiding Senior Section (Ranger Guides, etc)	20
Sea Cadets	13
Scout Network	4

Who are they?

The Scout and Guide movements cater for young people aged 6-25. Activities include developing personal skills, community service and outdoor skills.
http://www.scouts.org.uk
http://www.girlguiding.org.uk

The Boys' and Girls' Brigades are Christian youth organisations catering for young people aged 5-19. Activities include sports and games, crafts, music and holidays, and Christian teaching.
http://www.boys-brigade.org.uk
http://www.girlsbrigadeew.org.uk

Air Cadets, Army Cadets, Sea Cadets and Combined Cadet Forces are affiliated to the armed forces and include elements of military training.
http://www.aircadets.org
http://www.armycadets.com
http://www.sea-cadets.org

The Clubs for Young People organisation has over 3,000 clubs in the UK and reaches out to young people through community projects, arts and activities.
http://www.clubsforyoungpeople.org.uk

The YMCA Movement's purpose is to meet the needs of young people, regardless of gender, race or faith.
http://www.ymca.org.uk

The National Federation of Young Farmers is an association for young people aged between 10 and 26 who live in rural areas or have an interest in farming or the countryside.
http://www.nfyfc.org.uk

Source: Office for National Statistics; Social Trends 2007 © Crown copyright 2007

http://www.statistics.gov.uk

Tall tales

Q. Why have you lied about reading a book?

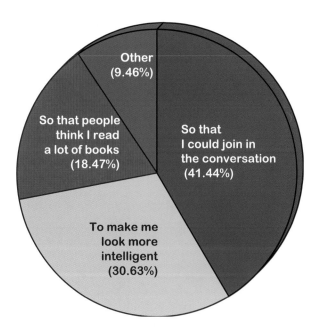

Other (9.46%)

So that people think I read a lot of books (18.47%)

So that I could join in the conversation (41.44%)

To make me look more intelligent (30.63%)

According to a survey of over 4,000 bookworms:

- One in ten men said they would fib about reading a certain book to impress the opposite sex

- 33% of adults confessed to reading challenging literature to appear well-read, when they haven't a clue what the book is about

- One in twenty men said they would lie about reading Harry Potter to give the illusion they're in touch with the latest trends

- Almost half of respondents said that reading classic titles like Jane Eyre or Pride and Prejudice makes you appear more intelligent

- Most people would lie to impress a new date, 15% have lied about what they have read to a new colleague and 5% have lied about their reading habits to their boss

Q. Which book would you most likely lie about reading? (Top five)

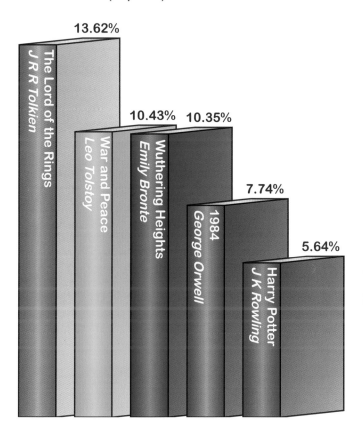

13.62% — The Lord of the Rings — J R R Tolkien

10.43% — War and Peace — Leo Tolstoy

10.35% — Wuthering Heights — Emily Bronte

7.74% — 1984 — George Orwell

5.64% — Harry Potter — J K Rowling

Photo: Neil Pettinger

Source: Book snobbery, Museums and archives council, 2007
http://www.mla.gov.uk

Need to read

Girls tend to have a more positive attitude towards reading than boys and Primary pupils more so than Secondary

Preferred reading materials outside class, by gender, %

■ Boys ■ Girls

Material	Boys	Girls
Magazines	71.1	82.9
Websites	65.3	63.4
Jokes	61.7	54.9
Comics	58.5	43.0
Text messages	55.1	69.5
Posters / signs	52.1	61.9
TV books / magazines	51.7	64.4
Fiction	50.7	54.1
Newspapers	50.0	44.3
Emails	47.7	58.8
Catalogues	39.4	55.4
Song lyrics	34.2	55.3
Manuals	32.4	24.1
Factual books	29.9	25.6
Teletext / Ceefax	29.9	21.9
Annuals	23.6	17.6
Graphic novels	23.0	15.3
Poetry	22.4	41.5
Plays	20.8	33.7
Encyclopedias	19.0	17.3
Travel books	18.3	21.2
Cookbooks	16.4	27.8
English as an additional language books / magazines	15.6	20.0
Audiobooks	15.5	12.7

25.6% of girls and 19.6% of boys said they enjoyed reading "very much".

42% of girls and 35% of boys said they read outside of school "every day or almost every day".

Girls were more likely to say they read for fun (50%) or to find out how other people live (43%), while boys were more likely to say they read as it will help them get a job (45%).

Both boys (51%) and girls (54%) saw reading as a skill for life.

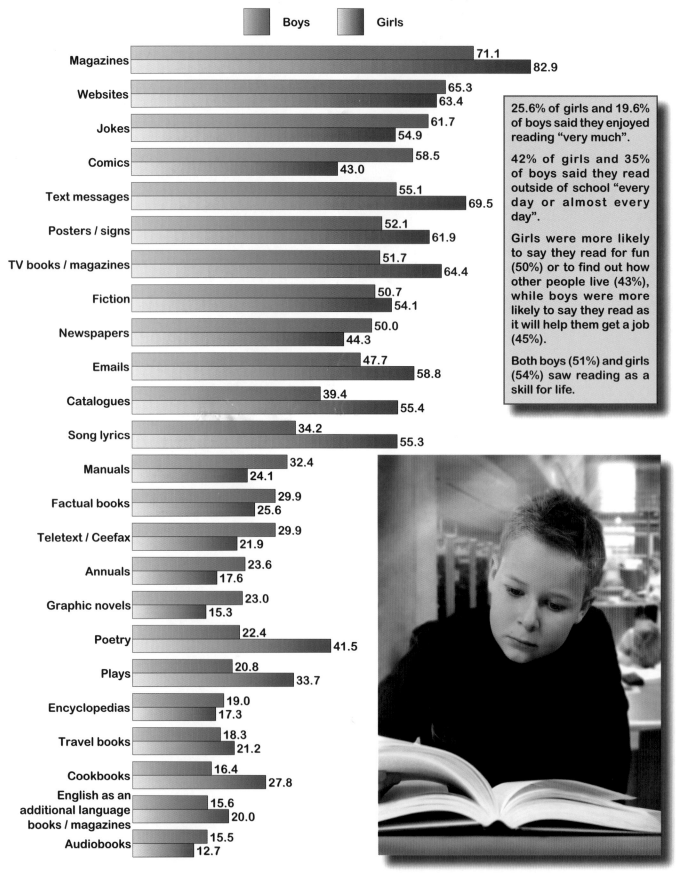

Q. How often do you read outside school? (%)

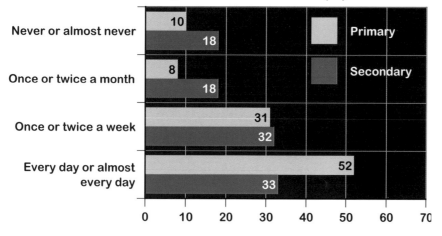

	Primary	Secondary
Never or almost never	10	18
Once or twice a month	8	18
Once or twice a week	31	32
Every day or almost every day	52	33

Both Secondary (43%) and Primary pupils (59%) say they would read more if they had more time; Secondary pupils would read more if they enjoyed it more (41%).

Primary pupils said playing reading games would help them to read more (62%); Secondary pupils said that designing magazines or websites would encourage them to read more (51%).

Q. Do you think you read enough? (%)

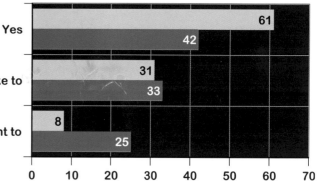

	Primary	Secondary
Yes	61	42
No, but I would like to	31	33
No, and I don't want to	8	25

Q. How much do you enjoy reading? (%)

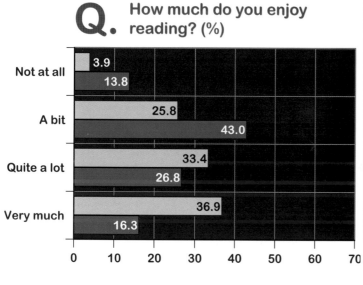

	Primary	Secondary
Not at all	3.9	13.8
A bit	25.8	43.0
Quite a lot	33.4	26.8
Very much	36.9	16.3

Source: National Literacy Trust: Children and young people's reading habits and preferences: the who, what, why, where and when © National Literacy Trust 2005

http://www.literacytrust.org.uk

Finders keepers

The Portable Antiquities Scheme records archaeological finds made by members of the public.

Method of discovery:

Metal-detector users	39,002
People field-walking	14,376
Chance find/ gardening	2,392
Building/ agricultural work	1,425
Archaeological investigation	146

These finds are an important source for understanding more about our history.

Finds recorded by period, England and Wales, 2005/6, %

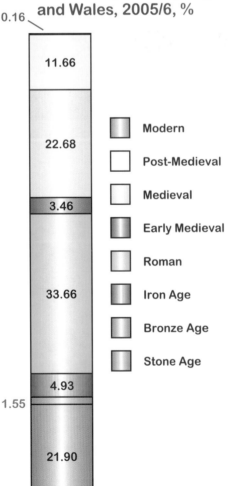

0.16

11.66

22.68

3.46

33.66

4.93

1.55

21.90

- Modern
- Post-Medieval
- Medieval
- Early Medieval
- Roman
- Iron Age
- Bronze Age
- Stone Age

Gold and silver items, and coins over 300 years old, must be declared as Treasure. The items may be given to a museum and the finder and landowner rewarded.

Treasure cases reported, England and Wales, 1996-2005

1996	1997	1998	1999	2000	2001	2002	2003	2004	2005
24	79	201	236	233	214	240	427	506	595

Source and images: Portable Antiquities Scheme, Annual Report 2005/6
http://www.finds.org.uk

Wider world

Population clock

Natural increase (births minus deaths), world figures, 2006

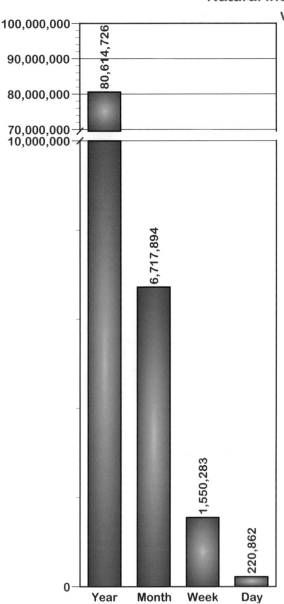

NB figures have been rounded

NEW YORK

TOKYO

LONDON

MOSCOW

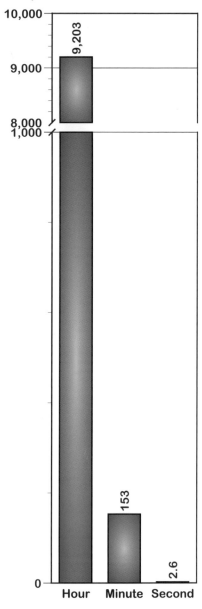

2006 world births and deaths

	Births	Deaths
per year	137,035,288	56,420,562
per month	11,419,607	4,701,714
per week	2,635,294	1,085,011
per day	375,439	154,577
per hour	15,643	6,441
per minute	261	107
per second	4.3	1.8

Source: Population Reference Bureau, 2006 World population data sheet

http://www.prb.org

Growing concern

Populations are growing most rapidly where such growth can be afforded the least

World population, in billions, 1950–2050 (projection)

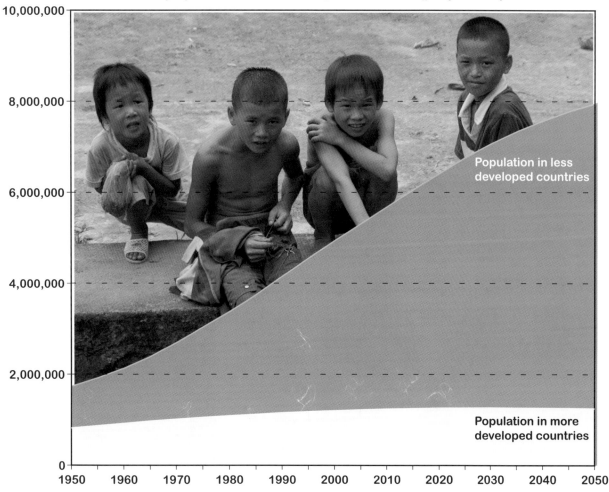

Population in less developed countries

Population in more developed countries

World's largest countries in population

2007	
Country	Population (millions)
China	1,318
India	1,132
US	302
Indonesia	232
Brazil	189
Pakistan	169
Bangladesh	149
Nigeria	144
Russia	142
Japan	128

80 million people are being added every year in less developed countries, compared with about 1.6 million in more developed countries

Population change is linked to economic development, education, the environment, the status of women, epidemics and other health threats, and access to family planning information and services.

All of these factors interact with every facet of our lives, regardless of where we live.

2050 (projected)	
Country	Population (millions)
India	1,747
China	1,437
US	420
Indonesia	297
Pakistan	295
Nigeria	282
Brazil	260
Bangladesh	231
Dem. Rep. of Congo	187
Philippines	150

Source: 2007 World Population data sheet, Population Reference Bureau

http://www.prb.org

Lifetime

Life expectancy at birth, EU-25, 2005

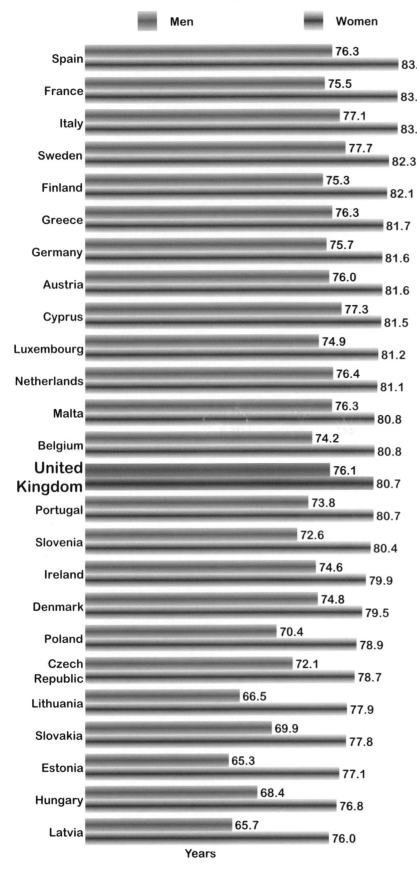

Men　　Women

Country	Men	Women
Spain	76.3	83.3
France	75.5	83.2
Italy	77.1	83.2
Sweden	77.7	82.3
Finland	75.3	82.1
Greece	76.3	81.7
Germany	75.7	81.6
Austria	76.0	81.6
Cyprus	77.3	81.5
Luxembourg	74.9	81.2
Netherlands	76.4	81.1
Malta	76.3	80.8
Belgium	74.2	80.8
United Kingdom	76.1	80.7
Portugal	73.8	80.7
Slovenia	72.6	80.4
Ireland	74.6	79.9
Denmark	74.8	79.5
Poland	70.4	78.9
Czech Republic	72.1	78.7
Lithuania	66.5	77.9
Slovakia	69.9	77.8
Estonia	65.3	77.1
Hungary	68.4	76.8
Latvia	65.7	76.0

Years

The European average life expectancy is **75.0** years for men and **81.4** years for women

By 2050, **one third** of Europe's population will be over 60, compared to **13%** who will be under 16

The number of Europeans over 60 will increase by **44%** between today and 2050. The number of "oldest old", aged 80+, is expected to grow by **180%**

Source: The state of ageing and health in Europe, International Longevity Centre UK and the Merck Company Foundation © ILC, 2006

http://www.ilcuk.org.uk

No rest...

People over 60 in full- or part-time work, top 10 countries, 2007, millions

Country	Millions
India	17.0
China	14.2
US	11.5
Japan	7.7
Russia	4.6
Germany	3.3
UK	3.2
Brazil	2.7
Mexico	2.0
Philippines	1.8

71% of workers worldwide who expect to continue working past 60 say it is because they want to, rather than feeling they have to

19% of people in their 60s and 70s worldwide do voluntary work; 15% of those give as much as half a day each week

UK voluntary workers over 60 give a total of 776.6 million hours per year which, calculated at a minimum wage of £5.35 per hour, is worth £4.2 billion to the UK economy

In the UK, those in their 60s and 70s contribute £59 billion to the economy in tax and voluntary work

Globally, more older people provide financial, practical and even in some cases, personal care, than receive it.

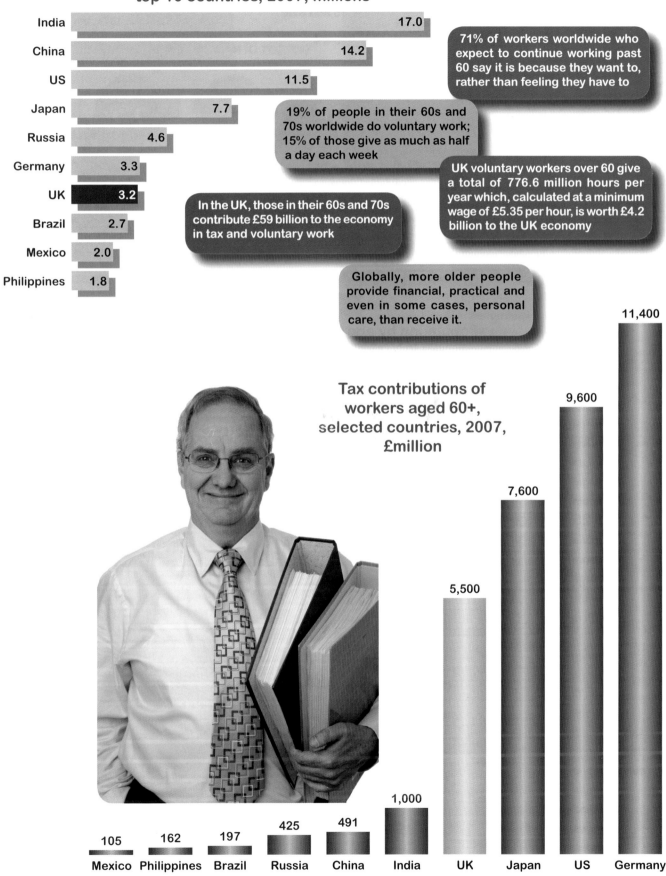

Tax contributions of workers aged 60+, selected countries, 2007, £million

Country	£million
Mexico	105
Philippines	162
Brazil	197
Russia	425
China	491
India	1,000
UK	5,500
Japan	7,600
US	9,600
Germany	11,400

Source: HSBC: The future of retirement: the new old age © HSBC 2007

http://www.hsbc.com

Coming to America

About one million foreigners legally enter the US each year. Immigration accounts for at least one-third of recent US population growth

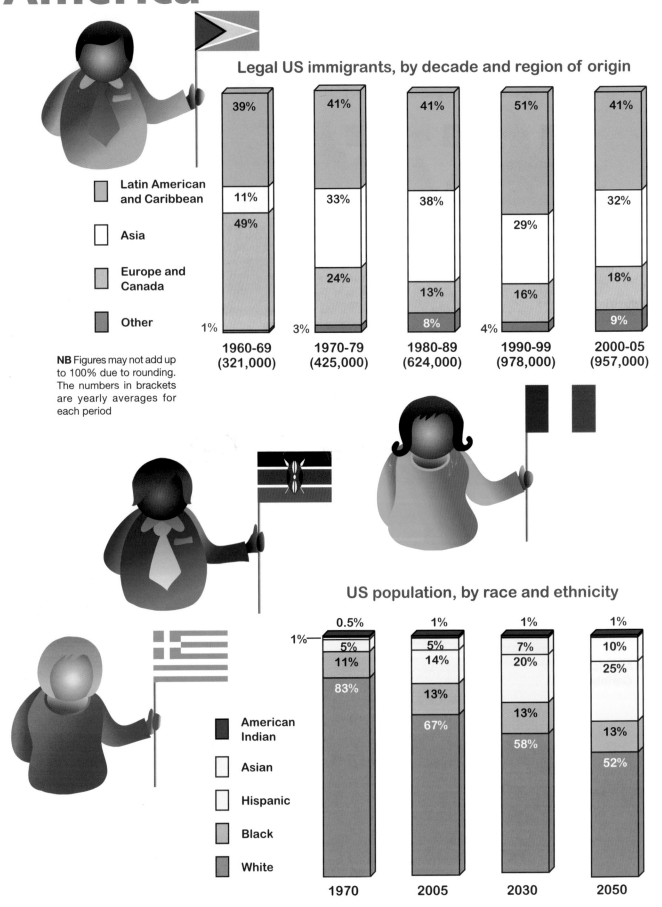

Legal US immigrants, by decade and region of origin

Legend:
- Latin American and Caribbean
- Asia
- Europe and Canada
- Other

NB Figures may not add up to 100% due to rounding. The numbers in brackets are yearly averages for each period

	1960-69 (321,000)	1970-79 (425,000)	1980-89 (624,000)	1990-99 (978,000)	2000-05 (957,000)
Latin American and Caribbean	39%	41%	41%	51%	41%
Asia	11%	33%	38%	29%	32%
Europe and Canada	49%	24%	13%	16%	18%
Other	1%	3%	8%	4%	9%

US population, by race and ethnicity

Legend:
- American Indian
- Asian
- Hispanic
- Black
- White

	1970	2005	2030	2050
American Indian	1%	1%	1%	1%
Asian	0.5%	1%	1%	1%
Hispanic	5%	5%	7%	10%
Black	11%	14%	20%	25%
White	83%	67%	13% / 58%	13% / 52%

Source: Immigration: Shaping and Reshaping America, Population Reference Bureau, 2006

http://www.prb.org

Two dollars a day

25 countries with the highest percentage of their population living on less than $2 a day

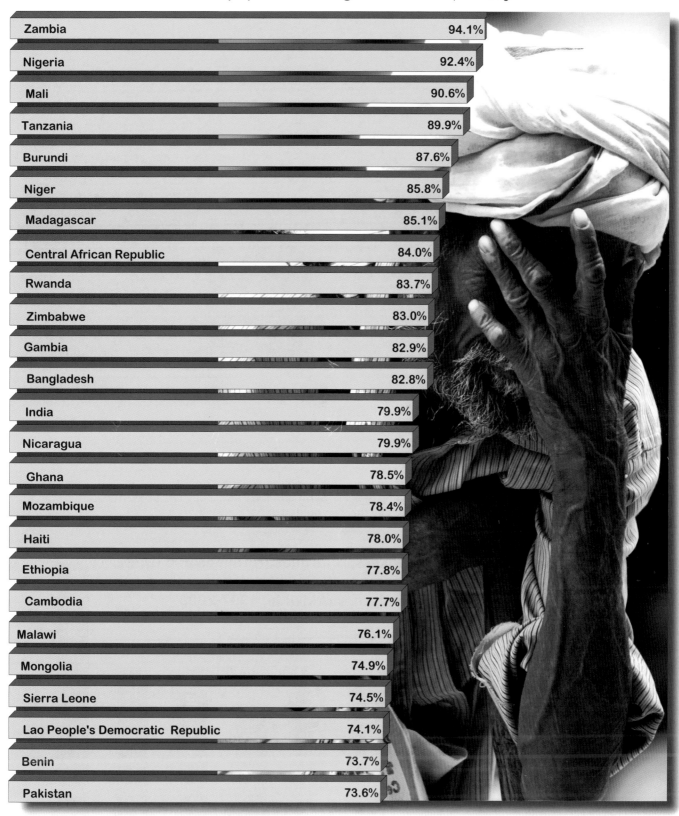

Country	Percentage
Zambia	94.1%
Nigeria	92.4%
Mali	90.6%
Tanzania	89.9%
Burundi	87.6%
Niger	85.8%
Madagascar	85.1%
Central African Republic	84.0%
Rwanda	83.7%
Zimbabwe	83.0%
Gambia	82.9%
Bangladesh	82.8%
India	79.9%
Nicaragua	79.9%
Ghana	78.5%
Mozambique	78.4%
Haiti	78.0%
Ethiopia	77.8%
Cambodia	77.7%
Malawi	76.1%
Mongolia	74.9%
Sierra Leone	74.5%
Lao People's Democratic Republic	74.1%
Benin	73.7%
Pakistan	73.6%

NB Data refers to the most recent year during the period 1990–2004

Under $2 a day means a daily total consumption of goods and services comparable to those that can be bought in the US for $2.

Source: Human Development Report 2006, United Nations Development Programme © United Nations 2006

http://hdr.undp.org/

Displaced

The number of refugees worldwide rose to nearly 10 million in 2006 – the first rise in five years – largely due to the violence in Iraq

Photo: Ricardo – DOD via pingnews

The UNHCR (United Nations High Commissioner for Refugees) provides protection and assistance to refugees and other people of concern.

These are civilians who have been forced to flee their homes through fear of persecution on grounds of race, religion, nationality, social group or political opinion. These include refugees, asylum seekers, refugees who have returned home but still need help in rebuilding their lives, local civilian communities directly affected by the movements of refugees, stateless people and people displaced internally within their own country.

The UNHCR report provides figures on how many people of concern they are aware of within the territories that they are responsible for. However, the actual number will be much higher. For example it does not include some 4.3 million Palestinian refugees in Jordan, Lebanon, Syria and the Palestinian Occupied Territories who are counted separately.

Refugees, asylum-seekers, returnees (refugees and IDPs), internally displaced persons (IDPs), stateless persons, and others of concern, worldwide, 1997-2006

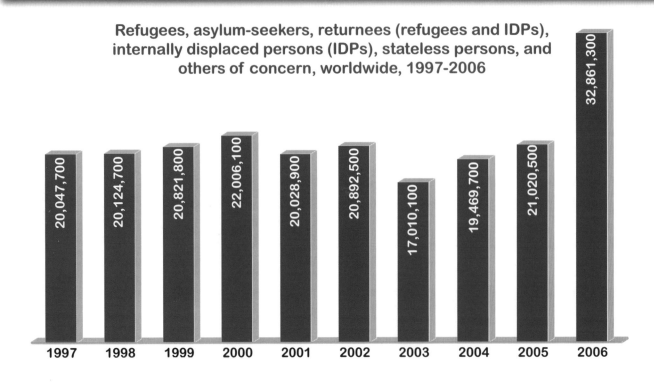

Year	Number
1997	20,047,700
1998	20,124,700
1999	20,821,800
2000	22,006,100
2001	20,028,900
2002	20,892,500
2003	17,010,100
2004	19,469,700
2005	21,020,500
2006	32,861,300

As the nature of war has changed in the last few decades, with more and more internal conflicts replacing interstate wars, the number of internally displaced people has increased significantly. The UNHCR report shows that in 2006 there were an estimated 12.8 million IDPs within UNHCR territories though the estimated global figure is 23.7 million.

Most refugees tend to settle in neighbouring countries.

Afghans continue to form the world's largest group with 21% of the global refugee population. At the end of 2006 there were 2.1m from that country in 71 different asylum countries, though mainly in Pakistan and Iran.

Iraqis now form the world's second largest group with some 1.5m now estimated to be living as refugees in other countries, mostly neighbouring Syria and Jordan. The Iraqi refugee number more than quintupled in the course of 2006.

The three other main source countries were Sudan with 686,000, Somalia with 460,000 and roughly 400,000 people each from DR Congo and Burundi.

Photo: Tracy Hunter

Major refugee hosting countries, the beginning and end of 2006

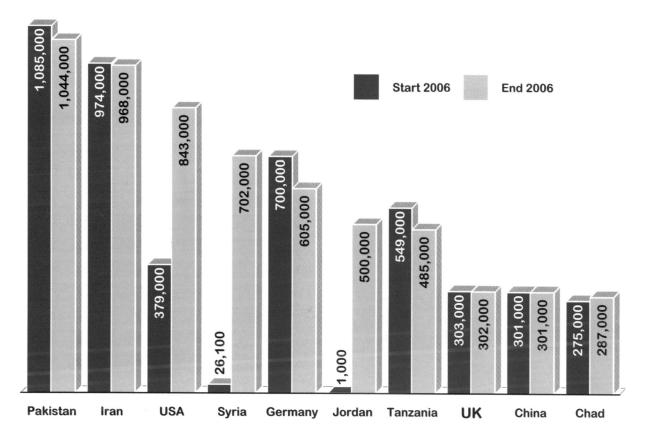

Start 2006   End 2006

	Start 2006	End 2006
Pakistan	1,085,000	1,044,000
Iran	974,000	968,000
USA	379,000	843,000
Syria	26,100	702,000
Germany	700,000	605,000
Jordan	1,000	500,000
Tanzania	549,000	485,000
UK	303,000	302,000
China	301,000	301,000
Chad	275,000	287,000

Source: 2006 Global Trends: Refugees, Asylum–seekers,
Returnees, Internally Displaced and Stateless Persons,
UNHCR The UN Refugee Agency 2007

http://www.unhcr.org

AIDS orphans

It is estimated that more than 15 million children worldwide have been orphaned as a result of AIDS. More than 12 million live in Sub-Saharan Africa

Estimated number of AIDS orphans in Sub-Saharan Africa, countries with the largest numbers, 2005

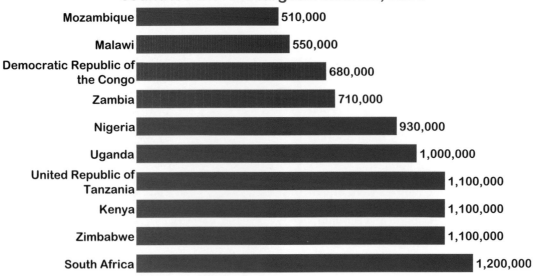

Mozambique	510,000
Malawi	550,000
Democratic Republic of the Congo	680,000
Zambia	710,000
Nigeria	930,000
Uganda	1,000,000
United Republic of Tanzania	1,100,000
Kenya	1,100,000
Zimbabwe	1,100,000
South Africa	1,200,000

Parental death from AIDS is greatest in southern Africa. In Zambia, for example, 20% of all children were orphans in 2005, over half of them due to AIDS. This has left a population of 11.7 million to support more than 1.2 million orphans. One-sixth of Zambian adults are currently infected with HIV, and only 25% of those who need it are receiving treatment. AIDS will continue to kill parents - it killed around 75,000 adults in 2005 - and increase the numbers of orphans for years to come.

UNAIDS/G. Pirozzi

Definition of 'Orphan'
A child under 18 whose mother, father or both parents have died from any cause.

Estimated percentage of AIDS orphans as a percentage of all orphans, Sub-Saharan Africa, 2005, 10 countries with highest prevalence

Country	AIDS orphans	Orphaned in other ways
Uganda	45%	55%
Kenya	46%	54%
South Africa	49%	51%
Zambia	57%	43%
Malawi	57%	43%
Namibia	62%	38%
Lesotho	64%	36%
Swaziland	66%	34%
Botswana	76%	24%
Zimbabwe	77%	23%

■ AIDS orphans   □ Orphaned in other ways

Source: Avert, Unicef 'Children affected by AIDS', 2006
http://www.avert.org
http://www.unicef.org/publications

Death penalty

Public opinion is still divided about the effectiveness of capital punishment

Only **67** counties worldwide retain the death penalty in their legal system and the number which actually apply it is very small. During 2006, at least **1,591** people were executed in **25** countries and **3,861** people were sentenced to death in **55** countries.

91% of executions were carried out in **6** countries:

1	China	**1,010**
2	Iran	**177**
3	Pakistan	**82**
4=	Iraq	**65**
4=	Sudan	**65**
6	USA	**53**

1,000 adults were polled in each selected country about their views on executions, of these only USA and South Korea make use of the death penalty.

Police officers and others view the scene as five convicted criminals are hanged in Iran, 1 August 2007. In the second round of collective executions in ten days, Iran publicly hanged 7 criminals convicted on various charges of rape, robbery and kidnapping.

Q If the death penalty were implemented in your country, do you think the number of murders would go up, go down or stay about the same?

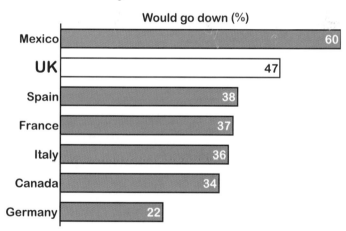

Would go down (%)

Mexico	60
UK	47
Spain	38
France	37
Italy	36
Canada	34
Germany	22

The execution of Saddam Hussein on 30th December 2006 started the debate again. Many people argued that the hanging appeared to be an act of revenge rather than justice. It also meant that he was never brought to trial for many atrocities.

In the case of Osama bin Laden, 62% of Americans felt that he should receive the death penalty if convicted of terrorism, compared to 40% in the UK and 23% in Spain

Q If the death penalty were abolished in your country, do you think the number of murders would go up, go down, or stay about the same?

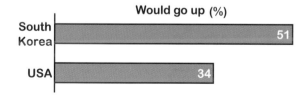

Would go up (%)

South Korea	51
USA	34

Q Which punishment do you prefer for people convicted of murder?
(Replies from UK only, 2007)

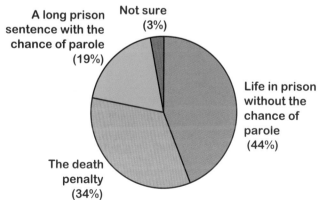

- A long prison sentence with the chance of parole (19%)
- Not sure (3%)
- Life in prison without the chance of parole (44%)
- The death penalty (34%)

Figures do not add up to 100% due to rounding

Sources: Amnesty International; Attitudes to the death penalty
Ipsos Mori 2007
http://www.amnesty.org
http://www.ipsos-mori.com

Cultivating cash

Worldwide, the estimated area under illicit opium poppy cultivation increased by 33% in 2006, mainly due to a sharp increase in Afghanistan

Global opium poppy cultivation (hectares), 2005-2006

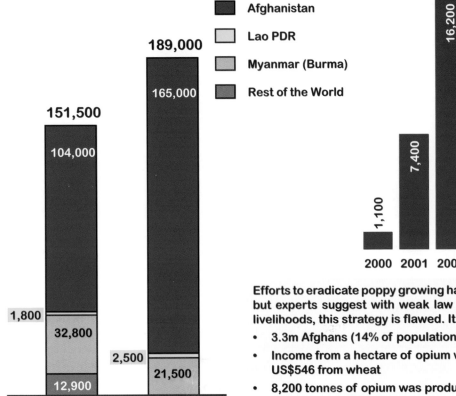

Legend:
- Afghanistan (dark)
- Lao PDR
- Myanmar (Burma)
- Rest of the World

2005: 151,500
- 104,000
- 1,800
- 32,800
- 12,900

2006: 189,000
- 165,000
- 2,500
- 21,500

Gross income of poppy cultivation in Afghanistan, US$ per hectare

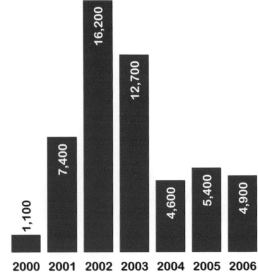

2000	2001	2002	2003	2004	2005	2006
1,100	7,400	16,200	12,700	4,600	5,400	4,900

Efforts to eradicate poppy growing have been targeted on poor farmers but experts suggest with weak law enforcement and few alternative livelihoods, this strategy is flawed. It is estimated that in 2007:

- 3.3m Afghans (14% of population) were involved in the drugs trade
- Income from a hectare of opium was US$5,200 compared to US$546 from wheat
- 8,200 tonnes of opium was produced (up 34%)

Where the worlds opium is produced, 2006 %

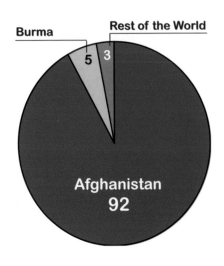

- Burma 5
- Rest of the World 3
- Afghanistan 92

Photo: poppies in Afghanistan by Koldo Hormaza

Opiate seizures reflect the levels of production and trafficking. There was a decline in opium and morphine seizures in 2001, the year of the opium poppy cultivation ban by the Taliban in Afghanistan.

The decline in heroin seizures reflects a delay of about a year between production of opium and the arrival of heroin on the market. Opiate seizures grew again strongly in subsequent years. Global opiate seizures in 2004 were 21% higher than in 2000.

Global seizures of opium and heroin & morphine, metric tons, 1994-2005

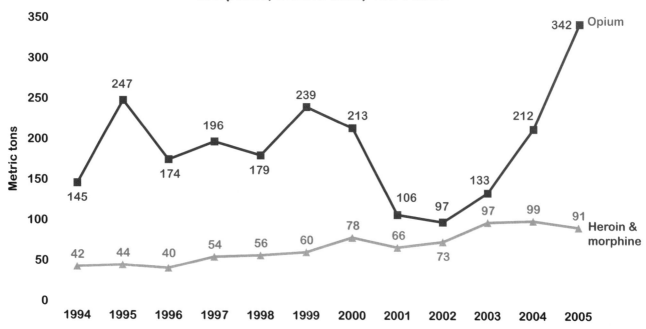

The drug route from Afghanistan continues to go mainly via Pakistan, Iran, Turkey and the Balkan countries to distribution centres in West Europe. The bulk of the seizures are close to the areas of production.

Seizures of heroin and morphine worldwide, 2005

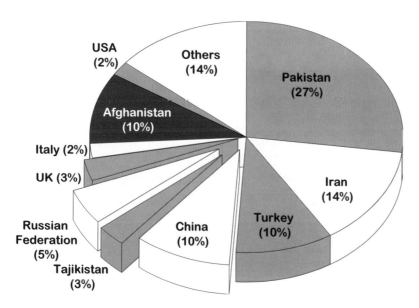

In 2006 the UK set up a new nationwide law enforcement agency, The Serious Crime Agency. In its first 12 months it seized 1.5 tonnes of heroin and 260kgs of opium.

Sources: Afghanistan Opium Survey 2006, Executive Summary, Opium Poppy Cultivation in the Golden Triangle, 2006, SOCA Annual Report 2006/07, World Drug Report 2007

http://www.unodc.org
http://www.soca.gov.uk

Tobacco tally

More than 10 million cigarettes are smoked every minute of every day around the world

Global cigarette consumption, 1880–2025
(projected)

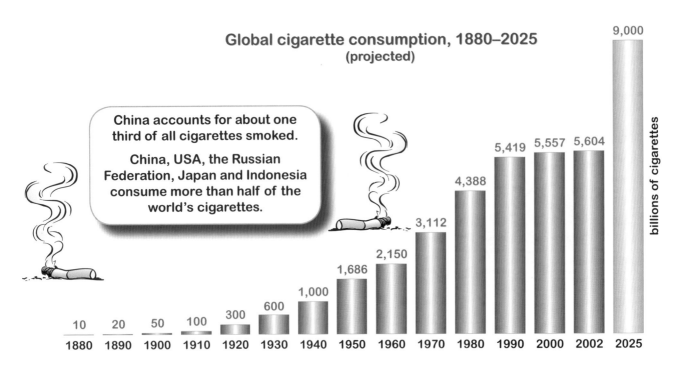

China accounts for about one third of all cigarettes smoked.

China, USA, the Russian Federation, Japan and Indonesia consume more than half of the world's cigarettes.

billions of cigarettes

Year	Value
1880	10
1890	20
1900	50
1910	100
1920	300
1930	600
1940	1,000
1950	1,686
1960	2,150
1970	3,112
1980	4,388
1990	5,419
2000	5,557
2002	5,604
2025	9,000

Top 10 countries Annual cigarette consumption per person
(latest available data)

3,441	Bulgaria
3,054	Greece
2,920	Japan
2,831	Spain
2,792	Russian Federation
2,718	Switzerland
2,631	Slovenia
2,609	Bahrain
2,566	Belgium
2,504	Bosnia & Herzegovina

NB Information not available from all countries

Research released in 2007 suggests that cancer deaths worldwide will hit 17m in 2030. The number of people diagnosed with cancer is expected to treble to 75m with poor countries shouldering the heaviest burden.

An ageing population will increase cancer rates worldwide, especially in developing countries where the number of people who smoke and drink is on the rise.

Shares of world cigarette sales, by region
(latest available)

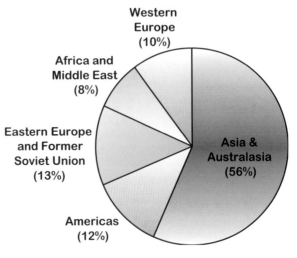

- Western Europe (10%)
- Africa and Middle East (8%)
- Eastern Europe and Former Soviet Union (13%)
- Americas (12%)
- Asia & Australasia (56%)

NB Figures may not add up to 100% due to rounding

Source: The Tobacco Atlas © American Cancer Society 2006; International Agency for Research on Cancer, 2007

http://www.cancer.org
http://www.iarc.fr

Stub it out

The proportion of people who have never smoked varies in the EU

	You have never smoked	Smokers	You used to smoke but you have stopped

Country	Never smoked	Smokers	Stopped
Portugal	64%	24%	12%
Slovakia	59%	25%	15%
Malta	57%	25%	18%
Cyprus	56%	31%	12%
Luxembourg	56%	26%	17%
Slovenia	54%	23%	23%
Ireland	52%	29%	18%
Finland	52%	26%	21%
Italy	51%	31%	16%
Latvia	51%	36%	13%
Belgium	50%	26%	24%
Czech Republic	50%	29%	21%
Lithuania	50%	34%	15%
Estonia	49%	33%	18%
Spain	48%	34%	17%
Hungary	48%	36%	15%
Austria	46%	31%	22%
Sweden	46%	18%	29%
Germany	45%	30%	24%
Poland	45%	35%	19%
UK	44%	33%	24%
France	43%	33%	24%
Greece	41%	42%	17%
Netherlands	40%	29%	30%
Denmark	39%	32%	27%
EU25	47%	32%	21%

NB In some cases complete figures unavailable or figures don't add up to 100% due to rounding

Countries who have recently joined

Country	Never smoked	Smokers	Stopped
Bulgaria	49%	36%	15%
Romania	57%	31%	11%

Potential candidate country

Country	Never smoked	Smokers	Stopped
Herzegovina	51%	33%	16%

0% 10% 20% 30% 40% 50% 60% 70% 80% 90% 100%

The most likely reason for European smokers to resume smoking after their attempt to quit is linked to stress (33%). Others reasons include: not being able to cope with the cravings (28%), having a friend or colleague who smokes (20%), finding pleasure in smoking (20%), missing the habit (17%), having a spouse or partner who smokes (9%) and putting on weight (6%).

*Source: Attitudes of Europeans towards Tobacco,
Special Eurobarometer, European Commission 2007*

http://www.ec.europa.eu

Euro-binge

One in 10 Europeans confesses to regular binge-drinking. A third of Irish drinkers consume five or more drinks in one sitting at least once a week

Amount of alcohol consumed on days when drinking took place, EU countries, 2006

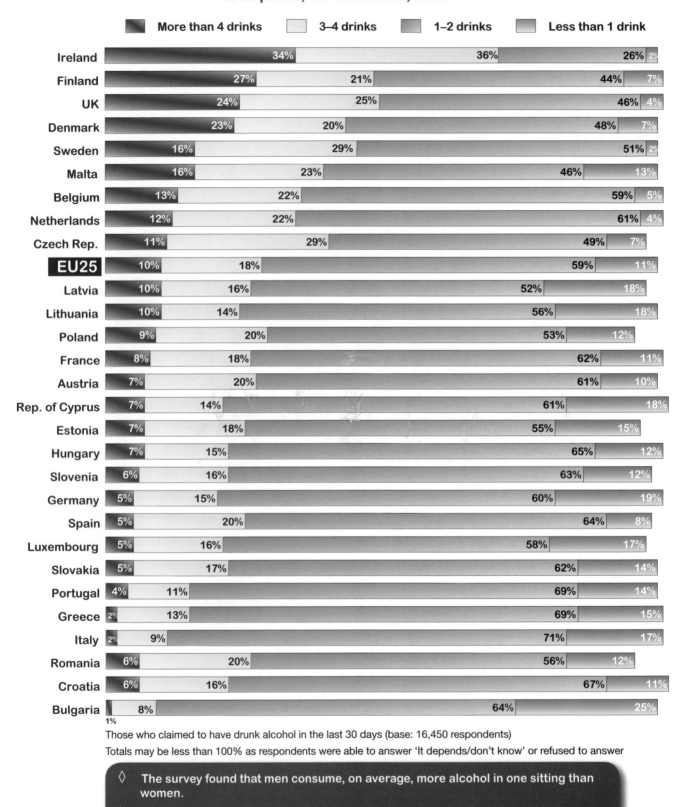

Legend: ■ More than 4 drinks □ 3–4 drinks ▨ 1–2 drinks ▨ Less than 1 drink

Country	More than 4 drinks	3–4 drinks	1–2 drinks	Less than 1 drink
Ireland	34%	36%	26%	2%
Finland	27%	21%	44%	7%
UK	24%	25%	46%	4%
Denmark	23%	20%	48%	7%
Sweden	16%	29%	51%	2%
Malta	16%	23%	46%	13%
Belgium	13%	22%	59%	5%
Netherlands	12%	22%	61%	4%
Czech Rep.	11%	29%	49%	7%
EU25	10%	18%	59%	11%
Latvia	10%	16%	52%	18%
Lithuania	10%	14%	56%	18%
Poland	9%	20%	53%	12%
France	8%	18%	62%	11%
Austria	7%	20%	61%	10%
Rep. of Cyprus	7%	14%	61%	18%
Estonia	7%	18%	55%	15%
Hungary	7%	15%	65%	12%
Slovenia	6%	16%	63%	12%
Germany	5%	15%	60%	19%
Spain	5%	20%	64%	8%
Luxembourg	5%	16%	58%	17%
Slovakia	5%	17%	62%	14%
Portugal	4%	11%	69%	14%
Greece	2%	13%	69%	15%
Italy	2%	9%	71%	17%
Romania	6%	20%	56%	12%
Croatia	6%	16%	67%	11%
Bulgaria	1%	8%	64%	25%

Those who claimed to have drunk alcohol in the last 30 days (base: 16,450 respondents)

Totals may be less than 100% as respondents were able to answer 'It depends/don't know' or refused to answer

◊ The survey found that men consume, on average, more alcohol in one sitting than women.

◊ Younger respondents and students claim to have had a drink on fewer occasions per month than the EU average. Binge drinking, however, is highest among the youngest respondents.

Source: Attitudes towards Alcohol Report 2007 Eurobarometer, European Commission

http://www.ec.europa.eu

A lot of bottle

Nearly 165,000 million litres of bottled water were consumed globally, an average of 25.5 litres per person annually

Consumption of bottled water, top 10 countries, million litres

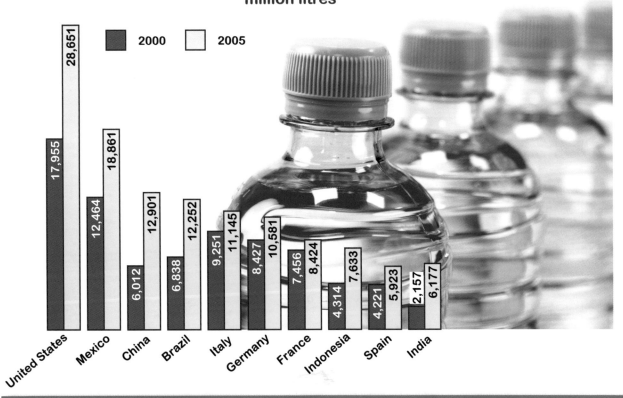

Legend: ■ 2000 □ 2005

Country	2000	2005
United States	17,955	28,651
Mexico	12,464	18,861
China	6,012	12,901
Brazil	6,838	12,252
Italy	9,251	11,145
Germany	8,427	10,581
France	7,456	8,424
Indonesia	4,314	7,633
Spain	4,221	5,923
India	2,157	6,177

Sales of bottled water are growing worldwide. It appeals to consumers in developed countries because it is seen as healthy, safe and convenient – although tap water is just as safe or safer.

Consumers often choose bottled water as an alternative to fizzy drinks, so it is not surprising that soft drink manufacturers – Nestlé, Pepsi-Cola and Coca-Cola – are also the major companies in this area.

In developing countries unsafe and unreliable water supplies have driven the growth in consumption. But many poorer people cannot afford the bottled version.

Drawing water for bottling can threaten local streams and groundwater and consumes energy in production and shipping, in addition about 2 million bottles made from oil-derived plastics end up in landfills in the US alone.

Consumption of bottled water, global, litres per person

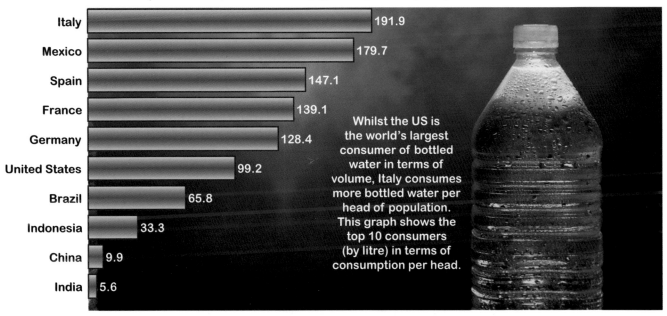

Country	litres per person
Italy	191.9
Mexico	179.7
Spain	147.1
France	139.1
Germany	128.4
United States	99.2
Brazil	65.8
Indonesia	33.3
China	9.9
India	5.6

Whilst the US is the world's largest consumer of bottled water in terms of volume, Italy consumes more bottled water per head of population. This graph shows the top 10 consumers (by litre) in terms of consumption per head.

Source: Consumption of bottled water, total and top 10 countries, 2000 and 2005, Worldwatch Institute and International Bottled Water Association © Worldwatch institute 2007

http://www.worldwatch.org

World wide

Overweight adults aged 15 and over, top 20 countries and UK, 2007, %

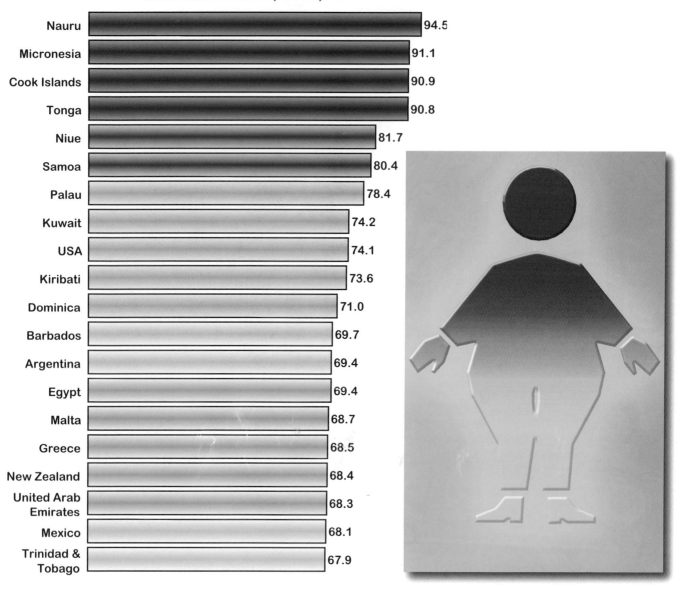

Country	%
Nauru	94.5
Micronesia	91.1
Cook Islands	90.9
Tonga	90.8
Niue	81.7
Samoa	80.4
Palau	78.4
Kuwait	74.2
USA	74.1
Kiribati	73.6
Dominica	71.0
Barbados	69.7
Argentina	69.4
Egypt	69.4
Malta	68.7
Greece	68.5
New Zealand	68.4
United Arab Emirates	68.3
Mexico	68.1
Trinidad & Tobago	67.9
UK	63.8

The UK is the 28th fattest country in the world

Overweight adults are defined as those with a Body Mass Index (BMI) greater than or equal to 25. Obese is defined as having a BMI greater than or equal to 30

Experts are not surprised that people across the globe are increasingly becoming overweight. They blame urbanisation and the influx of Western ways of life including numerous fast food choices, little exercise and stressful jobs. This change in lifestyle is most evident in the South Pacific, 8 of the top 10 fattest countries are in this region.

In the last 50 years this area has established significant economic ties with the US and New Zealand, causing a surge in Western imports and a significant change in diet. Studies conducted by the WHO Western Pacific regional office and by the International Obesity Task Force, have highlighted several other factors they say contribute to the region's high obesity rates.

These include the common belief that beauty is marked by a large physical size, the reliance on fatty, nutrient-deficient imported foods and a decrease in activity caused by less farming and agricultural work.

Elsewhere, developing countries are dealing with what many experts call a nutrition transition. Economies that are used to dealing primarily with undernutrition must now fight obesity as people fill up on things that have a high caloric value but little nutritional value.

Source: Forbes, World's fattest countries, 2007
http://www.forbes.com

Burgernomics

Worldwide it takes on average 35 minutes to earn the price of a Big Mac

2003   2006

Working time (in minutes) required to buy a Big Mac, range of cities worldwide, 2003 and 2006

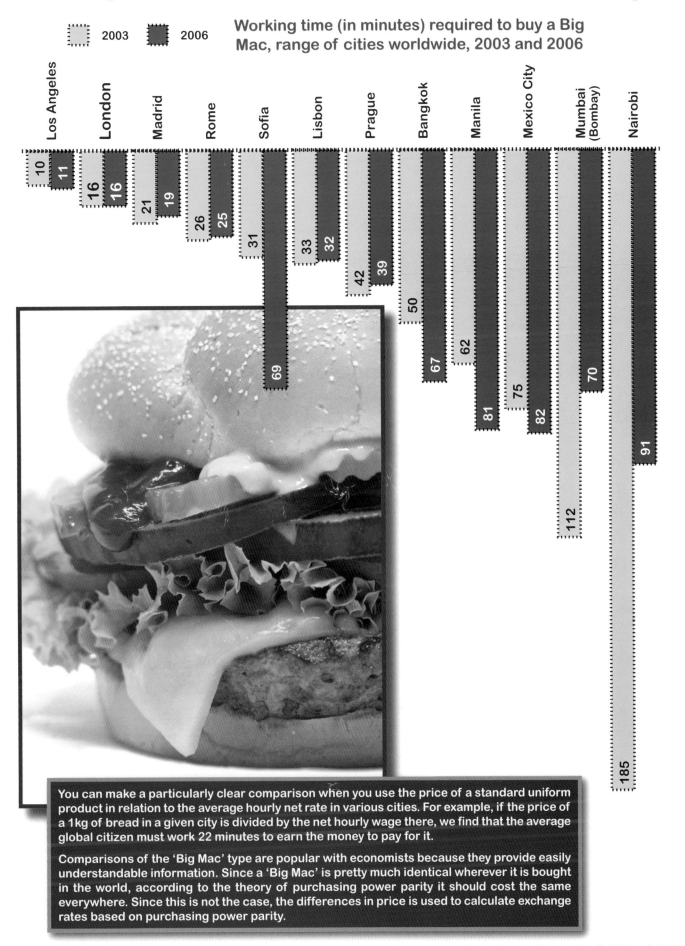

City	2003	2006
Los Angeles	10	11
London	16	16
Madrid	21	19
Rome	26	25
Sofia	31	69
Lisbon	33	32
Prague	42	39
Bangkok	50	67
Manila	62	81
Mexico City	75	82
Mumbai (Bombay)	112	70
Nairobi	185	91

You can make a particularly clear comparison when you use the price of a standard uniform product in relation to the average hourly net rate in various cities. For example, if the price of a 1kg of bread in a given city is divided by the net hourly wage there, we find that the average global citizen must work 22 minutes to earn the money to pay for it.

Comparisons of the 'Big Mac' type are popular with economists because they provide easily understandable information. Since a 'Big Mac' is pretty much identical wherever it is bought in the world, according to the theory of purchasing power parity it should cost the same everywhere. Since this is not the case, the differences in price is used to calculate exchange rates based on purchasing power parity.

Source: Prices and Earnings UBS (United Bank of Switzerland) 2003 and 2006

http://www.ubs.com

Take-away pay

Internationally the highest gross wages don't always result in the highest take-home pay

Gross and net hourly pay rates in selected cities worldwide, in US$, 2006
(% of taxes and social security contributions deducted from gross pay, in brackets)

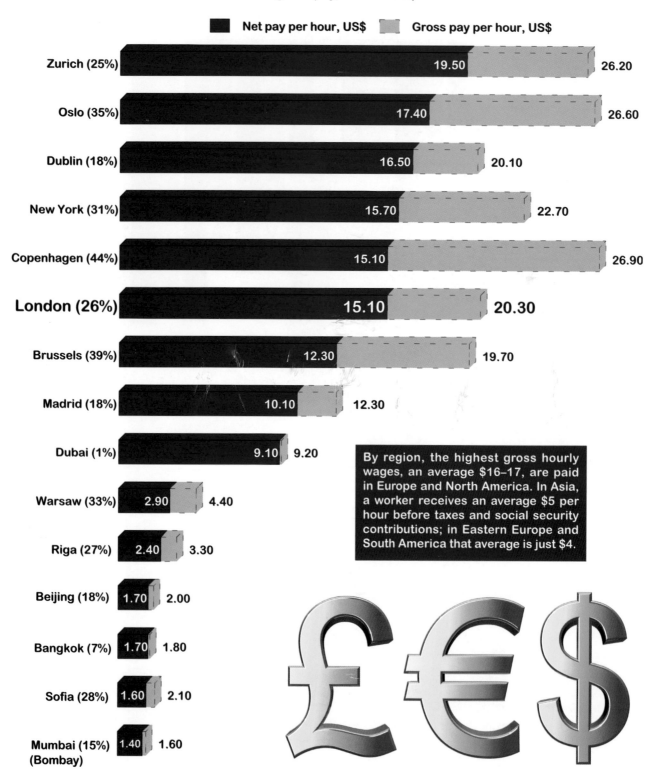

■ Net pay per hour, US$ ▨ Gross pay per hour, US$

City	Net pay	Gross pay
Zurich (25%)	19.50	26.20
Oslo (35%)	17.40	26.60
Dublin (18%)	16.50	20.10
New York (31%)	15.70	22.70
Copenhagen (44%)	15.10	26.90
London (26%)	15.10	20.30
Brussels (39%)	12.30	19.70
Madrid (18%)	10.10	12.30
Dubai (1%)	9.10	9.20
Warsaw (33%)	2.90	4.40
Riga (27%)	2.40	3.30
Beijing (18%)	1.70	2.00
Bangkok (7%)	1.70	1.80
Sofia (28%)	1.60	2.10
Mumbai (15%) (Bombay)	1.40	1.60

By region, the highest gross hourly wages, an average $16–17, are paid in Europe and North America. In Asia, a worker receives an average $5 per hour before taxes and social security contributions; in Eastern Europe and South America that average is just $4.

£€$

Source: UBS – Prices and Earnings 2006

http://www.ubs.com

Workplace whingers

UK workers came second in a global 'demanding workers' league table, mostly because of pay. This is despite what is, in global terms, a very good standard of living

Top 15 countries for worker complaints on pay and working hours

Country	Overall 'whinginess' rank	Pay			Working hours		
		% unhappy with pay	Actual income relative to cost of living	Pay whinge rank	% feeling working hours impinge on private life	Actual average weekly working hours	Hours whinge rank
France	1	43%	30,540	2	34%	34.5	6
UK	=2	40%	32,690	3	35%	36.4	7
Sweden	=2	35%	31,420	6	38%	35.7	4
USA	3	38%	41,950	1	31%	39.6	11
Australia	=4	30%	30,610	12	44%	34.8	2
Portugal	=4	42%	19,730	13	57%	39.1	1
Canada	=5	35%	32,220	5	28%	31.9	10
Greece	=5	40%	23,620	10	38%	39.8	5
Poland	6	55%	13,490	14	45%	39.8	3
Germany	=7	33%	29,210	8	28%	34.5	12
Spain	=7	41%	25,820	7	28%	35.2	13
Japan	8	38%	31,410	4	25%	42.2	19
Switzerland	9	18%	37,080	16	33%	36.1	8
Norway	10	23%	40,420	11	24%	34.9	17
Brazil	11	45%	8,230	21	35%	42.0	9

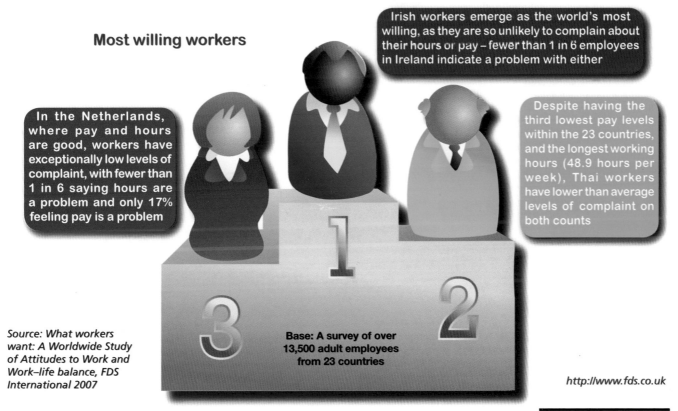

Most willing workers

Irish workers emerge as the world's most willing, as they are so unlikely to complain about their hours or pay – fewer than 1 in 6 employees in Ireland indicate a problem with either

In the Netherlands, where pay and hours are good, workers have exceptionally low levels of complaint, with fewer than 1 in 6 saying hours are a problem and only 17% feeling pay is a problem

Despite having the third lowest pay levels within the 23 countries, and the longest working hours (48.9 hours per week), Thai workers have lower than average levels of complaint on both counts

Source: What workers want: A Worldwide Study of Attitudes to Work and Work–life balance, FDS International 2007

Base: A survey of over 13,500 adult employees from 23 countries

http://www.fds.co.uk

Well-being

The UK has been accused of failing its children, as it comes bottom of a league table for child well-being across 21 industrialised countries

UNICEF, the United Nations Children's Fund, has conducted a report which attempts to measure and compare child well-being in 21 countries under six different headings or dimensions: material wellbeing, health & safety, education, peer & family relationships, behaviours & risks, and young people's own subjective sense of their own well-being. It draws on 40 separate indicators relevant to children's lives and rights.

Internationally, measurement and comparison gives an indication of each country's strengths and weaknesses. It shows what is achievable in practice and provides both government and civil society with the information to argue for and work towards the fulfilment of children's rights and the improvement of their lives.

Dimensions of child well-being (overall rank order)	Dimension 1 Material well-being	Dimension 2 Health and safety	Dimension 3 Educational well-being	Dimension 4 Family and peer relationships	Dimension 5 Behaviours and risks	Dimension 6 Subjective well-being
Netherlands	10	2	6	3	3	1
Sweden	1	1	5	15	1	7
Denmark	4	4	8	9	6	12
Finland	3	3	4	17	7	11
Spain	12	6	15	8	5	2
Switzerland	5	9	14	4	12	6
Norway	2	8	11	10	13	8
Italy	14	5	20	1	10	10
Ireland	19	19	7	7	4	5
Belgium	7	16	1	5	19	16
Germany	13	11	10	13	11	9
Canada	6	13	2	18	17	15
Greece	15	18	16	11	8	3
Poland	21	15	3	14	2	19
Czech Republic	11	10	9	19	9	17
France	9	7	18	12	14	18
Portugal	16	14	21	2	15	14
Austria	8	20	19	16	16	4
Hungary	20	17	13	6	18	13
United States	17	21	12	20	20	Question not asked
United Kingdom	18	12	17	21	21	20

A light blue background indicates a place in the top third of the table; mid blue denotes the middle third and dark blue the bottom third

OECD countries not included because of insufficient data: Australia, Iceland, Japan, Luxembourg, Mexico, New Zealand, the Slovak Republic, South Korea, and Turkey.

Dimension 1

Material well-being was based on:

» % of children living in homes with equivalent incomes below 50% of the national average

» % in families without an employed adult

» % of children reporting low family affluence, reporting few educational resources, and reporting fewer than 10 books in the home

Dimension 2

Health and safety was based on:

» number of infants dying before age 1 per 1,000 births

» % of infants born with low birth weight (<2,500g)

» % of children age 12 to 23 months immunized against measles, diphtheria, and polio

» deaths from accidents and injuries per 100,000 aged 0-19

Dimension 3

Educational well-being was based on:

» average achievement in reading literacy

» average achievement in mathematical literacy

» average achievement in science literacy

» % aged 15-19 remaining in education

» % aged 15-19 not in education, training or employment

» % of 15 year-olds expecting to find low-skilled work

Dimension 5

Behaviours and risks was based on:

» % of children who eat breakfast, who eat fruit daily, are physically active and % overweight

» % of 15 year-olds who smoke, who have been drunk more than twice, who use cannabis, who are having sex by age 15, who use condoms and the teenage fertility rate

» % of 11, 13 and 15 year-olds involved in fighting in last 12 months and % reporting being bullied in last two months

Dimension 4

Family and peer relationships was based on:

» % of children living in single-parent families

» % of children living in stepfamilies

» % of children who report eating the main meal of the day with parents more than once a week

» % of children who report that parents spend time 'just talking' to them

» % of 11, 13 and 15 year-olds who report finding their peers 'kind and helpful'

Dimension 6

Subjective well-being was based on:

» % of young people rating their own health no more than 'fair' or 'poor'

» % of young people 'liking school a lot'

» % of children rating themselves above the mid-point on a *'Life Satisfaction Scale'*

» % of children reporting negatively about personal well-being

Source: Child Poverty in perspective: An overview of child well–being in rich countries, Innocenti Report Card 7 © The United Nations Children's Fund, 2007

http://www.unicef.org

INDEX

Entries in colour refer to main sections